CLAY FOR THE POTTER

The Autobiography of Sarah Mitchell Gettys

WestBow
PRESS
A DIVISION OF THOMAS NELSON

Copyright © 2012 Sarah M. Gettys

All rights reserved. No part of this book may be used or reproduced by any means, graphic, electronic, or mechanical, including photocopying, recording, taping or by any information storage retrieval system without the written permission of the publisher except in the case of brief quotations embodied in critical articles and reviews.

WestBow Press books may be ordered through booksellers or by contacting:

WestBow Press
A Division of Thomas Nelson
1663 Liberty Drive
Bloomington, IN 47403
www.westbowpress.com
1-(866) 928-1240

Because of the dynamic nature of the Internet, any web addresses or links contained in this book may have changed since publication and may no longer be valid. The views expressed in this work are solely those of the author and do not necessarily reflect the views of the publisher, and the publisher hereby disclaims any responsibility for them.

Any people depicted in stock imagery provided by Thinkstock are models, and such images are being used for illustrative purposes only.

ISBN: 978-1-4624-0152-9 (sc)
ISBN: 978-1-4624-0151-2 (e)

Printed in the United States of America

WestBow Press rev. date: 06/07/2012

MY LIFE STORY IS DEDICATED TO ALL THE MEMBERS OF MY WONDERFUL FAMILY, TO ALL MY BELOVED IN-LAWS, AND TO THE MANY FINE FRIENDS ACROSS THE LAND, MUCH-LOVED FOR SO MANY YEARS. I REGRET THAT MANY HAVE GONE ON TO THEIR REWARDS. HOWEVER, EACH HAS BEEN A CONTRIBUTOR, IN HIS OR HER OWN WAY, TO MAKING MY LIFE TODAY A "TREASURE TROVE" OF HEART-WARMING MEMORIES.

In 1918, an unusually virulent strain of flu ravaged both Europe and the United States, leaving thousands dead in its wake. WWI was winding down, and I was born several weeks early, on Monday, May13, at 8:00 AM, in a one-room homesteader's shack on the barren prairies of Kit Carson County in eastern Colorado. I weighed in at approximately two and one-half pounds. Mother said they could have put me in a quart jar.

Mrs. Clementina Guthrie, born in Greenock, Scotland, was hurriedly summoned to assist at my premature birth, and undoubtedly, it is to Mrs. Guthrie that I owe my chance at life.

When Dr. Remington finally arrived from Burlington, twenty five miles away, he said I wouldn't live forty eight hours. He didn't know Mrs. Guthrie's experience with new babies— she had thirteen children, including two sets of twins, the first twins born in Kit Carson County—nor her dogged dedication to my survival.

She prepared an "incubator" in the corner behind the pot-bellied stove, using an orange crate for a crib, and kept the stove burning continually. She carried me on a pillow, as I was too small to handle, fed me (with an eye-dropper) milk pumped from Mother's breast, and I beat the odds against my survival. As an adult, I realize how very fortunate I am to have been blessed with a healthy body, and none of the physical ailments inherent in many premature births.

I regret that I never knew Mrs. Guthrie, though she lived until 1950 and died at ninety years of age.

"Surely the Good Lord wanted you to live for some reason," was a remark I heard my mother make many times during my life.

MY FATHER, VICTOR MITCHELL

I wish you could have known my father as a young man, as I knew him—a man of boundless energy and good nature, hard working, always an optimist, yet a very sensitive man with a big, tender heart. As a young girl, I was often embarrassed when his chin would quiver, his voice break, and his eyes mist with tears while reading, or telling, a "touching" anecdote. I'm sure that I have often embarrassed my own children in exactly the same way, for I inherited Dad's tender-heartedness.

Dad was fair skinned, blue-eyed, 5'10", weighed a solid two hundred pounds, and wore his thick, curly hair in a "pomp". Often he would say, as he patted his ample mid-section, "Nobody loves a fat man", but Dad was beloved by all who knew him.

Census data states that William Victor Mitchell was born in Phillipsburg, Kansas on September 25, 1886 to David LeRoy Mitchell (1858–1891) and Sarah Aracula Johnson (originally spelled Johnston, 1862–1905). Just why the family, with two other small children, would have been in Kansas at that particular time, we do not know, as their home was in LaRue, Ohio, where David was a barber and also an amateur musician who played several instruments. He also served as mayor of LaRue. A century later, my sister, Helen, researching genealogy records, found a beautifully penned letter from a representative of the LaRue community,

Dad & Mother • William Ramsey Mitchell (seated), My grandparents Sarah & David Mitchell (standing)

written to Sarah at the time of David's death at thirty-three years of age, giving him high praise for his service to the village of LaRue.

Sarah, 19, and David, 23, married in 1881. Ten years later David died from typhoid fever, leaving Sarah with three small children—Hoyt, 9, Alice, 7, and Victor, my father, 5 years old.

In that period of our history, women had few "civil rights" as we know them today. Most women were uneducated, except for the skills of homemaking, and there was no accommodation for them in the workplace. Sarah (Sadie to her friends) became a seamstress in an attempt to eke out a meager living for her family. However, since she had no visible means of support, custody of the three children was given to David's father, William Ramsey Mitchell, who lived in Bellefontaine.

Sarah moved with the children to Bellefontaine, probably at the insistence of her father-in-law. Also, she may have hoped that a seamstress would have more opportunity in a larger community. She found, however, that long hours of work resulted in few dollars, and the family lived poorly. William Ramsey Mitchell was evidently a man of some means, yet it is a sad commentary that none of the three children retained any adult memories of their grandfather's assistance, or influence, in their lives.

This true Christmas story, involving my father, related to us by Hoyt during the last years of his life, is both very sad and also joyous:

A Long-Ago Christmas

It was the custom in those days, on the night of the school's annual Christmas program, for each family to bring one gift for each of their own children and place it under the decorated Christmas tree, which usually stood, in all its glory, at the edge of the small stage at the front of the room. At the end of the program, "Santa" arrived with a merry "Ho Ho Ho" and sleigh bells ringing, stomping snow from his big black boots. He then distributed the gifts to the excited children.

Victor, 7, or 8, years old, was blessed with perfect pitch and had been chosen to sing the solos while the pageantry of the shepherds, the manger scene, and visits of the Magi were enacted on the stage. Victor knew that his mother would not be able to attend the program. Her sewing machine whirred late into the night so that they might have food on the table. He knew, too, that there would be no gift for him under the tree.

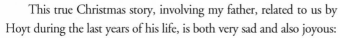

Sarah Mithchell • David Mitchell

On the night of the program, before leaving the house, Victor slipped the last three potatoes out of the bin in the kitchen, wrapped them in brown paper, put his name on the package, and carried it under the sleeve of his coat. When he arrived at the school, he quickly laid the small package under the tree, hoping that no one noticed.

During the program, Victor's sweet, true soprano brought appreciative applause many times and he had every right to feel proud. When Santa called his name, he walked with head held high to get his gift. In the excitement, no one noticed that he did not unwrap the package, but quickly laid it under his coat.

When the festivities ended, Victor, still holding the small package under his sleeve, trudged home through the snow, singing carols as he went, his soft, clear tones echoing in the night air. In the kitchen, he quickly took the three potatoes from their wrapping and returned them to the bin. Then excitedly, he hurried in to tell his mother about the nice Christmas program.

I have always considered that story a testament to Dad's ability, even as a child, to cope with adversity.

As a youngster, Dad lived with Aunt Lydia and Uncle Henry Hunt and helped on their farm near West Liberty. He was a happy youngster and a very bright student. He always said he learned to be good in math by playing dominoes with his teacher when he was in the seventh grade. Most of the students had to stay out of school to help their families with the sugar harvest, when the sap started running in the sugar maples. Dad and his teacher used that time to work sophisticated arithmetic problems.

Dad could add a column of four digit numbers and come up with the answer all at once, not adding each column singly. He always said he was "casting out nines", which I never understood, even though he explained it to me on several occasions.

Mother was a shark at algebra, but Dad could usually come up with the answer to a problem faster than she could, working it out in his head. My brother, Marvin, relates that Mother, when she was nearly eighty years of age and her eyesight rapidly failing, took a calculus course via correspondence. Once, she was "stuck" on a problem and Dad, looking

L. to R. Hoyt, Alice & Victor as adults

over her shoulder, gave her the solution. She never got out her calculus materials again!

Dad finished the seventh grade, passed the eighth grade examinations, and then went to work. However, his education continued throughout his life, as he was an avid reader.

Hoyt, four years older than Dad, went to work for the Corwin's, a family of some means who operated a cement plant near Rushsylvania. When Hoyt fell in love with their beautiful daughter, Belle, the family opposed the liaison. However, in spite of the opposition, Hoyt and Ada Belle Corwin were married when he was only nineteen years of age. They eventually had six fine-looking youngsters—Julia, Wellington, Wellman, Phyllis, Sherman, and Norman.

A second Corwin cement plant was to be built in Kansas, and Hoyt was put in charge of installing the concrete piers, which would later hold the heavy machinery. Therefore, in December of 1904, Hoyt, Belle, and little Julia, a year old, left for Neodesha, Kansas.

Dad, an eighteen year old, agreed to ride in the railroad car and supervise the transport of Hoyt's and Belle's few household belongings, plus their horse and buggy, from Rushsylvania to Kansas.

When Dad was in his eighties, I gave him a tape recorder and some blank tapes, and asked him to put on tape some of his memories of his early years. These are some of the things he remembered about that trip:

> It was the latter part of December and the ground was covered with snow when we were leaving Rushsylvania. In order to stay warm, I installed a stove in the railroad car, wiring it to the floor to keep it from tipping over. I fixed a board inside the door frame, so that the door could not accidentally close and crush the stovepipe, which was vented through the door.
>
> At a stop in Missouri the first evening, the brakeman asked if I needed coal. He'd already climbed up on one of the coal cars and got the coal he needed. My rail car was right next to the caboose, so I got enough coal to last for the rest of the trip. The next afternoon, probably at the St. Louis stop, a couple of young fellows asked if they could ride in the rail car with me. I told them they could. The next morning we arrived at Neodesha just about daylight. Without waking them, I jumped off the car and went to find where Hoyt lived. When Hoyt and I returned, these fellows were gone, but they had switched the car to the stockyards and had let the horse out, which was a big help to us.

Dad worked as a "feeder" at the cement plant with Harry Rudasill, also of Rushsylvania, who was in charge of lining the big kilns.

After being a widow for nearly fourteen years, Dad's mother, Sarah, married one Jacob Bentley, of whom we know very little. Soon after their marriage, she passed away (on October 22, 1905) from pneumonia and the trauma of a miscarriage. She was forty-three years of age. Dad, nineteen, and still working at the cement plant, was unable to return to Ohio in time for her funeral, which was held in Dayton, Ohio, on October 25, 1905. Her body was not interred until the next day, when he arrived home.

After their mother's funeral, Hoyt did not return to Kansas, as his job at the cement plant was finished. Dad, however, worked at the plant until a terrible accident caused the plant to be shut down. On the tape mentioned earlier, he says, "The throttle controlling the big 1632 h.p. steam engine, somehow got thrown wide open and the wheel (18 feet in diameter and rope-driven with 25 strands of 2 inch rope) literally ran away with itself. No piece weighing over 300 pounds was ever found."

Dad returned to Ohio where Belle's father backed him and Hoyt in buying a fifty-acre farm near Rushsylvania, in Logan County. This was not enough land to be profitable for two men, however, and Hoyt eventually took over the farm.

In June of 1908, Dad went back to Kansas to work on two farms near Emporia, which were owned by his Uncle Jim Mitchell and his Aunt Della Mitchell Pickett, brother and sister to his father. It was while he was there that he met Harry Loomis and got "homestead fever".

My Mother, Ruth Garrett

My mother, Ruth Naomi Garrett, was born in Denver, Colorado on September 22, 1889. Her father, John Fletcher Garrett (1848–1939), was born in Knox County, Illinois. On March 25, 1874 he married Rachel Asquith Fitts (1856–1894), also born in Illinois. They homesteaded near Cuba, Kansas before moving on to Colorado, probably in a covered wagon. They settled in Denver, where J. F. Garrett was a minister, and later Presiding Elder, of the Free Methodist Church.

Rachel died in Greenville, Illinois, while attending a church conference with her husband. She is buried in Cuba, Kansas. They no doubt made the trip from Denver in a wagon. Rachel was carrying another child, miscarried, and died at age 38, leaving four children—George 16, Mina 14, Grace 12, and Ruth Naomi, my mother, 5 years old.

On September 5, 1895, their father married his first cousin, Ella Garrett (born March 13, 1853), in order to provide a "mother" for the children. They were married in Davenport, Iowa as first cousins could not legally marry in Illinois. Ella was a fine lady, but sickly. She later became tubercular and died from that dreaded disease on April 14, 1928.

Due to the stepmother's ill health, Mina took over the running of the Garrett household. Perhaps Mother's memories of her childhood were inaccurate, but they were certainly not happy ones.

From childhood, Mother was burdened with very poor eyesight. I remember her telling about losing a handkerchief on their front lawn in Denver. It was evidently in plain view, but she could not see it. She was forced to look and look for it, while the older sister ridiculed her "stupidity" from the porch. Eventually the family realized she simply could not see. From that time on, she wore thick, "coke-bottle-lens" glasses.

Mother was the youngest child and, through the years, evidently took the brunt of her older sister's frustrations at being cast in the role of surrogate mother. All her life she suffered from eczema in her ears, which she always said was the result of Mina's merciless scrubbing of her ears with harsh soaps.

It is sadly true that many children, who are made to feel "different" due to a slight limp or thick glasses, withdraw into a world of their own, as an escape from the harsh reality they are forced to live in. Mother, a very bright child, escaped into a world of books and piano practice—a world that she could control.

In his position as Presiding Elder, J. F. Garrett was away from their home a great deal, traveling to visit various Free Methodist churches throughout the state. In the burgeoning frontier city of Denver, young George, lacking any male supervision, began to break away from the narrow confines of the home on South Washington Street, where Mina laid down the rules, and began habits that would create a lifetime of problems for him, and sorrow for those who loved him. Mother always resented the fact that her father thought it more important to be away, taking care of church affairs, than to be at home taking care of his family. She never forgave him for abandoning them for the sake of the church, and it affected not only her relationship with him, but also her feelings toward "organized religion" for the rest of her life.

It was a life-long sorrow to her that her only brother became a nomadic, and later an alcoholic barber who walked away from a fine wife (née Emma Desserage) and a fine young son, Emil George Garrett (September 23, 1918 to February 10, 1993), four months younger than I.

It is to their stepmother's credit, surely, that all three of the girls—Mina, Grace, and Mother—graduated from Denver University, in a day when few women went on to college.

J. F. Garrett (seated), Rachell Fitts Garrett, George, Grace, Mina (seated)
before mother was born

Mother was a small lady, not quite five feet tall, with swarthy skin, dark brown eyes, and blessed with a wonderful mind. She was a college graduate, an accomplished classical pianist, who gave her first concert in the Denver Auditorium when she was thirteen. Yet, she was essentially very shy.

It is hard to understand why this city-bred lady would even consider taking out a homestead on the eastern Colorado prairie. But Mother wanted the security of owning land. Her ancestors had come from England, where the "landed gentry" were in a class by themselves. Her father and grandfather had homesteaded in Kansas. Her great-grandfather was one of the earliest white settlers in Indiana, and later in the Illinois Territory. The fact that she was a city girl, unaccustomed to the hardships of the frontier, did not deter her from filing for a homestead in Kit Carson County.

Shortly before her death in 1973, she wrote the following account:

My father had gone out from Denver to Kit Carson County to preach. He knew I wanted to homestead and found a quarter section of land open for filing. I was fortunate to get a job teaching the school, located some two miles away.

Before school started my father went back to Kit Carson County, near Beaverton, and with the help of Willis Perkins, built a nine-by-twelve foot sod house for me. Drum, a dog belonging to Harry Loomis, dug a hole almost through the sod in the front wall of my soddy before I moved in.

When it was time for school to start, I rode the Rock Island Railroad train from Denver to Stratton. Mr. Perkins let my father borrow a team and wagon to meet me at the station. After my trunks, bed, and belongings were loaded, a drenching rain started, so we had to stay overnight in Stratton. The next day, after a drive of some twenty miles, we came past Beaverton, and on to the Willis Perkins' place.

For some reason, we slept at the abandoned Dickey place, and that night I was new bait for all the hungry insects in that house. By morning my face was a mass of ugly red bites and I looked horrible. That afternoon a whole buggy full of children came to the house to see the new teacher!

When I arrived at the school, also built of sod, I found the blackboard to be three boards about four feet long. At one time, they had been painted black. There was a small heater in the middle of the room, and the walls were unpainted.

It has always seemed incredible to me that this young lady, from a highly protective environment, would choose to leave a fast-growing city, where all kinds of wonderful oppor-

George, Mina, Mother (Ruth in the middle), Grace

tunities were developing almost overnight, and venture alone out to the eastern Colorado prairies, take out a homestead, and teach in a primitive, one-room school. But, Mother was never run-of-the-mill.

When Dad turned his share of the farm over to Hoyt and went back to Kansas to work for Uncle Jim and Aunt Della, he somehow met Harry Loomis, who was homesteading in eastern Colorado. Dad had grown up in other people's homes and had never owned much of anything himself. To be able to own land by "proving up" on it, as provided by the Homestead Act, sounded like the opportunity of a lifetime.

Congress passed the Homestead Act in May of 1862. It provided that any person over twenty-one years of age, who was the head of a family and a citizen (or an alien who intended to become a citizen), could obtain the title to 160 acres of public land if he lived on the land for five years and improved it. Or, the settler could pay $1.25 an acre in place of the residence requirement.

The Homestead Act attracted thousands of settlers to the West. However, through a series of additional laws, Congress granted much of the best land in the West to the railroad builders and to the states for the support of agricultural colleges.

In 1873, Congress passed a series of new measures that modified the Homestead Act of 1862, allowing people to acquire larger tracts of land. The chief beneficiaries, however, were land speculators and others who sought control of the West's rich natural resources.

The Homestead Act is still in effect today, but most homesteading efforts in recent years have been in Alaska.

On the tape I mentioned earlier, Dad tells that in April of 1910, he went from Kansas to Burlington, Colorado on the train. He spent the night in Burlington's small hotel and there he met an older man whose nephew and young wife lived in a dugout southwest of Burlington, near where Harry Loomis was homesteading.

Telephone lines rigged on the fences, with two-by-four "bridges" carrying the lines over gates, enabled the gentleman to call his nephew, who came to the hotel in Burlington to see his elderly uncle. Later he agreed to take Dad out to Harry Loomis' homestead.

Mother's sod schoolhouse

The trip by buggy was too long for one day, and Dad stayed all night with this young man and his wife. He says on the tape, "The dug-out was only one room and I had to step outside while they got ready for bed, then I went in and went to bed, too." No doubt he slept on the floor.

On April 10, 1910, Dad filed on his homestead, a half-section of grassland, thirteen miles south and one mile west of Bethune. George Gordon, a neighbor, helped him build a sod house to live in. He had two horses and a buggy. He spent the summer breaking ground and putting up fences. In the fall, in order to make a few dollars, he went back to Kansas to help with the harvest.

In the spring of 1911, he returned to his homestead and put up a sod barn. He bought a horse from George Gordon, and also a cow, in order to have milk. That fall he worked again in the harvest, both around Burlington and in western Kansas.

Part of his time in Kansas was spent working in the roundhouse for the railroad. Dad was a highly regarded, dependable workman and was offered a permanent job with the railroad. However, testing proved that he was color-blind and could not accurately interpret signals. Therefore, his career as a railroad man was short-lived.

In the fall of 1912, Mother came to teach in the sod school house that stood two miles west of her homestead, a quarter-section of land that lay approximately one mile north and one and one half mile west of Dad's homestead.

In those days young folks had to manufacture their own entertainment. The prairie young folks got together for what they called "sings". They would meet in some home where there was a piano, or an old pump organ, and spend the evening singing. Usually they would walk to the "sing", but sometimes they rode horses or came in a spring wagon.

Mother played the piano, or organ, at these get-togethers. Dad loved to sing and joined other settlers who gathered from miles around for these songfests. Thus, our parents met. Dad tells that when they were walking home after one "sing", he walked with Mother the first mile, as they were both headed east. When she had to turn north, he asked if he could walk her the rest of the way home. That was the beginning of nearly sixty years together.

The Colorado Rockies Gold Rush of 1858, which brought thousands of fortune hunters and spurred the growth of Denver from frontier town to business center, had dissipated by 1912. So, also, had the giant silver boom that brought great wealth to Leadville. However, many of the mines were still being worked to bring out tons of coal— "black gold."

Arthur Garrett, a cousin of Mother's, was working in the mines at Leadville. During the winter of 1912–1913, Dad joined Arthur in the mines. He returned to work on his homestead in the spring and summer.

Dad "proved up" on his land and made arrangements with George Gordon to take care of his livestock. Again, during the winter of 1913–1914, he worked with Arthur in Leadville. One day, while riding a coal car, a bolt of electricity went through him, knocking him off the car, and leaving him with a perfect "vaccination" mark about the size of a quarter, which he carried on his upper arm for the rest of his life.

Mother took advantage of the government regulation which allowed homesteaders to "buy out" a year or two of their homestead contract, rather than having to live on the land for the required term. The fall of 1913, she went to Leadville to teach, undoubtedly to be near her suitor.

On September 17, 1914, Victor and Ruth married in Denver, with her father, the Reverend J. F. Garrett, performing the ceremony. Their wedding certificate is signed by Harry B. Crawford, Mina's husband, and by her sister, Grace Garrett.

Harry's first wife had died, leaving him with a two-year-old daughter, Bertha, born in 1903. After Mina and Harry married, they had one child, Bradley, nine months older than I.

Grace went to Europe after college graduation to tutor two small German princes. Much of the time was spent in the Balkans, but she also visited Italy and several other European countries. After she returned home, she and some of her friends planned to hike up Pike's Peak. I'm not sure of the details, but she found at that time that she had a heart problem, which took her life at age thirty-two. She died a spinster. She used to say, "I don't know whether all the nice men are married, or whether marriage makes men nice."

I have, in my curio cabinet, a small porcelain figurine which a European suitor gave Grace after she rejected his proposal of marriage. It is an old maid, sitting on a park bench, book in hand, with a cup of tea on the bench beside her. All my growing up years, that figurine sat on our piano. Somehow, during the last years of Mother's life, the arms, holding the book, were broken off and lost. Even so, when both our parents were gone, and we four "kids" sat on their living room carpet, taking turns choosing from their cherished personal items, that figurine was the first item I chose.

Mother and Dad lived for the first three years of their marriage on a small farm owned by Grandma Garrett, near Erie, Colorado, in Weld County. There, on June 19, 1915, Helen Gail was born. Eventually Grandma sold that farm and in March of 1918, just prior to my arrival, they moved back to the homestead in Kit Carson County.

Helen was just two and one-half years old when they made that move, yet she retains vivid memories of the Erie home and of the trip to eastern Colorado in Dad's first

Grace Garrett

15

car. She remembers that each time they drove through a puddle in the dirt road, the exposed "coils" got wet, the engine stopped, and Dad had to get out and dry off the coils before he could start the engine again. Evidently that mechanical problem was not corrected for some time, as I remember that happening years later.

Again, I wonder why anyone would leave the piedmont at the foothills of the beautiful Rockies, and return to the barrenness of the undeveloped prairies of eastern Colorado. Mother always said that she feared Dad would be called to serve in the war, if they stayed where they were, and she was pregnant with her second child—me.

Prior to the move, Dad built a one-room building twelve-by-twenty four feet, of rough-hewn lumber, and it was there that I was born. Later, when a land survey was done, in connection with laying out the east-west road one mile north, which is still called the "correction line", they found that Dad's land had been improperly surveyed and this building actually stood on S. N. Rich's land. Eventually, Dad moved the building several rods south, onto his own land, but I was born while it stood on Rich property.

No doubt my premature birth was brought on by the trauma of the move, the long ride over rough, dirt roads, and the extra work of getting settled in such primitive surroundings while taking care of Helen, not yet three.

Pioneer settlers hauled water by wagon team, sometimes from great distances, until such a time as they could drill a well on their own property. Our well was two hundred feet deep and provided delicious soft water, which came up icy cold. It was years before I knew there was such a thing as "hard" water. In the west a constant wind blows, and it powers the windmills that bring water from various depths, through metal casings, to the surface. Often, in a high wind, some part of the windmill breaks. Many times Dad risked his life to climb the windmill's metal ladder, balance on a small platform many feet above the ground, and finally control a wildly turning wheel, the tail lashing out at him as if to kill. I shudder, still, remembering it.

When I was a toddler, Dad built a sod house with two good-sized rooms. He cut the sod from the west quarter section of his land and the scars left from cutting the sod were visible all my growing up years. The frame building, in which I had been born, became our granary-garage. Once, several years later, while we were at Keever's, we saw a funnel cloud coming from the west and feared that a tornado was headed for our place. It was. When we got home, the walls of this frame granary had collapsed inward, and the roof had been carried well over into the hog lot and set down so gently that there was not a shingle broken. The separator can, sitting on a table on the west side of the garage (in order to be "sterilized" by the sun during the day), was not even upset. Tornados are a freakish phenomena in nature.

If you have purchased sod to repair a lawn, you have some idea of the building material for a sod house. Furrows were plowed as deep as possible, and then the sod was cut cross-

wise into blocks about a foot square. The buffalo grass, indigenous to the western plains, held the sod together. Walls were formed by piling the sod squares, one on the other, row upon row, within the building's framework of two-by-fours, with spaces left for framing in windows and doors.

Our sod house, which we lived in for ten years, ran east and west, thus we referred to the "east room" and the "west room". There were no windows or doors on the north side of the house, a protection against the fierce winds of winter. The front door faced east, and there were two large east windows. There were also two west windows, and in each of the rooms there was a window on the south wall, as well as a back door in the west room. A partition, with an open archway, separated the two rooms.

In the west room, between the partition and the back door, was a fairly good-sized, square closet. It was here that Mother and Dad always hid the Christmas presents. Each year, the presents, most of which were ordered from the Montgomery Ward catalog, included three wooden buckets of candy—one of dipped chocolates, one of peanut brittle, and one of "ribbon" candy.

Under the west room was a small dugout cellar, reached through a trap door in the floor. Here we stored potatoes, squash, cabbage, and root vegetables for the winter. How I hated jumping down into that dank, musty hole to sprout potatoes, a dreaded spring chore.

Two double beds, with a dresser between them, filled the north wall of the west room. A coal cook stove, a round oak table, and a few nondescript chairs completed the furniture. One "chair" was really a fireless-cooker, an ingenious barrel-like object, with four-inch thick insulated metal walls, and a hinged lid that could be tightly secured. Two round soapstones, one for the bottom and one for the top, were first heated on the coal stove, and then placed under and over the food being prepared. They dispensed heat for several hours—enough to cook a fine meal. This was the original deep-well cooker, or crock-pot, and served as a food carrier for many a church picnic, as well as one of our "chairs" all my growing up years.

Our sod house. Sarah, Helen & Mother holding Marvin.

Those soapstones were in constant use during the winters as bed-warmers. Mother would put them on the stove in the early evening. When they were good and hot, she wrapped them in an old towel and put them at the foot of our beds, between the sheets. What a treat to feel that warmth when we got into bed on a cold night.

I spent many hours during my childhood on my knees on one of the double beds in the west room—the one that stood against the partitioned wall. On that wall was a slate about eighteen inches wide and perhaps six feet long, and under it, a shelf holding two good erasers and a plentiful supply of chalk. This proved a quiet haven for me during a lonely childhood. On that slate, I drew thousands of house plans while I day-dreamed about the beautiful home I would live in someday.

The walls of our sod house were approximately two feet thick. The window sills were the same depth—a favorite place for me to sit and

read. Dad had covered all the interior walls with chicken wire, then plastered over that. These walls had to be whitewashed regularly, as whitewash is a very temporary finishing touch.

The low peaked roof was braced with sturdy rafters, overlaid with wide, rough boards. Heavy tarpaper was stretched over the boards, and then a thick layer of sod, grass side up, was put on as the final layer. Sod houses were warm in winter and cool in summer. However, they were not as durable as adobe houses, which are made of sun-dried mud bricks.

Sparrows built nests in the sod, under the eaves. Rats, always prevalent where there are corn-cribs, burrowed their way through the thick sod walls. I still carry a scar on my right pointer finger where a rat bit me one night as I slept. Cows and horses, if not kept within fenced corrals, rubbed against the corners, wearing the sod away.

Once, just after Dad had whitewashed our walls, I sat on the floor in the corner behind the pot-bellied stove in the east room, and with a burned match, made dozens of black marks on the newly white wall. I was probably about three, but I remember it vividly, so was surely old enough to know better. Dad turned me over his knee and spanked me. I would not cry. He spanked me more severely. I refused to cry or to say that I was sorry. Helen still remembers that she wished I would cry so that Dad would stop spanking me. I was stoic at that time, but have remembered that punishment for nearly eighty years!

Helen (on the right) and Sarah

The east room served as both a living room and our parents' bedroom. Furnishings were the pot-bellied coal stove in the northwest corner, a fine rosewood upright piano and a revolving piano stool which stood along the partition-wall, a double bed in the northeast corner, an oak rocker with a brown leather padded seat, and a black leather, wooden-armed couch in the southeast corner of the room. The wide-plank floors were bare.

In the west room, between the closet and the back door, stood a round-topped steamer trunk. One of my favorite pastimes was looking through dozens of colorful postcards, which Aunt Grace had sent to Mother from Europe. There were pictures of ocean liners, passengers in fancy clothes dancing on the deck, and scenes of large, bustling European cities. They provided grist for my lively imagination. I loved to go to bed early and spend a long time daydreaming before falling asleep. My dreams were "serial" and continued night after night. I was happy each night to escape to this private, imaginary world. Someday, I would travel on a ship like the ones shown on the postcards. I would wear a soft, flowing gown and dance on the deck with a handsome man. There would be elegant food, served on beautiful china in a sunlit dining room. The waiter would have a white towel over his arm and would smile and bow. Someday! I believe I knew, even then, that it is good to dream, for dreams beget reality.

In that steamer trunk, Mother also kept treasures brought by missionaries who served in China, and who stayed in the Garrett home in Denver while on leave. There was a pair of tiny stuffed Chinese silk slippers, tasseled and in beautiful colors, showing the size of little Chinese girls' feet after they had been bound. As we looked at those tiny slippers, Mother would relate the stories she had heard the missionaries tell when she was a child—about the painful cries of the baby girls, hidden away in some isolated area so that the torture being imposed upon them wouldn't disturb their elders. I cried, too, listening, and even today I cringe at the thought that such abominable cruelty was once a common practice.

There was a small stuffed green silk frog, and a Chinese man in baggy pantaloons and a black silk "coolie" hat, his long black queue hanging down his back. Recently, Lowell Dunlap, a former fourth-grade student of Mother's, now ninety years of age, remembered her bringing those delicate Chinese souvenirs to school to share with the children.

In the top drawer of the dresser, Mother kept another bit of her past—a pair of white kid gloves. I remember her folding them, caressingly, in white tissue before laying them back in the drawer. Even as a very small child, I sensed her sadness as she looked lovingly at those gloves, a symbol, perhaps, of the life she'd left behind.

On October 18, 1921, when I was nearly three and one-half, my brother, Marvin Victor, was born. He and I were great buddies through our growing up years and remain so today. When we get together, we like to reminisce about the day our parents left us home alone while they went to Bethune for supplies. We took a Concord grape basket and gathered mushrooms from the back pasture, until our basket was full. In sautéing the mushrooms, we used all

the butter in the house. When Mother got home, she was furious—and well she might have been, too,—for they had taken all the cream to the creamery in Bethune and it would be days before we would have butter again. But we still remember how good those mushrooms tasted.

We also laugh about the time he chased me with a large white granite cup full of cold water, both of us running for dear life, barefoot, across a cactus-filled pasture. We have lots of fun memories from our growing up days.

The year I was five, Mother taught school at First Central, approximately six miles northwest of where we lived. Helen, then eight years old, started to school that year as a third grader. Even though she had not been in school, she knew how to read, do arithmetic, and write, as Mother had taught her at home.

Dad built a one-room "cook shack" for them to live in during the week. It sat up on blocks, just east of the First Central School, near the old Church family grocery, known earlier as Beaverton. Marvin and I stayed with Dad. We would go each Friday after school and bring Mother and Helen home for the weekend, then take them back to school on Monday morning.

One Friday, Dad took Marvin and me down to Okie Carpenter's. He and Okie contracted to harvest government-owned land and were co-owners of harvest machinery and equipment. Marvin, I suppose, was out with the men. I was in the house with Okie's wife, Laura. Laury, as we called her, was a big woman who had no children, and I was half afraid of her. During the day, my thick plait of hair, which had never been cut, came unbraided. Laury took her kitchen scissors and cut it off even with my ear lobes. You can imagine how blunt and ugly it looked. On the way over to pick up Mother and Helen that afternoon, I pushed my stubby hair up under my

J. F. Garrett, Ella Garrett (stepmother), Mina, Mother (with glasses)
George, Grace in the back • Marvin during WWII (medical corps)

20

stocking cap, hoping no one would notice it. However, Mother knew immediately that something was amiss and jerked off my cap. I will never forget the expression on her face. I saw my mother mad many times during the years, but never madder than on that day.

At that time, we had an open touring car, a Dort, one of the heaviest cars ever made. One Monday morning, Mother had gotten us kids ready and we were in the car, waiting to take her and Helen to First Central. In those days, cars had to be cranked. Dad had just begun to turn the crank when Mother, approaching the car with her arms full of school materials, dropped something and stooped to pick it up. Perhaps two year old Marvin had toyed with the gear shift while we waited, as we were both in the front seat. In any case, as Dad turned the crank, the car jumped into gear, lurched forward, and knocked Mother beneath it. Both the front and back wheels ran over her upper body. I can see her yet, as she writhed there on the ground in agony. Dad, agile enough to jump out of the way, had to run to stop the car, as we kids were still in it.

Helen ran to the Grave's, a mile east of us, for help, jumping the lister ditches in the newly plowed field, her coat billowing out behind her.

I do not remember how Dad got Mother up off the ground and into the house. No doubt he lifted her, as he was a big strong man and she was a small lady. Today, paramedics would move her very carefully on a gurney. Her injuries were severe. Many, if not all, of her ribs were broken. Years later, chiropractors refused to work on her back or neck because of cracked vertebrae. It is a miracle that she lived.

I have forgotten how long Mother lay in bed in the east room of the soddy, unable to move. I remember her drinking Welch's grape-juice through a bent glass straw, because she could not raise her head. It was a sad time at our house.

Eventually, she could be out of bed for short periods of time and one of the first things she did was some much-needed mending. I remember her, sitting on Dad's lap, while he treadled the White sewing machine for her as she mended an accumulation of well-worn clothing. She never fully recovered. Though she lived to be eighty-three years of age, she suffered from those injuries for the rest of her life.

Sarah, Helen & Marvin

Not long after the accident, Mother had another heavy burden thrust upon her. Her stepmother was ill in Phoenix, where they had moved after Grandpa Garrett retired from the ministry. They wanted her to come. Dad arranged for Jim Conkey, who later married Lois Perkins, to live in our house and take care of the livestock. In October of 1924 we headed for Phoenix. Today, such a trip can be made in a short time, but at that period in our history, it was like going to the end of the world. There were no good roads. Cars were not dependable. Tires were poor. There were no Holiday Inns along the way. In fact, there were few garages or filling stations.

Dad drove what he always referred to as the "Dodge Commercial", as it resembled a dog catcher's vehicle, a paddy wagon or an early-day van. The sides were diamond-shaped metal screens, with heavy canvas tarps rolled at the top on the outside, to be let down for shelter, if needed. The door was in the back. Our parents laid a mattress on the floor of the vehicle—a bed for us three children. Mother packed an assortment of foods which could travel.

The first night, we got as far as a small town in New Mexico. Dad pulled his Dodge into what appeared to be a small park. We kids were happy to stretch our legs as Mother put together something for us to eat. It was getting dusk when a man in a beat-up truck stopped. He was an unsavory looking character and seemed to be asking a lot of questions. Dad was alerted to danger. As soon as the man drove off, Dad got us all back in the van and drove a few blocks to the town garage. He asked the owner if he could pull our vehicle into the garage and spend the night there. We were grateful when the garage owner said he could.

We had a small puppy with us and there was no place for him to ride inside the vehicle. Dad fixed a bed for him on the running board and secured him with a safety harness fastened to the side screen with a small rope. We kids could keep an eye on him and talk to him as we traveled. Somewhere in the wilds of New Mexico, we lost the puppy. It is a grief I have never forgotten.

One evening we stopped along a river. Mother was trying to prepare food and needed water. She took a pan and went to the river's bank. I can see her yet as she leaned over the bank, stretching, trying to reach the water below. What if she had fallen? No one in the family knew how to swim. That scene haunted many childhood years for me.

Mother bought jam in half-gallon buckets, which we later used for school lunch buckets. Bread and jam was an easy snack, no doubt, for three bored, hungry youngsters during the long trip. I got so sick of jam on that trip that I would not eat it again for many years.

After a long trip, we finally located Deerwood Place, the street where Grandma and Grandpa lived, on the outskirts of Phoenix's southeast side. Beyond it were cotton fields, grapefruit orchards, and truck gardens full of head lettuce.

In Grandpa's back yard grew a lemon tree, a pear tree, and a grapefruit tree. He also had a goat. I loved to watch him milk her, but I did not like the rich, rank taste of the goat's milk.

Grandma was very ill with tuberculosis. She looked so frail as she lay on her small cot, on the porch that looked out onto the street. I loved being out there with her and would hold her thin, bony hand in mine, and trace the blue veins that stood out against her white skin.

The beautiful covered bowl on my mantle is the one she always kept on her dining room table with soda crackers in it. Crackers were a treat we seldom had at home. Grandma would let me climb up on a chair and reach across her table and get crackers from that bowl. Today, a piece is broken from the lid, but that bowl holds cherished memories for me.

From Grandma's porch I could see the huckster wagon turn down the street. The huckster would call loudly, in a sing-song voice, "P-i-e-s, c-a-k-e-s, p-u-d-d-i-n-g-s, b-u-n-s, do-nuts." He always ended with his voice on the upswing. When the children on the street heard him coming, they gleefully fell in behind the wagon and followed him. I soon learned to join them. We always hoped that along the way he'd find some kind of a treat for us. Usually he did.

Mother and Dad found a sparsely furnished house on Deerwood Place, just a few doors from Grandma. It seemed like a mansion to me, after the soddy. I'm sure it had no more than three or four rooms, for I remember that Helen and I slept in the living room. There was a garden in back of the house, and an "out house". A nice neighbor to the south of us often saved a piece of their breakfast toast for me, a treat that we seldom had at home. My best friend was a little girl name May, who lived across the street from our house. When we left Phoenix, I hated so to leave her that, for a long time, I pretended that my middle name was May.

Mother let me start to school, even though it was late October. I had no trouble catching up with the others, and when we left for home in early May, I had a workbook with "stars" on every page, which I forgot to retrieve from my desk. Leaving that prized workbook was such a sorrow that I have remembered it all these years.

The name of my school was Longview and only grades one through three went there. In the schoolyard were lots of pomegranate trees. At recess and noon, the little

boys would shinny up the trees and bring us down ripe fruit. I loved the pomegranates. Why do the ones I buy today never taste as delectable as those that grew in our schoolyard in Phoenix?

Across the street from Longview School was an Indian School. I loved watching the Indian girls, with papooses strapped to cradle boards on their

Grandma & Grandpa Garrett

23

backs, riding the merry-go-round during their playtime.

Longview was possibly three or four blocks from where we lived. As I walked to school, I passed a large cotton field, crossed an irrigation canal, and just beyond that, a small store sat on the left side of the street. In the afternoons when I returned home, an Indian buck, with a long black braid down his back, would usually be walking down that street. I loved to walk behind him and watch his heavy braid, entwined with bright red ribbons, swing back and forth as he walked. I was never afraid of him. I knew he liked me because he would stop at the little store and buy me a long, twisted black licorice stick for a penny.

Once he did not have time to stop at the little store and, instead, gave me the penny. I did not buy a licorice stick, but took the penny home and hid it in the Bible, which was always on the lower shelf of the library table in the front room. I told no one about the penny. I was sure it would be safe there. When I went to get it, it was gone. No doubt Mother, who read her Bible every day, salvaged the penny, but I still remember the disappointment of that loss.

It was in Phoenix that I saw my first movies—*The Ten Commandments* and *A Christmas Carol*, both silent pictures. I would not see another movie until I was ten, when Vi Campbell took our fifth grade class to Burlington to see *Uncle Tom's Cabin*.

While we were in Phoenix, Dad worked as a carpenter. I often wonder how different life would have been, had we stayed in Phoenix.

When spring came, we packed our few belongings and headed home in the old Dodge Commercial. For some reason, Dad wanted to go via Lordsburg. The differential went out of the Dodge and we had to wait there a week while the garage sent for parts. It was a long week.

Grandma (Ella) Garrett, Grandpa holding Marvin, Helen behind him and Sarah beside Grandma • Grandma & Grandpa Garrett

To farm the vast expanses of the prairie, a tractor was an essential. Mother agreed to teach a year in order to save money to buy one. For that reason, she and I spent the next school year north of Flagler, where she taught the upper grades in a two-room school. Helen and Marvin stayed at home with Dad. Mother and I lived in a one-room basement "apartment" which had been fixed for the teacher. The other half of the basement housed the coal furnace and the winter's supply of coal.

During the summer, the school grounds had been used for raising a flock of chickens. The flock had been removed just prior to our arrival. One young rooster, however, had somehow fallen into the pit of the outdoor toilet marked GIRLS. He was frantically trying to escape the muck that threatened to engulf him and squawked loudly for help. In spite of all our efforts, the depth of the pit made it impossible for us to rescue him. That memory still makes me feel sad.

In the northeast corner of the school grounds was a small barn, where the children who rode horses tethered them during the day. I remember that barn especially, because I could have broken my neck, when I once jumped from the roof on a dare.

The basement "apartment" Mother and I lived in during that school year, is as clear in my mind as if I were in it yesterday. At the south end of the room, two beds, side-by-side with only a narrow aisle between, were concealed with a curtain, which slid back and forth on a wire at the ceiling. At the opposite end of the room, in the kitchen area, there was a small table, a stove, and a cupboard. As a little girl of seven, I loved to empty everything out of the cupboard drawers, clean them, and lay everything back in neatly. It was the first inkling, I suppose, that I would be a "neat-nick" housekeeper.

Mother bought dried cod fish in a wooden box and my favorite meal was baked potatoes with creamed codfish.

My teacher's name was Miss Ella Robb, a plump lady with a round face. She had grades one through four in the west room. Mother had grades five through eight in the east room. Mother got her hair "bobbed" during that school year. Only very daring women bobbed their hair at that time, and her father was sure she had one foot in Hell and the other on a banana peel.

One of my little playmates lived in a dugout—really a basement used as a place to live until the rest of the house could be completed. Often, the dugout ended up as the permanent home when money failed to materialize to build the rest of the house.

Northwest of the school was a fenced pasture, containing one of the largest prairie dog towns I've ever seen. Several thousand prairie dogs lived there. I often crawled through that fence and ran kitty-corner across the pasture to go to a little friend's house to play. We learned early to dodge the prairie dog holes, as to step into one was to break a leg. They are an ever-present danger to horses. I always hurried home before dusk, as burrowing owls share prairie dogs' homes and, at dusk, they stand stoically on the mounds, heads turning from side to side, making the scary, mournful sounds that owls make.

When the school year ended, and Mother and I were back home, Dad got his first tractor—a Hart Parr, a big awkward contraption that scared the animals half to death, but did cover the fields faster than a team of horses.

Dad loved the farm animals and developed a special relationship with most of them. He had a way of putting his two "pinkies" together, between his lips, and blowing a shrill, piercing whistle that would bring the horses to the barn, from the far side of the pasture.

Our surly boar, however, was never placated by kindness. Once, while Dad was feeding the hogs, this boar took after him at a gallop, with Dad running for the nearest fence. He got one leg over, but the boar tusked the other thigh, laying it open to the bone, a gash about eight inches long. Dad carried that scar the rest of his life.

Rural people had no electricity at this time in our history. Dad built a "refrigerator" on the north side of our sod house, in the shade. He dug a pit about four feet square and five feet deep, framed it above ground with a wooden collar, and fitted it with a hinged lid. In the bottom he put sand to a depth of two feet. Each morning we poured two buckets of cold water on the sand. This made a "cooler" for keeping perishable foods, such as milk, butter, eggs, and meat. It served us well all my growing up years. I was an agile youngster and it usually fell my lot to jump down in the "cooler" to get out and put away the foods.

The flat wooden lid also served as a cool, shady spot to place the churn when we churned butter. Our crockery churn held three gallons of cream. The churn lid had a hole for the dasher handle, and the bottom of the dasher was the shape of a cross. After a half-hour to forty-five minutes of constant churning, yellow butter particles began to separate from the buttermilk. With a small, wooden butter paddle, we collected the butter particles and lifted them out into a large bowl. We then "worked" the butter with cold water again and again, to get all the buttermilk out. When that step was finished, the butter was lightly salted, placed in molds, or small crocks, and put in the "cooler". Mother used lots of butter in food preparation, so churning was a weekly task at our house.

Mother made an especially good chocolate cake. As soon as she took a cake from the oven, she'd cut a square piece from one corner, spread the warm cake with lots of butter and eat it. I never saw anyone else do that.

In the days before rural electrification, we used coal oil lamps. They smoked profusely, gave off a very poor light, and the glass chimneys were easily broken. Once, when I was about seven or eight, I spent an overnight with a little friend, Frances Church. We were playing with a ball and I bounced it into the lamp, breaking the chimney. The next day Mrs. Church came to our home and collected twenty five cents to pay for the damage. As a child I received, and no doubt deserved, frequent punishment.

Doing the family laundry in those days was a major undertaking. First the water had to be pumped, then carried in buckets and poured into the copper-bottomed boiler, which covered two "holes" on the coal stove. Of course, laundry day used a lot of fuel, as the stove had to be kept burning for hours at a time. In the winter we appreciated the heat, but in summer the constant heat, in the confines of the small room, was unbearable.

We grated bars of Fels Naptha or homemade lye soap into a pan, added water, and heated it to dissolve the soap before pouring it into the boiler. Detergents, of course, did not exist at that time. When the sudsy water was hot, it was poured into a round metal tub. We washed out in the yard on nice days, but winter laundry had to be done in the kitchen. Clothes were scrubbed on the washboard, with special care being given to collars and cuffs, knees of pants, and sock feet. Dirtiest clothes were often put to soak in the hot sudsy water in the boiler. When the clothing, or bedding, or towels, had been scrubbed sufficiently, they were run through the wringer. The wringer was a hand-cranked contraption, which was screwed to the rim of the round metal washtub. Two revolving rubber rollers squeezed the water from the clothes as the crank was turned. However, if something was too thick to go through the rollers, a spring would snap open, leaving the rollers unable to turn. Then you had to pull the offending piece back out, re-set the rollers, and start again. If several tubs of clothes were being washed, hot water was added to the tub from the boiler, again and again during the process, to keep the water hot enough, and soapy enough to clean well. When the washing part was done, the clothes went through the wringer into another tub, which was filled with fresh water to rinse the clothes. The rinse water did not have to be hot, but warm water rinsed more soap out than cold water did, so usually the first rinse, at least, was done with warm water. After two rinses, liquid "bluing" was added to the final rinse water to help whiten the clothes. After the last rinse, with the clothes wrung as dry as possible, they were ready for the clothesline.

Clotheslines were a permanent fixture in the yard. On the west side of our house, Dad had set two posts in cement, perhaps sixty feet apart, with braced two-by-fours at the top. Four strong, smooth wires were strung between the posts. These wires had to be cleaned off with a wet cloth each time before hanging clothes on them. Even then, they sometimes left a mark on the clothes. We kept all the clothespins—Mother liked the "pinch" kind—in a large colorful bag on a hanger, which we hooked over one of the lines. We took great pride in hanging out a nice-looking wash. Sheets, for example, were folded in half and the hems kept straight as they were pinned with at least four pins to keep them from sagging. Towel edges were stretched straight, then hung by three pins.

The weight of the wet clothes would, on occasion, cause a line to break, letting the wet clothes touch the ground. This was a tragedy, as when that happened, the wash had to be done over.

I mentioned earlier, the constant wind in eastern Colorado. If you have ever tried to hang out wet clothes in such a wind, with towel corners or long-john legs hitting you in the face, you know it is not a pleasant experience. And during the dust storms in the 1930s, many times big clouds of dust rolled in just when a fresh wash had been pinned to the lines.

I remember hearing Isaphene Dunlap Lesher tell about an experience she had during the dust bowl era when Ila, her daughter, was a little tot. She set her on a blanket on the ground while she hung freshly washed clothes on the line. Just as she finished, she saw a huge dust cloud rolling in from the west. Quickly, she jerked the pins out, stuffed the wet clothes back into the basket, and hurried inside with them, so that the wash would not have to be re-done. When she dashed out to retrieve Ila, she could hardly locate her, as the cloud of choking dust had simply enveloped her and blocked her from sight.

In winter, the clothes would freeze stiff, almost before you could get them pinned to the line. Fingers could freeze just as fast. Then, the stiffly frozen clothes had to be carefully removed from the line and hung indoors around the stove in order to get them dry enough to iron. My elderly friend, Dr. Harm Harms, one of five brothers raised in Nebraska during this era in our country's history, tells that they would bring in their frozen long-johns, stand them up against the wall, around their kitchen stove, and then bet on which set of long-johns would "fold" first!

Ironing was done with "flat irons", which were heated on the coal stove. There was always danger that a black smudge of soot, or stove blackening used for polishing the stove, would be

transferred from the stove to a white shirt collar. Mother kept three irons in service all the time—two on the stove heating while the third was in use. The handle, which clamped into the top of the flat irons, was used interchangeably.

In most households, Monday was washday and Tuesday was ironing day. In each case, those tasks were all-day jobs. Wash and wear fabrics were unheard of at that time, so everything had to be ironed, including sheets and pillowcases.

The round galvanized metal washtubs also served as bathtubs. Water for baths was heated in the same way as for the laundry. Each of us took our turn, throwing out our bath water, wiping the tub clean for the next user. Saturday night was bath night and shoe polishing night in most rural homes, as families prepared to look their best for church on Sunday.

During my early childhood, our mail was delivered only once a week and we had to drive nearly two miles east of our house to get it. Helen drove old Nellie hitched to our buggy. I always begged to go along in spite of being afraid. Before we got to the road where our mailbox was, we had to pass an area where a steam engine had exploded and left huge pieces of the wreckage lying on the open prairie. I was terrified of those big pieces of gray metal and covered my eyes as we passed. Sometimes I peeked out between two fingers, always fearful that something was going to jump from behind those huge relics and "get us".

Sarah standing behind Dr. Harms on his 100th birthday.

The road was a graded dirt road with many ups-and-downs for the buggy, and each "dip" gave me that sinking feeling in the pit of my stomach. I always asked Helen to go slow over those "edie-down paces." What I was trying to say was "easy-down places", but I could not talk plainly. One day Mother said to a visitor, "Sally can't say one word plain." I quickly retorted, "I tan, too. I tan say mud pane." I heard that related many times through the years.

I remember distinctly the day we got our first radio—an old Atwater Kent, a hand-me-down from Uncle Harry Crawford. Dad brought the battery in from the car and set both battery and radio in the southwest corner of the kitchen, behind the round oak table, on a set of bookshelves he'd made. Tommy Davis, who owned the garage in Bethune, was there for some reason and he helped Dad get the radio hooked up. I was drying my hands on the roller-towel (the roller was mounted on the back of our kitchen door) when the first sound came over the radio. I can still feel the "thrill" in the pit of my stomach, the kind you get when you make a sudden drop on the Ferris Wheel, when that first radio voice came into our kitchen.

The radio could be used only when the car did not need the battery, but it was a wonderful addition to our home. Many a night I hurried through my milking in order to rush in and listen to The Lonesome Cowboy or The Renfro Valley Barn Dance. And evenings with Fibber McGee and Molly, or Amos and Andy, are still fun to remember. Every time I hear the song "You Light Up My Life", I think of that radio. It brought some of the outside world to us and truly lit up our lives.

Bill Yearson owned the first grocery store in Bethune. During my growing up years, it was a typical general store, with shelves lining the walls from floor to ceiling and a pot-bellied stove at the back where the town's men gathered in the evening. Bill used a ladder on rollers and long-handled tongs to reach the items on the upper shelves, as customers asked for them.

We very seldom got to go to town, especially at night. But one night, when I was perhaps four or five, I was in Yearson's grocery with Dad. At the front of the store was a bushel basket filled with beautiful Red Delicious apples, piled high and nearly running over. Apples were, and still are, my favorite fruit. Probably, at that time, the whole basket could have been bought for $1.00. I'm sure Dad would have "treated" me to an apple if I'd asked for one, as it would have cost no more than a penny.

I was wearing a gray plush coat, a hand-me-down from one of Mother's Denver friends. The coat was too large for me and had big patch pockets. While Dad and Mr. Yearson were busy at the back of the store, I put a shiny red apply in my pocket.

I intended to eat it during the fourteen mile ride home. I sat in the back seat, not up in front with Dad, in order to do so unobserved. However, on the way home, the enormity of what I had done overwhelmed me. I had stolen something. I was a thief. I was afraid of being found out and punished. Carefully, I unbuttoned the side curtains of our touring car and threw the apple away, without ever taking a bite. No one ever knew I stole that apple—neither Dad nor Mr. Yearson. But I knew. And nearly eighty years later, I have not forgotten.

I will always believe that the Good Lord allowed me that experience, so that I could "pass it on" during my years as a first grade teacher. Most little children take things that don't belong to them, at one time or another. When children in my classroom took something that didn't belong to them, I would hold them on my lap and quietly tell them my story. No other punishment was ever needed, as tears of regret always flowed easily.

The year I was a third grader stands out in my memory as a very special year. Helen and I attended the Midway School, one mile east and two miles north of our home. This true story, which I wrote and was published by *Colorado Homes & Lifestyles Magazine*, tells of one memorable incident that occurred that year:

First Blizzard

The 1927 day dawned clear and icy cold. Snow blanketed the Eastern Colorado prairie a foot deep. As usual, the sun shone brilliantly, offering no warning of the perilous day ahead.

I was one of twenty-eight students—ranch children all—who attended Midway School in Kit Carson County. Midway was little different from dozens of other one-room country schools, which dotted the western plains. Thirty yards behind the main building stood the coal house, flanked on either side by toilets, one marked GIRLS, the other BOYS. In the schoolyard were a merry-go-round, two teeter totters, and a swing set. For most of the year, we had a huge ring for playing Fox-and-Geese—the hub, spokes, and rim growing constantly wider and deeper as winter progressed.

Midway had acquired a reputation as a hard-to-teach school, mostly because it was made up of grades one through eight, with pupils ranging in age from six to sixteen.

When Miss Nielson, the new teacher, arrived, many ranchers were quick to voice doubts about her ability to handle boys like Verlin and Raymond—tall as men, experienced ranch hands, and tough as leather. She was just out of normal school and hardly more than a girl herself. Besides, she was very pretty. Her hair was a brown cascade, curling over her shoulders. Her eyes were keen and blue and looked out at us with a warm smile. Against the drabness of the prairie, Miss Nielson was beautiful.

"Which of you big boys would like to carry the water for us this morning?" she would ask, looking pleasantly at Verlin and Raymond, or "Which of you big boys would like to bring in another bucket of coal?" Suddenly the trip to the Perkins' well, a quarter-mile down the road, or to the coal house out back, were no longer dreaded chores. We were quick to respond to her kindness. Miss Nielson was more than our teacher; she was also our friend.

When the school bell rang this particular winter morning, we trooped in from the playground, snow-blind at first, stomping snow from our boots. We hung our coats, caps, and scarves on the hooks in the entrance hall. We stretched our mittens and put them under the stove to dry. The school day had begun.

We did not know, in those days, about "progressive groupings", "work areas", and "special education". But, now that I look back on it, I know they were all there in Miss Nielson's well-organized routine. The little ones recited to her. The older ones worked together. The more advanced helped those who needed help. We were warm, busy, and happy.

I suppose that is why we did not notice at once that the wind had changed. Suddenly, a shadow filled our room. We rushed from our seats to the west wall and the high west windows. The sky had turned a frightening gray. A strong northwest wind was bearing down fiercely across the prairie. The rising wind whipped fine grains of snow against the panes. It sifted through the cracks between the sashes and the ill-fitting frames.

"Let's all go back to our seats," Miss Nielson directed calmly. "Verlin and Raymond and I are going to bring in some extra fuel. Get your wraps on quickly, boys, please. No one else is to leave the room." Her voice was firm. Quickly she snatched a light rope from the box behind the curtains on the stage.

Verlin pushed the door open against the force of the wind. Miss Nielson tied the rope end securely to the outside door knob, then the three of them disappeared into the swirling, stinging snow, holding their collars up to protect their faces. The other end of the rope was tightly clutched in Miss Nielson's hand. The room seemed desperately empty after the wind slammed the door shut behind them.

Finally, they were back, carrying two buckets of coal between them as they clung to the rope for guidance. We knew that they could not go out again. What had been a sunny winter day only hours before, was now a roaring, savage, biting storm.

"Blizzard," Verlin said when he had caught his breath. He did not need to say it. We all knew. We had seen blizzards before and the very word struck terror. It meant freezing cold, hard biting wind, piercing snow driven into every crevice. It meant frostbitten flesh and dead livestock and impassable roads. It meant hardship and loss for every rancher in the area.

"How will we get home?" one of the little ones asked. It was a question on all our minds.

"We will not get home this afternoon," Miss Nielson answered brightly, quelling our fears. "I'm sure none of us want to leave the warmth and safety here and go out into this blinding storm."

The pot-bellied stove in the center of the room glowed red, but the room grew increasingly chilly. Miss Nielson turned the damper off and closed both drafts. "This scant fuel must last," she said softly. For how long, we did not know.

"Each of you save some of your lunch for tonight," she cautioned.

We ciphered. We chose up sides and had a spelling bee. We played a states-and-capitals game. We sang. Miss Nielson played the piano and I guess we sang every song in "The Golden Book of Favorite Songs." We sang rounds—the boys singing "Old Solomon Levi" while the girls sang "A Spanish Cavalier." The hours passed.

Finally, Miss Nielson stood before us quietly. I do not remember that she was either embarrassed or shy. She said forthrightly, "I am sure many of you need to use the toilets. It is impossible for us to get out to them, so we will have to do the next best thing. Will you boys please stay at the far end of the room?" She paused a moment. "Thank you, boys. Now, girls, come up on the stage with me, please." Then she closed the flimsy stage curtains. Behind the piano she set an empty bucket. She played loudly and we all sang loudly as each girl took her turn. When we finished, Miss Nielson ushered us off the stage and directed the boys to follow a similar procedure, without piano accompaniment. I do not remember that there were any snickers or snide remarks. We each felt that we had helped a friend meet an emergency in a manner satisfactory to us all.

The blizzard continued with increased ferocity. Night fell early. We lit the Coleman lanterns. The fire burned low. Only one lump of coal was laid on the firebox at a time and we hovered around the stove like chicks around a brooder. We ate what lunch we had saved. We were still hungry.

The wind howled. We told stories in the flickering light of the lanterns—old stories, made-up stories, blizzard stories, ghost stories. Then we heard a sound outside, a sound other than the driving wind and pelting snow.

The door opened slowly and Mr. Snelling was literally blown inside by the force of the wind. He carried a heavy milk bucket. Miss Nielson rushed to him. He set the bucket, piled high with snow, on the floor. She took the gloved hand he held out to her and carefully pulled the frozen, ragged, bloody glove from his hand. Neither of them spoke. We children stood without a word and watched as Miss Nielson got water and washed the frozen blood from the jagged, torn palm.

"Barbs," Mr. Snelling said finally. We knew what he meant. The Snelling ranch lay one mile south of Midway School. The section of land between was fenced with four strands of barbed wire. Carrying the bucket in his left hand, he had held to the barbed wire with his right hand and had guided himself to us through the blinding storm. "Took nearly two hours, that mile," Mr. Snelling said, still breathing heavily, as he glanced at the big wall clock.

The snow on top of the bucket melted in the warmth of the room and then we saw the purpose of his coming. The bucket was full of hard-cooked eggs. Mr. Snelling had risked his life to bring us food.

I do not remember how long our benefactor remained with us. I do remember that we hated to see him start out again into the night. The wind would be to his back going home. He would hold to the fence with his left hand and would have no heavy bucket to carry. He would make it. "Drifts are up to the eaves on the west, ma'am," Mr. Snelling said, as he left. "By morning we'll have to shovel you out. But don't you worry, ma'am."

I don't believe Miss Nielson worried. At least she did not let us see that she did. "Will you bigger folks help arrange the benches so that we can get the little ones bedded down for the night, please?" she asked after we had eaten the eggs. The older ones got their coats and spread them over the smaller ones. The talk grew quiet. The howling wind forced its way through every crack and crevice and the room grew increasingly colder. We sat huddled close to the stove and to each other. Someone laid another small lump on the coals. Some slept well, some fitfully, some slightly, and some, like Miss Nielson, not at all. She walked among the sleeping children, covering feet, adjusting an arm, tucking a collar up around a shoulder, making each a bit more comfortable on the hard benches.

Morning came. Drifts covered our windows. We could not see outside, but we knew the wind had died. The coal was gone. The stove felt warm to the touch, but it gave off no heat. The room was cold. One by one the children wakened. Backs and necks were stiff. Throats were sore. All were hungry.

We tried to open the door. Mr. Snelling had been right. We were snowed in.

Miss Nielson again took calm command. "Let's tidy up the room," she said. "Someone will be coming soon and we will want to be ready." She tried to start some singing as we pushed back the benches and arranged the desks in ordered rows. But somehow things were different. What had been adventure last night was reduced to cold, uncomfortable reality this morning. We went through the toilet routine. We put on our wraps. We clapped our hands and stomped our feet to delay the cold that waited to grip us. And then we heard it—the wonderfully welcome sound that someone was outside. Someone was shoveling the drifted snow. After what seemed like a long, long time, we heard the shovel strike the door. More shoveling. More scraping. Finally the door was forced open and we were released from our cold, dank tomb. We rushed, shouting, into the bright Colorado sunshine.

Leaning on his shovel and squinting into the dazzling brightness of the sun reflected on this white, white world, was Bill Keever. The Keever ranch lay one mile west of Midway School. Mr Keever opened up a gunnysack he had set down on the snow—a gunnysack full of shiny red apples.

I'll never forget those apples—juicy, red, cold apples. We ate. We laughed. We talked all at once. The drifted snow made the flat prairie resemble rolling hill country. We ran over the fences, over the merry-go-round, over the stile as if it were all level ground. We slid down eight-foot drifts. We made a new fox-and-geese ring. The storm was over. The earth, stretching as far as the eye could see, was clean and new and beautiful, sparkling like a million diamonds in the bright sunshine. The thermometer registered zero, but the sun was warm. And we were safe.

Our bus driver came across the prairie, not in a big yellow bus, but behind a team of plodding horses hitched to a big farm sled. During the day, amid much rollicking laughter, we were all delivered to our homes.

I stood beside the driver as he slowed the team in front of the ranch home where Miss Nielson boarded. "I hope you know how we all feel," the driver said, as he helped Miss Nielson down from the sled. "I speak for all the ranchers when I say we think you're the best teacher Midway School ever had. We sure appreciate the way you took care of our children during the blizzard."

"Thank you," Miss Nielson replied, as she smiled down at me. For the first time I noticed how very tired she looked. "It was really the children who took care of me. You see, this is my first blizzard."

It was not to be her last. Before another school term began, Miss Nielson married a local rancher and became a permanent resident of our community. Their home, through the years, was the neighborhood gathering place. Even today, on long winter evenings, when snow blankets the Eastern Colorado plains a foot deep, ranchers like to get together and reminisce of long ago. During any such evening, the talk is sure to turn to the Big Blizzard. And someone is bound to ask, with a wry smile, "I wonder, do they still bring apples to the teacher?"

This article I had published by the *Cincinnati Enquirer*, also concerns that year:

The One Room Country School
Recently I visited one of today's ultra-modern schools. Students assembled "in the round," researched class projects in a quiet, carpeted library surrounded by walls of shelving stocked with seemingly endless sets of the latest reference materials,

and created graphics for their school's year book on a color monitor computer. At noon, we ate an attractive lunch served from a sleek, stainless steel cafeteria.

I could not but wonder if today's students have any concept of the one-room country schools that served America for more than a century and played a significant role in developing the firm foundation upon which this nation stands—schools that many of their ancestors attended.

As I look back on the years I spent in one such school, in eastern Colorado during the mid-1920s, I'm amazed at the education for living that was taught (and caught) there.

The one-room school wore many hats. Its main purpose, of course, was to serve as a place to educate the children of the early settlers, but it was much more than that. The Literary Society, school and community programs, box socials, pie suppers, square dances, and last-day-of-school picnics held there made it the center of community activity.

Our teacher, Miss Nielson, like many teachers at that time, had only "normal school" training. However, she loved children and loved teaching them. Otherwise she would never have subjected herself to the isolation, the hardships, and the responsibilities of the one-room school. Teachers, in that era, were expected to serve as janitor, playground supervisor, and hold many other "titles", for meager remuneration. Usually, they roomed and boarded with some family in the community, sharing a bed with one of the children or, sometimes, with a grandmother.

Our school, called Midway, consisted of one large room with a cloak- room at the entrance, where we hung our wraps and lined our overshoes against the walls in winter. A slate chalkboard covered the north and east walls of the room. Six tall windows, side by side on the west wall, made the room light and airy. At the front of the room a small stage, elevated about a foot above floor level, provided a space for privacy; faded curtains hung from a tightly stretched wire and could be drawn when necessary. Shelving on either side, at the back of the stage, housed a small assortment of well-used library books.

The teacher's desk and a long "recitation bench" stood on one side of the stage. An upright piano, its ivory keyboard yellowed with age, on the other. In the middle of the room towered a pot-bellied stove, centered on a large square of heavy metal to protect the oiled floorboards from sparks. Rows of desks, each desk accommodating two students, ran from front to back, with the larger desks at the back.

Just inside the door, a waist-high wooden bench held a galvanized water bucket, filled each morning at the Perkins' well, a quarter-mile down the road. All of us, in grades one through eight, drank from the same tin dipper and washed with cold water in the chipped enamel basin before we ate our lunches.

Above the chalkboard on the front wall, a large Seth Thomas clock faithfully proclaimed the time of day. On either side of the clock, handsome prints of Rosa Bonheur's "The Horse Fair" and Winslow Homer's "The Fog Warning" provided a quiet haven for a sensitive soul. Attached to the chalkboard molding, a set of roll-down maps—one of Colorado's sixty-three counties, one of the United States, one of each hemisphere, and one of the world—opened grand vistas for us.

On the east wall, just above the slate, a Palmer Method alphabet, approximately a foot high, challenged us daily to learn to write both capitals and lower case letters perfectly.

Out back, a small "coal house", flanked on either side by toilets—one marked GIRLS and the other BOYS—held a winter's supply of fuel. On the east side of the school building, a large play area witnessed intense rivalries before school, at noon, and recesses, as regularly chosen teams competed in games such as Dare Base, Last Couple Out, Two Deep, and Steal Sticks. In winter, we tramped a huge wheel—rim, spokes, and hub—into the snow for our favorite game, Fox and Geese. Our playground also boasted a swing set, teeter-totters, and a merry-go-round.

The students who attended Midway School ranged in age from six to sixteen. We came from isolated ranch homes which had none of the modern conveniences we take for granted today—no phones, no electricity, no indoor plumbing. School was a drop of water in our desert.

Miss Nielson grounded us firmly in the basics. Our day began with the Pledge of Allegiance to the flag of the United States of America. Each youngster proudly stood at attention, with right hand over heart. We then sang the "Star Spangled Banner," which, in March of 1931, became our national anthem. We not only sang it, we learned all the verses, and how to write them, with punctuation and spelling correct.

Background noise in the one-room school was a geography lesson about the giant pyramids in Egypt, the explanation of a problem in long division, or how to diagram a simple sentence, showing the subject, predicate, and object. Slower learners profited from the repetition. Quick learners absorbed material far beyond their years. "I can write the Roman Numerals to one hundred," I bragged to my parents one day, when I was eight. They doubted I could do it. I could. I had absorbed an older group's lesson.

We learned to be participators. Spelling bees, ciphering matches, states-and-capitals contests, and debates—we considered them games. "How can Carl be learning so much?" his mother asked Miss Nielson. "He says all you do is play games." It was true. Without realizing we were studying, we acquired arithmetic skills, knowledge of geography, and a good understanding of the fine contributions made by such men as Thomas Jefferson and John Adams in the formative years of our Republic.

On the playground, we always chose teams before playing games. We learned early that each individual was important to the team and was expected to be a contributor. Every youngster was included. School sports were not reserved for a few gifted athletes with the rest being merely spectators. We played outdoors, vigorously, in all kinds of weather. On warm days we ran barefooted. In winter we ran in four-buckle "Arctics" through the snowdrifts. Playing fair, taking turns, learning to be good losers as well as winners, all were part of our school day.

We learned to work under a code of honor. With twenty-eight students and a wide range of grade levels, self-discipline was necessary, and it was expected and nurtured. Miss Nielson well knew the old saw, "A pat on the back is worth two on the rump." She complimented us often. Her motto was, "Anything that is worth doing at all is worth doing well." She made us feel proud to be dependable enough to work on our own, quietly, neatly, and to the best of our ability. "You know what is right to do. You don't need Miss Nielson to tell you". I can hear her yet.

We learned respect for authority. In that day, parents held teachers in high esteem, therefore, children did, too. In fact, any youngster getting into trouble at school feared most the punishment at home when the parents heard of it. We were taught that team captains, cloakroom monitors, and playground supervisors were representatives of the teacher, and therefore, were to be treated with the same respect as the teacher.

Our appetites were whetted for the fine arts. Miss Nielson had a portfolio of large sepia prints of many of the Old Masters—Rembrandt, Monet, Millet, Bonheur, Van Gogh. Each Friday afternoon we gathered around her in a circle, the smaller children sitting cross-legged on the floor, and studied the life of one of the artists and one of his paintings. For three cents, as I remember it, we could purchase a wallet-size print with a brief of the artist's life on the back. That small "art gallery" was a prized possession for many years and enriches my life even today.

Miss Nielson trained us in the performing arts. Everyday classroom activity included oral reading. We learned to read clearly, accurately, and expressively. We memorized poetry, everything from "A Leak in the Dike" to "Evangeline." We learned to recite before our peers without experiencing stage fright. On Halloween, Thanksgiving, Christmas, and the last day of school, we put on programs for the entire community. We practiced songs, recitations, and dramatic skits for weeks under the patient coaching of our teacher. Every youngster participated and every parent came to enjoy and applaud.

The one-room school also gave us social training. Hiring a "sitter" was unheard of in that day. Children accompanied their parents to all events and were expected to behave. Families set standards for their children and trained them from infancy to meet those standards. The community was an extension of the family—each family felt an acute responsibility for its own members, yet felt an almost equal responsibility for the whole. To have needed a policeman to patrol a community school would have been the ultimate shame.

Today, ever-increasing tax levies provide school environments undreamed of a century ago. Teachers are highly trained, many with Master's degrees from our finest universities. Yet, we read of consistently falling test scores, frightening examples of discipline problems, and "graduates" whose basic skills are so mediocre that they fail to meet the requirements of our nation's work force.

"You can take the girl out of the country, but you can't take the country out of the girl," goes an old saying. I believe it, and thank God for that truth. The many practical lessons learned in a one-room school in eastern Colorado have been the springboard for many successes in the life of this country girl.

Our parents' best friends were Bill and Letha Keever. They lived two miles north of us and the two families were often together. Minta was between Helen and me in age; Loren was just older than Marvin. The Keever's house was a very small, two-room frame house, yet Letha always made us kids feel welcome.

We had to crawl across two beds to get from one side of their bedroom to the other, but we loved to play hide-and-seek in that room. On one side of the room was a closet; on the other, Letha had a tall "banana" basket, which she used as a dirty clothes hamper. Both made wonderful hiding places. I marvel, today, at her patience with us.

Letha was an excellent baker and it was always a real treat to get to her house when she was taking a pan of beautifully browned loaves of bread out of the oven. I can smell that sweet aroma yet. She would break off the crusts (cutting mashes fresh-baked loaves), spread them with her delicious tomato butter and give them to us to eat—food for the gods!

Letha was a very neat housekeeper. Her cast iron skillets hung on nails pounded into the two-by-fours behind her kitchen stove. Once, I saw her lift a skillet off its nail only to find a young rattlesnake curled up in it. It had found a warm place to hibernate.

The Keever's and the Mitchell's shared so many birthdays, Thanksgivings, and Christmases, as well as scores of ordinary days, that we were crushed when we learned that they were moving to Kansas. It was an especially sad time for Mother. Letha was like a sister to her. Mother would never again have such a dear friend.

Another sadness gripped us during that summer. Our beloved teacher, Thelma Nielson, married a young man named Armstrong, and while on their honeymoon in Kansas, he drowned in an unfortunate swimming accident.

Thelma's replacement, as Midway's teacher, was Susie Bogart, young and inexperienced. The only memory I retain of my fourth grade is being wrongly accused of throwing an apple core on the playground during lunch. I did not have an apple in my lunch that day, yet Miss Bogart had received this report from a student "playground monitor", and rules were rules. She insisted that I stand in front of all the students and admit my guilt and apologize. I stood in front of the room, head down, twirling the sash on my dress with nervous hands, but I would not speak. The longer I stood, disobeying, the more severe the punishment became— one recess detention, then two, then three. Finally, when the detention had grown to two full weeks, I was allowed to return to my seat, without ever having said a word. I served my "time" and to this day have strong feelings for the accused. What if he, or she, is not guilty?

In winter, I had to wear long-legged, drop-seat underwear to Midway. If you have never worn long underwear, you have no idea how impossible it was to pull the legs tight enough to avoid having a big bulge in the back of your stockings, just above your high-top shoes. The heavy ribbed black cotton stockings we had to wear were bad enough, but the long underwear was an unbearable embarrassment.

Before the school bell rang to begin each day, Inez Perkins and I ran to the outdoor toilet and rearranged the way our mothers had dressed us for the day. We'd pull down our black stockings (which were held up by tight round garters just above the knees), pull up the legs of our long underwear, and roll them neatly under our bloomers. Then we'd pull the black stocking up, roll the garters into them just above our knees, and not have those ugly bulges in the backs of our stockings. We were not as warm, but we thought we were a lot more stylish.

The year I was in the fourth grade, we had to drill a new well at home. On the way to school one morning, Dad stopped at a neighbor's well and filled a ten-gallon milk can with water for our use. He hoisted the can to the back of the truck, where I was riding. When we reached school, I hurriedly jumped from the back of the truck, and pulled the can of water off the truck with my coattail. It landed on my back.

I have mentioned before that our parents were not people who ran to the doctor. Dr. Remington, the only doctor in the entire area, was 25 miles away. Usually Dad "doctored" us with the liniments he used on the animals. Cuts were soaked in blue vitriol, or turpentine. I have no memory of ever going to a doctor as a youngster.

Years later, when I was newly pregnant with Rock, Dr. Brehm, Columbus, Ohio was giving me a thorough physical exam. First, he asked me a good many basic health questions. Then he took measurements and did an X-ray. "Why didn't you tell me you'd had a broken vertebrae, or at least a cracked vertebrae, in your back?" he asked, after viewing the X-ray. It was news to me, but it undoubtedly happened when I pulled that ten-gallon can of water down on me from the back of the truck.

When the well drilling was finished, several extra lengths of pipe needed to be returned to Stratton. Dad was a very strong man, with large heavy-muscled shoulders and neck. He squatted down, lifted the heavy pipes across his shoulders, behind his neck, with both arms raised over them to hold them steady, and started walking toward the truck.

Marvin, a little tyke, had been "fixing" a small wagon and had taken off its wire wheels. Dad tripped over the almost invisible wheels and fell with a thud, his face hitting a piece of well casing. All the weight of the pipes came down hard on the back of his neck. Most men would have suffered a broken neck from such an accident. It is a miracle that he did not.

His nose was broken and his face swelled immediately so that he was unrecognizable. Later that afternoon, after his nose stopped bleeding, and he somewhat recovered from the shock of the accident, he made the trip to Stratton to return the pipes. I went with him. Due to his mangled face, neighbors passed him on the street without recognizing him. Not until they saw me, did they realize who he was.

One of my early childhood memories is of mother becoming so sick while working in the garden that she lay down between the rows and vomited over and over into the ground cherries. She was a victim of migraine headaches. Doctors know very little, even today, about what causes migraines. They do know they tend to run in families. That same ailment would plague me for nearly fifty years.

Our land lay on the border of two school districts—Midway and First Central. Before another school year began, Dad got permission from the county to transfer to the First Central District, which boasted a four-room, and eventually a five-room school, with many more advantages, including a high school.

My fifth grade teacher was Violet Campbell. Of all my teachers, only two stand out in my memory as real influences in my life—Thelma and Vi. I am pleased that the Blizzard Story was published while Thelma was still alive and able to enjoy it. I have seen Vi several times in recent years and she is just a dear as ever.

I had my first "boyfriend" during the year I was a fifth grader. I was ten years old. (I always had a boyfriend and Mother told me a thousand times that I was "boy crazy".) The Taylor's lived just west of the school and had a family of five boys—Eugene, Wesley, Vaughn, Vance, and Shelby, and one little girl, Darlene. Vaughn, who we called "Soupy", was in my class. He was a bright student and often he and I were chosen to be "team captains" for ciphering contests or spelling bees.

The Taylor's went to Stratton every Saturday night and on Monday morning, without fail, Soupy had a candy treat for me. He always put it in my desk, "on the sly", sometime before the school day started. I grew to expect it.

One night, after a meeting at school, I went to get my coat from the cloakroom. A big bull snake had crawled in from the cold and was comfortably stretched out on the cloakroom floor. When you grow up with rattlesnakes, you do not fear a harmless bull snake. I picked it up by the tail, took it to the main door, and flung it out into the dark. I did not realize that Soupy and some other boys were standing out by the flagpole. That bull snake wrapped right

around Soupy's neck. I got no more candy for a long time.

In the spring of that year, Vi arranged to take our whole class-room, grades four, five and six, to Burlington to see the movie, *Uncle Tom's Cabin*. Mother said that I could not go. I was absolutely crushed as we had few such occasions to look forward to. I have no memory of why she changed her mind, but, eventually, she consented to let me go with the understanding that Helen would go along to "see that I behaved."

Helen, bless her, was one of those naturally good girls who never had to be punished for anything in her entire life. She always knew what was the right thing to do and did it. She was an excellent student, very dependable, and never caused our parents one moment of worry. I was definitely "cut from a different bolt of cloth" and that fact was difficult for Mother to deal with.

For Helen to be put in such a position was certainly unfair to her. I am happy to say that as adults, she and I are very compatible and love each other dearly.

The big day for going to the movie finally arrived. In honor of such a special occasion, most of the boys came to school in a clean pair of overalls. Jimmy Hodge came dressed in gray wool pants, a white shirt with the starched collar turned up at the back, and a pair of new shoes. I dropped Soupy like a hot potato. Jimmy and I sat together during the thirty-mile ride

to Burlington, and he sat with his arm around me during the movie. Helen, the appointed guardian, was seated a row or two behind us and gave the expected report when we got home. The tongue-lashing I got from Mother never dimmed the joy of that day.

During my early school years, I became an avid reader.

First Central School • First Central Students. Sarah is 2nd from left in the 2nd row. Vi and Thelma at back.

We were twenty-five miles from the small library in Burlington, and the number of books in any classroom at school was minimal. Still, much of my childhood was spent reading, as Mother had collections of classics, most of them far beyond my immature understanding. I read them anyway, everything from Ben Hur to Mother India. If it had not been for books, I'm sure I would have died of loneliness. Books were my friends. They were also my teacher. This article, which I wrote was published in the *Cincinnati Enquirer*, and says a great deal about what books have meant to me:

Books Are Passports

Do you long to travel, yet feel you cannot afford such luxury? Do you desire romance, but currently lack any intimate relationship? Do you crave adventure, yet find yourself bogged down with the mundane tasks of everyday, both at home and at work? Why not experience these pleasures vicariously, through the treasures that await you in great abundance on the shelves of any public library?

I consider myself fortunate to have grown up in an era when radios were a rarity and TV did not exist. My entertainment came, of necessity, from the printed page. I've had a life-long love affair with books.

At seven I became friends with Lucy Fitch Perkins' "Twins", beginning with *The Little Dutch Twins*, which I practically memorized before I learned that "to read a book" did not mean it had to be read all at one sitting! I visited *The Japanese Twins*, *The Eskimo Twins*, *The Mexican Twins*, and many more of the 25 "Twins" series, all wonderfully well-written and beautifully illustrated.

I devoured the Thornton Burgess books, feasting upon the lore of field and forest as described so intimately in *Jimmy Skunk*, *Reddy Fox*, and Burgess' many other books. I was fascinated by Dr. Doolittle and his ability to talk to the animals.

Through the years, Rudyard Kipling's *The Jungle Book*, and his *Just So Stories* delighted me over and over—how the leopard got his spots, and how the elephant got his trunk down by the great, gray, green, greasy Limpopo River all set about with fever trees. Albert Payson Terhune's *Lad: A Dog*, and *Silver Chief, Dog of the North* provided thrilling adventures for me as a youngster. And I was touched by the pastor's children and their sensitive care of *Beautiful Joe*.

During my growing-up years, I loved *The Keeper of the Bees*, *The Secret Garden*, and *Lorna Doone*. I wept each time I read Helen Hunt Jackson's sad story of ill-fated love as told in *Ramona*. Books such as *So Big*, *Mother India*, *Ben Hur*, *Quo Vadis*, *Magnificent Obsession*, *The Silver Chalice* all provided memorable experiences during my teens. During one hot Colorado summer, I read Peter Freuchen's *Arctic Adventure* and its realism had me shivering and goose-pimply in the grip of Greenland's icy cold. *The Rivers Run East* provided me a seat, front and center, on a most exciting journey down the Amazon, starting at Iquitos in Peru, and ending on the Atlantic shore.

Of the literally thousands of books I have read—from Zane Grey to Pearl S. Buck to James Michener— the late Irving Stone's biographical-historical novels stand at the head of the class. They are painstakingly researched and through them I have had the privilege of knowing intimately men and women, who lived in centuries gone by, yet contributed greatly to our appreciation of the arts, the sciences, and to the ever-evolving political entity that is our nation. His works are, indeed, a treasured legacy.

Who would dare to put a value on Andrew Carnegie's gift to America—the endowment of our public libraries? Most of us live within a few blocks, or at most a few miles, of a fine library. Each houses a wealth of knowledge waiting to be shared with readers; knowledge and experiences that open up new horizons through the medium of the printed page.

Books allow us to travel to lands which we may never actually see. They allow us to participate, vicariously, in adventures we may never actually experience. Books are the tools of learning. They exist in great abundance in every community throughout our land. They are free and may be used over and over again.

Why, then, in the United States of America, should the specter of illiteracy hang like a pall over any household, or any community? Most of our greatest leaders have been self-educated. The desire to learn is a more basic factor in becoming an educated person than skillful teachers or modern classrooms. Self-education is a challenge; it is also the responsibility of each and every normal individual, no matter what the circumstances.

Books are a magic carpet. Jump on. They'll give you a "ride to remember", and you'll enjoy the trip.

Vi passed me from fifth grade into the seventh grade, skipping the sixth altogether. (It is good that I later taught sixth grade and learned the rudiments of percentage!) I was the only girl in a class of boys, and it was probably during that time that I learned to prefer boys as friends.

Clyde Barr was one of the boys in my class. His mother was our Sunday school teacher. Once she invited us all to her home for Sunday dinner and an afternoon of play. Mother had made me an especially pretty dress. It was pink with a light green pattern through it, trimmed in green bias tape, and with panties to match. The dress was sleeveless, had a swirly skirt, and I loved it.

For Sundays, however, I always had to wear a dress of dark blue dotted Swiss, trimmed in white lace. I hated that dress. It was see-through material and to this day, I dislike any type of see-through material and lace trim.

The dotted-Swiss dress, freshly ironed, was hanging on a hanger ready for Sunday. I wanted so much to wear the pink one to Mrs. Barr's that I tore a place in the back of the dotted-Swiss dress. When it was time to get ready for church, I showed it to Mother. "I don't remember seeing that tear when I ironed it," she said. She didn't have time to mend it before we had to leave for church, so I got to wear the pink dress with the matching panties. Joy for a moment, as often happens, has been a long-remembered shame.

After Grandma's death, Grandpa Garrett came to live with us. The "cook shack", which Mother and Helen lived in that year at First Central, was moved home and put on a cement

foundation just south of the soddy, to serve as our kitchen. It was not connected to the soddy, but we cooked and ate our meals there.

Dad dug a cistern, really an underground water-storage tank, between the well and the kitchen. It was cemented up the sides and shoulders, covered with a heavy cement lid five-feet square, and kept filled with good fresh water pumped into it through a pipe from the well.

Dad also installed a sink and a pitcher-pump in the southeast corner of the kitchen. The drain pipe, perhaps ten feet long, sloped from sink level inside the house, to approximately two feet above ground outside, where the water drained into the yard and quickly disappeared into the dry soil. Many times, as I ran through that area, I jumped that drainpipe. Once, however, my feet slipped and I landed straddling the pipe, injuring my coccyx severely. For many years, it painfully reminded me of my careless childhood antics.

Colorado is seldom without wind, but occasionally there would be a spell when the wind did not blow. When all the water was used out of the cistern, we would clean it before re-filling it. Dad tied a bucket to a long rope and lowered me, barefooted and with a large stiff-bristled brush, down to the bottom of the cistern. He'd haul the bucket back up and send me down many buckets of fresh

7th graders at First Central. Left to Right: Russel Glad, Howard Beeson, Sarah, Edgar Geist, Clyde Barr • The Boys. "Soupy" 1st row right. Dale Lesher in glasses.

water to wash and rinse, wash and rinse, wash and rinse. When the floor and walls of the cistern were nice and clean, and the rinse water all removed, I'd wipe down the walls with a clean towel and then ride the bucket back to the surface. Usually, the cistern cleaning took place on a dry, hot summer day and so I quite enjoyed it, as the cool dampness of the cistern was a welcome relief from the parched air. As I relate this, I realize that my tendency toward claustrophobia must have developed in later years.

One time when several days had gone by with no wind to turn the windmill to pump water, all our water tanks were dry. The cattle needed water desperately and were sadly lowing their misery. Helen and I decided to drive the herd down to a small creek that ran through the old Steven's place, which bordered our south pasture. It was about a mile and a half from our house, as we had to drive the herd around the perimeter of our pasture, outside the four-wire barbed fence.

There was seldom enough rainfall for this little creek to have any water in it, but at this particular time, it contained a few shallow pools of water.

The still air and merciless sun made the temperature 110 degrees and there was no shade along the way. We finally got the herd to the creek and they drank eagerly, even though the shallow water was muddy. It seemed an eternity before they'd slaked their thirsts. Helen and I were both beginning to suffer from lack of water ourselves. Eventually, we got the animals rounded up and headed for home. By this time, my mouth was so dry I couldn't speak. We were only halfway home, but Helen, bless her, told me to run across the pasture to the house, where I could get water. She brought the herd the rest of the way by herself. I was never more grateful for a kindness.

Whenever I hear the western song about the tumbling tumbleweeds and the "cool, clear water", I remember that day. I know how dreadfully fast one could die of thirst, with the tongue thickened and choking in the throat.

One night, after we'd eaten our supper over in the "new" kitchen, Marvin, a pre-schooler, got sleepy at the table, laid his head over on a chair, and went to sleep. No doubt I had gone to bed early to get on with my "day-dreaming". Eventually both our parents and Helen went to the soddy and went to bed, forgetting Marvin, asleep behind the table. In the middle of the night, he reminded them!

Fuel on the prairie was hard to come by, as there are no trees. Dad always raised a great number of hogs and one of our fall chores was to collect the dried corncobs from the pig lot and store them in the brooder house in order to have dry starter-fuel during the winter. I have carried hundreds, probably thousands, of bushel baskets of corncobs. I can still smell the stench of the hog lot, remembering it.

We often took Dad's header-barge (a wide wagon-bed, with one side considerably higher than the other) and went out onto the surrounding, open grazing land to pick up barge loads of dried cow chips, which make excellent fuel.

Of course, each winter Dad bought coal for the cook stove in the kitchen and the pot-bellied heating stove in the "east room." I hated the coal pile, black and ugly, and dreaded each year to see the coal unloaded in our yard. However, as soon as the first snow fell, the entire landscape was blanketed in white. The bright Colorado sun made everything, including the now white mound of coal, sparkle beautifully, like a million diamonds.

I went to church all my life and became a Christian when I was eleven. I had often heard the hymn..."though your sins be as scarlet, they shall be as white as snow." One day in the mid-seventies, I was alone in our living room, listening to a fine Christian pastor on TV. His practical message so touched me that I literally fell to my knees, with my face to the carpet, and wept. On the screen of my mind, a parade of incidences from years gone by flashed before me—most so trivial I had never even thought of them as "sins." Each visualization seemed to be like a big chunk of ugly black coal, "held up" for me to see, then tossed over on the ever-growing ugly, black pile. Suddenly, the black pile became snow white and glistened like a million diamonds, just like ours long ago had glistened in the bright Colorado sun, after the first snowfall of winter. I like to think that a loving Savior was again reassuring this "child" of His promised "blanket of forgiveness."

It is almost impossible to bank a coal stove so that live embers last through the night. I still shiver when I remember getting up in a frigid house, before daylight, to go milk by lantern light in a cold barn on winter mornings.

My dear friend, Lucy Jones, says, "Unless a woman has scrubbed clothes on a washboard, she cannot fully appreciate an automatic washer." I add to that: "No one really appreciates the comforts of electricity, automatic furnaces, hot showers, and all our other modern conveniences, unless he or she had grown up without them." Each morning as I stand under the hot shower, I thank the Good Lord for the many conveniences we have today that make my life so comfortable.

Dad purchased twelve head of purebred heifers during my early childhood, the start of a herd that eventually numbered more than sixty. That was long before the advent of milking machines. Our milking was done in the barn or in the corral, sitting on a one-legged milk stool, a galvanized bucket between the knees, and probably a cat sitting nearby, begging for a playful squirt of milk. I was Dad's "right hand man" when it was milking time.

Before I was old enough to accept such responsibilities, Helen drove a four-horse team in the fields and did such chores as hoeing the sweet corn in the truck patch. She always protected herself from the fierce Colorado sun by wearing a sunbonnet to shade her face and long sleeves to protect her arms. It had not yet become fashionable to be bronzed by the sun. Eventually, however, I did more of the outside chores with Dad, while Helen helped Mother in the house. I never worried about the sun and, each summer, I got as brown as a berry.

One summer, when Marvin was a youngster, he and one of the Iseman boys decided to see who could get the brownest. Marvin, having inherited the Garrett swarthy skin, ran and played without a shirt and soon was bronze as an Indian. The Iseman boy, reddish haired and freckled faced, immediately got so badly burned on his back that they had to lift him out of bed by his head. It was an uneven contest.

Probably the summer of 1930, the soddy was torn down, due to the deterioration of the outside walls and supporting frame structure. Before that occurred, Dad built a room on the west side of the kitchen and an enclosed porch on the east side. Wood siding was nailed to two-by-fours, and covered on the outside with tarpaper. The inside of the rooms remained unfinished. In the west room, approximately twelve-by-twelve feet, the walls were lined with the dresser, a double bed where Helen and I slept, Grandpa's bed, the White treadle sewing machine, the piano, and the leather-seated oak rocker. A curtained shelf was our clothes closet and hid the tall banana basket used as a dirty clothes hamper.

Above, where the roof had been extended to incorporate the new room, "attic space" served as a storage area for Mother's music and her treasured books.

Under the west room was a cellar—the cellar door and steps down located outside, just under the west window of that room. Dad dug an earthen shelf about a foot deep and head high all around the walls of the cellar. Here Mother stored her jars of canned goods... green beans, carrots, corn, and tomatoes.

Dad butchered a beef each fall and much of that meat was canned. He also butchered a young hog, usually twice a year. Mother rendered out the lard. Sausage patties, which had been seasoned and browned, were packed in a big crockery churn, with the hot lard poured over them to preserve them through the winter. Hams were smoked and hung on rafters in the garage.

Once we lost a ham. Someone came during the night and stole it. We never had proof, but after that night, our unusually good collie dog would never allow one neighbor to enter our gate until Dad literally forced him to.

Once, I brought Inez Perkins home from school with me to spend the night. Mother, who had worked hard all day and was exhausted, was pouring hot lard over the sausage patties. Just as we entered the kitchen door, the crockery churn broke and hot lard began to ooze slowly over the kitchen floor, seeping under the edges of the linoleum. It was not an auspicious time to have brought home a guest.

On the earthen floor in the cellar were crocks of sauerkraut and also small crocks of pickles. Mother was expert at making a variety of delicious pickles. During the long winters, when we did not have any fresh produce, those pickles added a delightfully crisp goodness to our meals. The cool cellar, of course, replaced the old sand-bottomed "refrigerator".

On the east side of the kitchen, Dad laid a cement floor, nine-by-twelve feet, a step down from the kitchen floor, and sided the room up about five feet. He screened in the top half. Later the screen was covered with heavy isinglass to keep out the wind and some of the cold. This room, which we always referred to as the "porch", contained a double bed, which stood along the north wall and in which our parents slept, a cot for Marvin, a tall storage cupboard, and the "Sharpless" cream separator.

Each morning and night, after the milking was done and milk was saved for the family's use, great buckets of fresh, foamy milk were poured into the separator's tank. Dad turned the handle and cream came out one spout, skim milk out the other. The skim milk was fed to the hogs. The cream was used for making butter. Whatever was in excess of our needs was sold in Bethune at the creamery, along with dozens and dozens of eggs from our large flock of chickens.

When I was a pre-schooler, Mother hatched her baby chickens in incubators in the soddy, keeping the eggs warm for twenty-six days, turning them over every day. Hatching time was an exciting time. Eventually, however, Dad built a chicken house with a brooder house on the south side. Then, the incubators were placed out there.

Later, Mother gave up incubating her own eggs. Each spring she ordered baby chicks and turkeys from a hatchery. They came by mail, in square perforated boxes about four inches deep and a yard square. She bought several hundred of them, although usually more chicks than turkeys. I can hear their "cheep-cheeps" yet, as by the time they were delivered to us by our mail carrier, Ted Knodel, they were all crying for food.

For the first few weeks, they were kept warm by small heaters in the brooder house, and their main food was hundreds and hundreds of crumbled, hard-cooked eggs.

Baby turkeys are more delicate than baby chicks and we always kept them in a separate location. One year we had several hundred baby turkeys in Dad's big header barge, which was off the wheeled chassis, sitting on wood blocks on the ground. I was in the barge, crumbling dozens of hard-cooked eggs for the little turkeys to eat. They were little balls of gray fuzz scrambling around my bare feet, and I accidentally stepped on one. I still remember the sickening feeling of squashing that baby turkey.

As they grew, the chickens were separated into two groups, future layers and fryers. We could hardly wait for the fryers to mature enough to start eating them. The fryers I grew up on were a far cry from the commercially force-fed pap that is passed off as chicken in today's modern grocery.

To catch a young fryer, we used a long stiff wire with a hook on one end. One quick movement and the hook was around the fryer's legs. A wooden block with a small axe stuck in it, served as the guillotine. One sharp blow and the head was severed. If you have never seen a chicken beheaded, you would no doubt be surprised to see that for several minutes, he jumps and jerks as it he were still alive, sometimes covering quite a bit of territory.

A very hot "hot water bath" made plucking the feathers easy. However, I was blessed with a very sensitive sense of smell and always hated the odor of those wet chicken feathers.

Mother was expert at frying chicken in her big cast-iron skillet with the domed glass lid. It was a good thing, as Dad, gregarious soul that he was, often unexpectedly invited folks for dinner. She fried her chickens in lard, which was always in plentiful supply. Our diet was based on chickens, eggs, milk, butter, and cream. Today there is an on-going debate as to whether such foods are healthful or harmful. I feel that we four Mitchell "kids" are evidence that they are all good foods.

Mother made her own bread, of course, as did all farm women of that day. This was a twice a week task. I can see those loaves rising yet, greased on the top and with cheesecloth over them. And her cinnamon rolls were truly food for the gods. I wish I knew where I could get such superb fare today.

Each fall, Mother culled out her non-layers and took them to town to sell. The money from those fat old hens paid for the yards of material she needed to make new school clothes for us. I often think of the nice job Mother did, making not only our clothes, but often having to make her own patterns, as well. Pioneer women became "masters" of many trades.

Turkeys were a cash crop just before Thanksgiving. The whole family worked together. The turkeys were hung by their feet from a rafter in the garage, stuck, plucked, cleaned, packed in barrels of ice, and shipped to markets in Chicago. That is the only time I ever remember our parents keeping any of us out of school.

Dad always planted a big truck-patch just south of the hog lot. One of the chores I hated was picking up potatoes in the fall, after the weather turned cold. He'd plow up row after row of potatoes. Then, as soon as we got home from school, we'd start picking up potatoes, sacking them in big burlap bags, hauling them in the wagon, and storing them in the cellar, along with the Mother Hubbard squash. Potatoes were a staple food all year long. We ate them mashed, baked, scalloped, and fried, as well as in soups and stews. One of my favorite meals was fried potatoes—sliced and fried to a golden brown in bacon grease in Mother's big cast-iron skillet—and served with "over-easy" eggs.

Our parents always arranged for us to have some source of money for buying Christmas gifts. Usually, early in the spring, Dad would take us down to the Johnson sheep ranch, southeast of us, beyond Dunlap's, and we would get three or four orphan lambs to bring home and bottle-feed. When it came time to sell them, we'd all be heart-broken, as, by that time, the lambs were beloved pets. I remember Mrs. Johnson often gave us watermelon pickles to eat, a rare treat, as Mother did not make that kind of pickle.

We got very attached to all the animals on the farm. Calves were taken from their mothers almost immediately, since our livelihood depended on our milk cows. The calves had to be taught to drink from a bucket. We would take the warm milk out to the holding shed, straddle the calf's neck, and hold his head down to the milk. Sometimes, we had to immerse one hand in the milk and let the calf suck a finger to get him started drinking. All new calves learned to drink from the bucket. Each animal had a name, usually the name of one of our teachers.

Christmases were an exciting time, even though we were poor. Mother and Dad always got a tree and hid it in the loft above the garage. After we children were in bed on Christmas Eve, they'd bring the tree in and decorate it with ropes of popcorn and cranberries, and garlands cut from red and green construction paper, which we had made during long winter evenings prior to Christmas. Candles in small metal holders, like clothespins, were clipped on the tree's branches, but were lighted only under strict supervision because of the danger of fire.

Late at night, Dad would put on his big rubber boots and make tracks in the snow on the roof and down the lane. Long after Marvin could tell who gave him each gift, he still believed that Santa had left those boot tracks in the snow.

Usually there was one large gift for each of us—a sled for Marvin, perhaps, or Bye-Lo Baby Dolls for Helen and me. Sometimes, however, there was only one large gift for the three of us, like the Red Flyer wagon we used for many years.

We each had a stocking—one of our regular school stockings—and in the toe there was always a beautiful orange, a real winter treat in the days before refrigerated railroad cars. Also, each stocking held a pack of Wrigley's gum, a jawbreaker, a Hershey bar, and a set of jacks. Many an hour, we played jacks on the wide floorboards in the soddy.

I mentioned that Dad and Okie Carpenter contracted to harvest many acres of grain grown on government land, as well as their own. Dad would go into Burlington and hire a crew of men who had arrived on the Rock Island train, hoping to work in the harvest. We always had several harvest hands to feed and bed down for the night. These men worked from daylight till dark for $1.00 a day. The stacker, Mr. Bigelow, was with the crew for several years, and Dad paid him $2.00 a day, as he was an artist at stacking the wheat or barley so that it was still in perfect shape at threshing time.

At noon, the harvest hands came in from the field tired and dusty. They wore red bandanas around their necks to keep the grasshoppers out of their shirts. Prior to going to the fields, Dad would place two sawhorses with wide boards on them, out under the big willow tree by the well. Mother brought several washbasins, bars of soap, and towels out for the men. They took turns washing in cold water before coming in to a "harvest-hand meal" of fried chicken, mounds of mashed potatoes, gravy, probably green beans or corn, hot bread, and two or three kinds of pie. At night they expected a similar meal. As I reminisce, I marvel at Mother's ability to do all the things she had to do, under very difficult circumstances, with absolutely no modern conveniences.

Indian John worked for Dad for a long period of time. He was a full-blooded Navajo. Once when he came back from a visit to his hogan in Arizona, he brought Helen and me each a pair of beautiful, beaded moccasins. They were a prized possession for years and I have often wondered whatever happened to them.

During all the years that we had harvest hands and corn huskers to feed and bed down for the night, I do not remember hearing a cuss word spoken, an off-color joke told, or a suggestive remark made. I consider that a tribute to our parents and the standards they set for conduct in our home.

Helen was an excellent checker player, even as a very young girl. In the evenings, she would play checkers with the men and I remember that she could usually beat them. As an adult, she is a tournament bridge player, having won all her "gold" points. Is the saying "Men are only boys grown tall, they have not changed much after all" also true of women?

Once Dad hired a young Tom Mahan to help him for a few days. The Mahan's lived just north and a bit west of First Central School. Since they were not church-going people, we did not know them very well. On a day when the weather kept them from work in the field, young Tom bummed a ride into Bethune with our neighbor, Maynard Dunham. After several hours, they returned and Tom sat down by our kitchen stove. The warmth of the small room soon had him nodding and alerted Dad that he reeked of liquor. Dad woke him abruptly and said, "Tom, there has never been a drop of liquor in this house and my children have never seen a drunk man. Get your things. I'm taking you home." And he did.

When we were growing up, we entertained ourselves. No inane (or depraved) television programs dulled our natural creativity. We played hide-and-go-seek in the cornfields, using the shocks as good hiding places. We played ante-over, throwing the ball over the house or garage, and then running to tag the other players. We made playhouses by "roofing" the long tines of Dad's rake with layers of redroot, and crawling under it for shade. We played thousands of games of hopscotch, jumped rope, and walked miles on stilts. We played circus, jumping from the barn rafters onto the backs of horses. (It's a wonder kids ever grow up.) We even rode the young shoats. And Dad always had a nice swing for us somewhere in the yard.

One of our favorite daredevil games was placing a wagon-bed, with the ends removed, on an over-turned barrel, then running to the top and riding it dangerously to the ground. I still have scars on my knees from falling and grinding stones into the flesh. When we wanted to play with neighbor kids, we rode horseback to their place, or to meet them if they were coming to our place to play.

Colorado winters, in those days, were much more severe than they are today. Many times we had big drifts of snow that never melted from fall to spring. These made great slides, with or without a sled. As we got older, we ran many a mile playing Fox and Geese, our favorite winter game.

Two churches furnished a great many of our activities all my growing-up years. The Nazarene church stood just a mile north of our house. Services were first held there in the basement, but, eventually, a good frame building was built. (That building is still in use as a church today, having been moved into Burlington.)

Our family went to the Evangelical Church, which met in the First Central School building, six miles northwest of where we lived. We often attended services at the Nazarene Church, however, as we could walk there if the car wouldn't start, or if the roads were drifted. Grandpa attended there regularly, always walking, and he used to preach there on occasion, when the regular minister was ill or away.

One Sunday, after services, Helen, Edith Beeson, and another older girl, perhaps Isaphene, I'm not sure, were in the back seat of a car in the Nazarene churchyard. It was a very hot day, yet I had on a coat—a beautiful navy blue coat with rose-colored lapels and patch pockets, sent by one of Mother's Denver friends. I had never seen a "spring coat" before, as we were lucky to have coats in winter, when we needed them. Today, church rummage sales, and consignment stores like Snooty Fox, have made wearing previously used clothing an acceptable practice. But, when I was a child, it was a real disgrace to have to wear hand-me-downs. These older girls called me over to the car and asked me where I got the coat. I told them Mother bought it for me in Burlington. They continued to bait me with questions, and I continued to lie to them. Later, I learned that Helen had already told them where the coat came from. I remember to this day the embarrassment and humiliation. It was a lie to last a lifetime.

In my childhood, I felt that I was the only child in the world who ever told a lie. After working with first graders for many years, I know that most children sometimes tell things that are not true—either out of fear of too harsh punishment or out of too lively imaginations.

I always taught the children that a lie is a foolish thing. "You can say a hundred times, 'I didn't hit Billy. I didn't hit Billy.' But you did hit Billy. His nose is bleeding and several of the other children saw you hit Billy. Isn't it foolish to keep saying you didn't? Wouldn't it make you feel a lot better to tell Billy you are sorry you hit him and that you won't do it again?" I always found that children respond well to good common sense. I never punished a child if he told the truth.

The "selective" memory of children would make an interesting study. Why are some experiences remembered in great detail and thousands of others are lost to memory? One Sunday, when Edith Beeson was learning to drive, her father let her come to our house to take Helen for a ride. Edith's little sister, Midge, and I were good friends and I begged to go along. Edith finally consented and told me to get in the back seat. She drove around awhile, then, coming down our lane, she stopped the car and asked me to pick her a bouquet of sunflowers, which were blooming in great masses just across the fence. I was delighted to be able to do something nice for this much admired, older girl, and quickly jumped from the

car. I had barely started to pick the flowers when she drove off laughing, leaving me to walk the half-mile home.

I remember, as if it happened yesterday, how absolutely stunned I was. Hard lessons are learned from life's hurts and disappointments, and teach us the wisdom of the Golden Rule.

Dad was leader of the Sunday school for many years, ordering all the materials from the David C. Cook Publishing Company. He also served as janitor, arriving early to build the fires in winter, and staying late to be sure the hymnals were put away and the rooms left orderly for school the following day.

Dad always liked to dress up. He had one good suit and one pair of dress shoes most of my growing up years. He was a big man, but light on his feet, and very easy on his clothes. During the years of the Great Depression, however, his one suit finally wore out. There was no money to replace it.

For everyday, he wore blue denim bib-overalls. Since getting a new suit was out of the question, he bought a pair of bib-overalls that were gray and white stripe, like bed ticking, and kept that pair for church. I can see him yet, standing in front of the congregation, head

held high, wearing those "Sunday" overalls.

One Sunday morning, the roads were badly drifted from a heavy snow, yet Dad drove us to church. Several times, he had to get out and shovel snow from the road in order to get through. Thelma, our beloved teacher (who had married Arthur Lowe after his wife died, leaving him with four small children, including a set of twins), saw us go by their house. She said to Arthur, "If Victor Mitchell can bring his family six miles in this weather, we can surely take our family one mile." They got the children ready and came. The Lowe's and the Mitchell's were the only ones at church that Sunday.

Vi, Thelma and two other teachers. • Thelma and First Central students.

Mother often played the piano for services or taught a Sunday School class. However, there were many Sundays that she did not go to church. I'm sure she needed that quiet time, at home alone, after caring for six people all week in three small rooms.

Mother was an avid student of the Bible and tithed her cream and egg money faithfully. Once, she used some of her tithe money to take a classmate of mine, Dale Lesher, to her eye specialists, Carpenter & Hibbard, in Denver. We made the trip on the train. In later years, when she didn't have to be so careful with her spending, she bought overalls, shoes, and eyeglasses for many needy children, always anonymously.

Our parents never started a meal without prayer. Usually Dad asked the blessing, but sometimes he called on Mother or Grandpa to do so. And no matter how cold the room, they never crawled into bed at night without first kneeling beside their bed to pray—a legacy I consider far more valuable than the money left us at their deaths.

One summer, hail devastated crops in our area. As the storm raged, Dad stood in the doorway of our porch, fervently thanking the Lord for protecting our corn crop. When the storm finally abated, our field of corn stood unscathed, yet just across the fence, hail lay piled so deep that we gathered great tubs of it, made ice cream, and took it over to share with the Keever's.

On Halloween night in 1929, Mother gave birth to a stillborn boy. They named him Hoyt. Guy McArthur, our neighbor to the south, made a small wooden casket for him. He was buried beneath the currant bushes at the west side of our garden, with Grandpa performing a short service. None of us three children were allowed to see the baby or attend the burial. I have always felt that was a mistake.

1929 was the year of the stock market crash and the beginning of the great Depression. It was also the year that I became a Christian. These two articles, written years later, concern that time in my life.

Encounter on a Milk stool

Would God, Creator of heaven and earth, deign to come to a dusty, smelly barnyard and "speak" to a little girl while she milked a cow?

When I was a child our church was made up of a motley group of ranchers' families, who scraped a meager living from the dry plains of eastern Colorado, aptly called The Great American Desert. Services were held in the community schoolhouse. On Sundays, the church families often shared a basket dinner under the lone shade tree that grew in the barren schoolyard. In the days before good roads, reliable automobiles, and rural electrification, ranchers were an isolated lot. Few even owned a battery-operated radio. The basket dinner, therefore, filled a basic community need, as it provided a time for fellowship before evening chores had to be started.

One summer Sunday in 1929, when I was eleven, the basket dinner celebrated the close of a week-long revival service. Dr. Bartsch, the visiting evangelist, was our guest. We all circled the table, holding hands, our heads bowed, while he asked the blessing, as was the custom. There was much good food and relaxed camaraderie and the afternoon passed too quickly. Soon, it was time to carry tables and chairs inside. Each family packed its belongings and hurried home to get chores done in time to return for the final evening service.

I went to the barnyard with Dad to do my share of the milking. Our barnyard, like every other barnyard throughout the western plains, was barren. Not a blade of grass escaped the twisting, sharp hooves of the milling herd of cattle. Our red bull, bellowing and pawing the ground to show his prowess, sent great clouds of dust mushrooming into the dry air.

I was balanced on a one-legged milk stool, a galvanized bucket held firmly between my knees, my forehead pressed against the cow's flank, when Love enfolded me with such warmth and intimacy that, more than a half-century later, it is as fresh in my memory as if it happened only yesterday.

As I milked, a panorama of rarest beauty began to pass before my eyes— gently rolling hills and verdant valleys, lovely green trees providing cool shade; acres of blossoms in great masses of color, wafting a soft fragrance into the air; a cool, clear stream with a gurgling spring and a tumbling waterfall; an azure sky tufted with soft cotton-ball clouds. Such scenes kept flowing before me, as if from a slow-motion film.

How long the "vision" lasted, I can't be sure, but when I came back to the harsh reality of the ugliness of the barren barnyard, I knew, beyond any doubt, that this child of the prairie had been shown the handiwork of God, the Creator of all things beautiful, the magnificent Artist. It was, indeed, for me a rainbow.

When chores were finished we returned to the schoolhouse for the evening service. After the hymns and a sweet message depicting a loving God, Reverend Bartsch asked the pianist to play the familiar hymn "Just As I Am". She began softly. "If you would like to meet our Lord personally," he said, "come quietly to the front of the room and kneel at one of the oak chairs placed here for you." I was the first one out of my seat. I knelt at an old oak chair and wept. Wept at the wonder of being made new, at the miracle of feeling clean all over, at the intimacy of God's love as He wrapped me tenderly and securely in His great loving arms—a loving Father who would come to a dusty barnyard in order that a little girl might see and believe. It was many years before any real growth took place in my knowledge and understanding of the Lord, but during those years, this childhood experience anchored me firmly to the "Faith of Our Fathers".

Our God is a Practical God

I grew up on a cattle ranch on the plains of Eastern Colorado. The summer that I was eleven, I severely injured my foot, which swelled to the size of a football. I was unable to wear a shoe. Therefore, I was at home alone while the rest of the family made the weekly trip into town, fourteen miles away.

They were no more than out of sight when our herd of cattle, some sixty head, started in a bee line across open grazing land, toward Dunham's field a mile away. I was especially alarmed, as this neighbor had planted a border of cane around his corn. Cane is a quick poison to cattle.

The field was protected by a four-wire barbed fence, common on the western plains, yet cattle, intent on getting through, always succeeded. There was not a minute to lose. Quickly, I stuck a hammer and pliers in the hip pocket of my overalls and hobbled toward the barn, trying desperately to protect my badly swollen foot. Somehow I managed to get astride my horse, without a saddle.

Before I could reach the field, however, the cattle had worked their way through the barbed wires, and were noisily munching on the first rows of cane. Two raging bulls—McArthur's white bull, dragging a chain hooked to a ring in his nose, and Wellman's red bull—had joined our herd. Both were pawing the ground, throwing great clouds of dust and bellowing menacingly. I was scared to death.

I managed to force the four tightly stretched barbed wires down to about a foot above the ground and drove a large staple over them into the fence post to hold them. However, my horse, wire-cut as a colt, refused to cross the fence. For me to hobble precariously over the loose dirt would be a futile effort. Yet there was no one else to get the cattle out. I was helpless.

"Lord," I prayed. "Please help me." It was a prayer of desperation.

At that very moment, a team of horses, pulling a wagonload of hay, crested the small rise in the terrain a quarter-mile away. The driver was a neighbor lad, Carl Snelling. I will never forget the absolute amazement I felt. How quickly God had responded to a little girl's cry for help.

Carl unhitched one horse from his team, jumped on, and rounded up our cattle. He patiently urged them back over the fence, across the steeply graded ditches on each side of the road, and headed them toward our open grazing land.

You say God had nothing to do with it? The boy and a team of horses just happened along? Perhaps. But ordinarily, he would not even have been on that road, coming from where he was coming from and going to where he was going.

"Something just told me to come this way," he said, as I thanked him sincerely. Something or Someone?

During the fall of 1931, we were startled to see a young lady wearing spike-heeled shoes walk through our barnyard, past our front yard, through our north gate, and keep right on walking north. Mother recognized her as the wife of Davy Wright, a young man who had worked for Dad, and who lived about two miles south and east of us in a one-room shack on the old Flanagan place.

The Wrights had four small boys, all pre-school, including a fairly new baby. The baby had been in a Denver hospital due to a severe rupture and had just been brought home. As soon as Mother saw the woman walking north, she said, "That mother is abandoning her children."

Quickly we hitched a team to our spring wagon, and drove to their shack. I will never forget the pitiful screams of that baby nor the masses of huge black "horse flies" swarming about those frightened children. There were no screens on the windows.

The mother may have ordered the older children to go to the field where their father was working, but they had stayed with the baby and were gathered around his makeshift crib, trying to comfort him.

Because of the rupture, his little tummy had been bound with wide tape. Evidently, in anger, the mother had ripped the tape off, taking great patches of skin with it. All around his little body were open sores as large as a quarter, all of them covered with large black flies.

Mother took all four of the little boys home with us in the wagon. I'm sure we let Davy know, somehow. I may have run back to the field to tell him, but I have forgotten that detail. I remember that he came in a wagon, later that afternoon, and got the three older boys. Mother kept the baby and cared for him until his sores were healed and he was on the road to good health. We had him for nearly two months, during which time we all got so attached to him that it was hard to give him up. Mother always said she would have kept him had she not known she was newly pregnant with Jean.

As I remember it, Davy had relatives in one of the Dakotas. All four of the boys were eventually put in an orphanage there, and each was adopted into a different home. We always felt sad to think about the separation of that little family.

Riding the range at 11 years old.

Helen graduated from high school in 1932. Our country's economy had collapsed and there was no money to send her to college. She worked part of the following year as baby-sitter and housekeeper for one of the teachers at First Central.

The years of the Great Depression coincided with the years of the Dust Bowl in eastern Colorado. Thousands of acres of topsoil were blown as far as the Gulf of Mexico. Depression was not an adequate word to describe the devastation, the helplessness and hopelessness of the families in the area.

Dan Rather, a few years ago, did a TV special about that period in our history, which he called "Trouble on the Land". After watching his program, I wrote an article, which was published in the *Cincinnati Enquirer*, in which I said, "I watched and wept." That TV special brought back many wrenching memories for me.

It is a credit to our parents, and to many other parents in our community, that we did not go hungry during that time.

On April 15, 1932, just before my fourteenth birthday, I was helping Mother make a batch of lye soap. She sat on a low octagonal stool, which I have in my home today, and stirred a crock of the soap mix with a large wooden spoon. I noticed for the first time that she looked pregnant. The next morning, our baby sister, Alice Jean, was born. Dad wanted to name her Jean Alice, but I said she would be nicknamed JAM.

Today, when girls of 14 are having out-of-wedlock babies, it is hard to believe that I was so naïve. But Mother was short, rather thick through the middle, and she always wore an apron. She had never mentioned to me that she was expecting a baby. Being "in the family way" was not a topic of conversation in those days.

Mother was forty-three years old. A change-of-life baby was undoubtedly unplanned, but when Marvin was in service during WWII, and Helen and I were both married and busy with our own families, Jean proved to be a real blessing to our parents. And during the ensuing years, she has been a great joy to us all.

I remember well the first time we ever took her to church. She was two weeks old and I got to carry her in from the car. I was so proud. And at the end of each school day, I'd hurry off the bus and run to be the first to reach her. She brought great joy to our family at a sad time in our history.

Sarah's older sister, Helen.

All my growing up years, Mother looked forward to the Round Robin. She and eleven of her friends from college days started the Round Robin as a way to keep in touch after graduation, when marriage or careers separated them by many miles. Each agreed to keep the Robin no longer than two weeks, during which time she would take out her old letter and include a newly written one, before sending the Robin on. Twice a year this large pack of letters and pictures arrived with news from the Robin "girls" in Leadville or Steamboat Springs or Pueblo or Denver.

One morning in 1933, Ted Knodel, our mailman, brought a suitcase—a good, sturdy suitcase, costing probably $2.95 at that time. In it were a variety of practical things that a young college girl would need-undies, a slip, nightie, robe, blouse, sweater, and skirt. And in the "pocket" of the lid, was a $100 bill. At that time, when grown men worked from daylight to dark for $1.00 a day, that was a lot of money. This generous gift from the "Robin Girls" enabled Helen to start to college in Greeley. Later, after she was teaching, she helped me go to college. It was a gift that changed all our lives.

When Mother passed away at eighty-three in 1973, she had just received the Round Robin. It contained only two letters—her own, written earlier, and one other. The Round Robin was sixty years old. I wonder if that is a record?

My high school days at First Central were filled with baseball, basketball, and track. Ours was such a small school, with so few students to choose from, that I was always on the school's teams, even as an eighth grader. We had only an outdoor basketball court, resulting in many skinned knees. When we went to Bethune to play against their team, we invariably got beat. I don't remember that we ever won a game, but Mr. Otis Ross, our coach, was very patient with us.

Ella Storrer and I were evidently fairly good guards. One day, the basketball coach from Stratton came to talk to our parents about letting us play on Stratton's team. He had arranged for living quarters for us, at no expense to our families, and the school board had agreed to dispense with the usual tuition fees. We both felt our parents were very cruel when they refused to let us take advantage of what we thought was an exciting opportunity. Later, that Stratton coach was dismissed for getting one of the team members pregnant.

In order for us to have enough players for two teams in baseball, we girls always chose up sides with the boys. I was usually one of the first ones chosen. I remember feeling embarrassed for those who were left to the last, and then chosen only reluctantly. I wonder if that sort of cruelty is still practiced on school playgrounds today?

I loved the track meets held in the spring. I was not the fastest runner in school—both Dorothy Hodge and Ella Storrer could out-run me. But, I was always on the relay team, and won the high jump, standing broad jump, and running broad jump—called long jump today—regularly.

In the spring of my junior year, I threw my right hip out of joint during the high jump. Mr. Ross re-set the joint, but that injury bothered me for many years and kept me from participating in sports my senior year.

I often wonder what happened to all my blue ribbons (and a few red or white ones) that I won at track meets. I kept them in a special little box—an oval metal box, about three inches high and four and one-half inches long. It was pretty, green enamel with white stars all over it. When I first saw it in a drugstore in Burlington, when I was about eight or nine, it was filled with small pillow mints and cost ten cents. I wanted that box more than anything in the world. I ran to find Dad and begged him for a dime. He finally gave me one with the admonition that I could not spend more than five cents of it. I was to bring him back a nickel.

I ran right back to the drugstore and bought the green box. I wanted it so badly that I knew I could bear any punishment I would get for disobeying. (I think I got by with only a scolding from dad.) I loved that box and had it for many years. As I got into high school I stored all my track ribbons in it, each one curling around the oval so as not to get mussed. I regret that in one of our many moves, it got lost or discarded.

During my high school years, I gave readings at various programs held at the school, and participated in several three-act plays. I always learned all the parts, in addition to my own, and never could understand why some of the "actors" needed constant cuing from a prompter.

I also participated in lots of music activities both in school and at church, as I sang a fair alto. Mr. Ross, our coach, had a lovely tenor voice and he and I sometimes sang duets together.

During the early spring of the year, as the snow melted, deep tracks developed in the schoolyard where the two school buses pulled in for loading and unloading. One day during my junior year, after the bell rang ending recess, Cloyd Storrer and I continued to play catch as we walked slowly to the schoolhouse. Walking backwards, I stepped into one of those ruts, fell and broke my right wrist.

I did not realize, at first, that I was really hurt. I sat down at my desk, but could not raise my arm up to get my geometry book out for class. By this time, Mr. Ross had noticed me. He came back to my desk and with concern in his voice said, "What is wrong? You are as white as a sheet."

Eventually, he placed the bowl of a big wooden spoon in my hand and bound me firmly, but not tightly, from hand to elbow with gauze. He checked the binding every day to be sure there was no swelling. It was not easy writing essays for English class or doing shorthand with my left hand, but I got by and eventually the "cast" came off. As I have already mentioned, a variety of home remedies served us well.

In high school, I continued to get into occasional trouble. Inez Perkins and I were good friends and sat together at a double desk. One day during Mrs. McEwen's class, I noticed a blackhead in Inez' left ear. I took a bobby pin and tried to dislodge the blackhead. Inez had a roll of thin candy wafers in her hand, each wafer with a short message printed on it. After putting up too long with my futile attempt to squeeze out the blackhead, she held up a wafer that said, "Are you done?" Needless to say, we burst out laughing until Mrs. McEwen finally had to separate us, for we couldn't stop giggling.

Once in hygiene class, Mrs. McEwen made the statement, "I'd just as soon someone would use my toothbrush as my comb." In an aside to Inez, I said, "She must have purebreds." Mrs. McEwen heard me and did not think that was funny.

During the spring of 1934, our junior class planned a "banquet" for the seniors. It could not have been anything very elaborate, as we had no cooking facilities at the school and dancing was not allowed. I have little memory of the affair except that Helen Magnuson, bless her, let me wear her new white high-heeled shoes, as I had no decent shoes of my own.

I was allowed to go on only one real date during my first three years of high school. Norman Smith, who I had a real crush on, took me to a square dance somewhere between First Central and Stratton. Another couple was with us, but I do not remember who they were. In fact, I remember absolutely nothing about the evening except that during "Buffalo Girls", the elastic in my under-panties gave way and they slid precariously down on my hips. Each "dosey-do" thereafter was flirting with disaster, until I finally got to the ladies' room with a borrowed safety pin.

That was the last time I ever saw Norman until nearly sixty years later when he attended a neighborhood reunion in a park near Denver. I would never have recognized him, and he didn't remember me, as he was in the early stages of Alzheimer's disease. Very sad.

The summer after my junior year, I went to work for a family in Bethune. I have forgotten their name, but there were five pre-school children, including a set of twins. The mother was bedfast, recovering from a serious kidney operation.

The father worked on the railroad. I had to get up early and make him a breakfast of biscuits, fried potatoes, and gravy, pack his lunch, and get him off to work. I had full care of the invalid mother who had large incisions across her back and could not get out of bed. And, of course, I had complete charge of the five little ones all day. I was paid three dollars a week and had to wait on that.

The first night I was there, I could not sleep. I itched all over and kept sitting up in bed to scratch. I had never experienced anything like it, for I'd always slept like a log.

Dad was full of fun and had a repertoire of funny rhymes and crazy songs. He used to sing one about "the bedbug has no wings at all, but he gets there just the same, all night long, all night long." That was my entire knowledge of bedbugs. Well, at this house, I got educated.

When I finally could stand it no longer, I got up and turned on the lights. Bedbugs ran from the children's beds and from mine (we were all in the same room), toward the walls. The walls of that house were literally alive with bedbugs.

The next morning, the lady of the house instructed me to fill cans with kerosene and stand the legs of each bed in the kerosene. I also had to take all the bedding outside, hang it on the clothesline, and paint the coils of the bedsprings with kerosene.

I had not worked there very long when, for the first time in my life, I began to have "heartburn". I don't remember how long it took me to get sick, but I went home with yellow jaundice—called hepatitis today—as a result of those filthy bedbugs. Medical research has proven that rats carry this dread disease. I can assure them that bedbugs can carry it, too.

Mother made me strip and take a good tub bath, before letting me into the house. She put all my clothes in a boiler full of hot water. She made me take everything out of the suitcase. Nothing was brought into the house until it had been gone over thoroughly, sprayed, and then washed. Thankfully, I brought no bedbugs home with me.

I had always been a very healthy young girl, had hardly been sick in my life, yet I could easily have died from that illness. I lay in bed on the porch, too sick to care. My skin and the whites of my eyes were as yellow as the bedspread. I was 5'8" tall, and got down to 104 pounds. It would be over a year before I would bounce back to anywhere near normal, and the damage to my liver would be with me for the rest of my life.

Before I was able to be up and around, we got word that Uncle Hoyt, Aunt Belle, their daughter, Phyllis, and Wellington's wife, Ruth, were coming from Ohio for a visit. I felt I had to get up and help Mother. I was ashamed to have them see the house we lived in. If only we could trade houses with the Graves for a few days. The Graves' house had only three rooms, too, but it was a much nicer house than ours.

The visitors arrived. I have no idea how Mother took care of four extra adults in our three small rooms. Undoubtedly Phyllis and Ruth slept on the floor with us kids. Phyllis, a registered nurse, was immediately concerned about my physical condition. She gave me a glass of Epsom salts as "medicine." I simply could not drink it. When she was not looking, I set it down in the kitchen. That night, after supper, while washing up the dishes, she put it in her dishpan, thinking it was a glass of water. The salts immediately turned the water hard. She found out I had not taken her "medicine" and I learned that there was such a thing as hard water.

During the years of the Dust Bowl and the Depression, farmers planted crops and did not harvest, for without moisture nothing grew. Dad, who had always raised a lot of hogs, took a truckload of young shoats to market and brought them home again. No one had money to buy them, nor food to feed them.

Government agents came through the area and bought up starving cattle for a few dollars a head.

By September 1934, our parents had lost everything to a combination of depression and drought. They told almost no one they planned to leave eastern Colorado, and, in fact, left "between two days" to avoid saying goodbye to their friends of many years. They had intended to move several weeks earlier, prior to the beginning of the school year, but my illness delayed them, as I was too sick to travel.

Dudley Swann, a neighbor to the south, drove his car and Grandpa, Mother, Jean, and I rode with him. Dad and Marvin came in the farm truck, loaded with our few household belongings. Helen was already in Greeley in college.

The farm that Dad had arranged to rent, near Greeley, belonged to some of Aunt Emma's family, and was known as the Dougherty place. Undoubtedly, the crops had not yet been harvested and it was not available to us immediately. We lived temporarily in two other houses before we could move to the Dougherty place.

The first house, in Windsor, had not been lived in for a long time and grass and weeds were head high when we arrived there. We no more than got it cleaned up and livable when we had to move again, this time to a place outside of town. This move was undoubtedly necessary so that we could keep a cow and have milk for the family. I remember that Marvin and I rode the bus to school from that house.

No doubt it was due to my poor physical condition, plus the trauma of moving, that my menstrual cycle completely shut down. Mother, always expecting the worst, accused me of being pregnant. I had heard it whispered that you could get pregnant by wearing a man's overalls. I had worn Dad's overalls to do the milking, and was horrified to think it might be true. Still jaundiced, with yellow skin and eyeballs, and thin as a rail, sleepless nights were not what I needed at that time.

When we moved to Lima, Peru, Ronda, a junior in high school, had exactly the same experience. I took her to the doctor, who said, "Uterus collapse in young girls is very common and is usually due to emotional trauma. Give her time to adjust. There is nothing to worry about. She will be fine." She was. Years later, when she asked, "Did you worry that I might be pregnant?" I was glad I could truthfully tell her I had not.

The Dougherty place was three miles north of Severance. There was no high school in that district, so Dad made arrangements for me to work in Windsor and finish my senior year of high school. I worked at the town's bakery, owned by Mr. and Mrs. Sawyer, and lived with them in a large two-story brick house adjoining the bakery, fronting on Main Street, directly across from the theater.

The Sawyers were well past middle age, with two grown sons. Their older son, Paul, was a doctor in Denver.

Mrs. Sawyer had come to America from Scotland at age eighteen and still spoke with a thick burr. Mr. Sawyer had a lame leg and it was not easy for him to get around. However, he was an excellent baker. He got up at four o'clock every morning to stoke the fires, which heated the large (approximately nine feet square) brick oven. He had two long-handled paddles that he used to lift the hot pans containing breads, rolls, or hot cross buns from the oven and place them on the myriad cooling racks in the back room.

I have wished many times that I had been interested enough in cooking to take advantage of the opportunity to learn from him, for he was an artist in his work—just one of many opportunities I failed to take advantage of in my lifetime. "Too soon oldt and too late smardt."

My job was to keep the glass show cases clean, the floors mopped, and to wait on customers. I also worked in the house—a big, old, musty house that needed a good airing. The front parlor and the large dining room were "off limits" except for keeping them clean, as was one "guest" bedroom. The three of us lived in the small kitchen, slept in our separate bedrooms, and passed each other in the dark passageway that connected the house and the bakery.

Shorty and Marion, a very nice young married couple rented an apartment upstairs. Down the hall from them, a middle-aged man rented a single room. I had to clean his room and the hall bathroom, a job I hated, as everything reeked of that stale, musty smell that old, unaired houses have. I always made sure he was nowhere around before I went up those stairs.

The Sawyers were very nice, but it was a lonesome existence for a sixteen year old. I don't know what I would have done had it not been for Barbara and Dorothy (Dukie) Yancey, daughters of Mrs. Sawyer's younger sister, Jean, who was a registered nurse. They were a year or two younger than I, but they lived only a few blocks away and we became good friends. I regret that I lost contact with them after I went to college.

It was the last of September when I entered Windsor High School. Everyone else was well established in his or her classes by that time, of course. I was living away from home for the first time, was physically below par (my skin and eyeballs remained yellow for months), and I had to take chemistry, for which I had absolutely no background nor liking.

Windsor is a German town. At that time, the Great Western Sugar Company operated a large plant there and the thrifty German families all lived well. My classmates came to school in "Sunday" dresses, high- heeled shoes, and silk stockings. I had one pair of practical brown oxfords and a mish-mash of ill-fitting hand-me-downs from the Robin girls. Comedian George Gobel has asked, "Did you ever feel that the world was a tuxedo and you were a pair of brown shoes?" Oh, yes, George, yes.

Due to my physical condition, I was subject to a lot of illnesses during that year, a first for me. Blood poison, from a wire-scratch, could have cost me my right arm. A severe case of red measles caused me to miss two full weeks of school, which put me behind the eight ball in Chemistry Lab. There were several bouts of my hip slipping out of place, making the nerves near the hip joint burn like fire. On our "Senior Day" excursion to Gem Lake, I got so ill that I slept through the movie in Loveland on the way home, and was out of school for two weeks with a severe case of tonsillitis. Nurse Jean Yancey, bless her, took care of me during each illness, without charging anything for her services. Mrs. Sawyer even let me use the "guest" bedroom during that end-of-school illness.

Emma Lehr sat right behind me in study hall and was my best friend at school. I really didn't learn to know anyone very well, however, as I never got to attend the games or other school activities because of my work at the bakery. Jerry, Emma's older brother and I became good friends during the following summer and remained so during the years I was in college and teaching in Colorado.

On graduation night (I ranked third in a class of thirty-three), I wore the floor-length yellow taffeta dress I'd gotten for the prom, since it was the only thing I had that was new. The other girls all wore street-length dresses under their gowns. I was so embarrassed that I forgot to change the tassel on my cap to the other side, when I received my diploma. It was a year to forget.

In 1985, I went back to Windsor to attend our fiftieth year class reunion. The reception I got from my classmates still warms my heart. They had many nice memories of my year with them. A table of memorabilia included the class poem I'd written for the school's Yearbook. There were dozens of pictures of our Senior Class Play, "Diggin' Up The Dirt", in which I had the leading role. I was shocked to think that for fifty years, I'd remembered only the bad and none of the good. Perhaps my senior year was not such a bad year after all.

Having to move to a new school my senior year had been such a traumatic experience for me that I swore I would never move my children during their junior or senior year in high school. We moved all three of them—Rock from Guam to California, Ronda from California to Lima, Peru, and Reva from Ravenna to Cincinnati.

During the summer of 1985, after returning from Colorado where I attended our fiftieth class reunion, Paul and I drove to Marlinton, West Virginia to help Reed and Mary Davis celebrate their fiftieth wedding anniversary. I was talking to another guest, a doctor friend of theirs from Denver, who had come for the occasion. I mentioned that I'd just been in Windsor. He said, "The doctor across the hall from me in our medical building in Denver is from Windsor. His parents used to own the bakery there." Dr. Paul Sawyer. I kept their little toddler and his Pekinese dog for two weeks the summer of 1935, while they went on vacation in the Northwest. I still remember the wonderful halibut, packed in dry ice, he sent to his parents while on that trip. It's a small world.

During the year that I worked at the bakery, unions were getting well organized. One day two union "goons" from Denver came to persuade Mr. Sawyer that he should join the union—"if you don't want to find your big glass display window broken and your glass showcases smashed." They scared me half to death, but Mr. Sawyer was not intimidated by them. Thankfully, none of their threats ever came to pass.

I grew up knowing what it was to work hard. However, I worked harder the summer after my senior year in school than I'd ever worked in my life. Beets for the sugar factories were the cash crop for farmers in the area. Mexican beet workers came to plant in the spring, to thin the beets in early summer, and to work in the beet harvest in the fall. Our parents had no contacts for obtaining Mexican labor, which had to be contracted for well in advance. Nor did they have money to pay for such labor. We all worked in the beets. Mother took Jean, three years old, and put her on a blanket with some toys. We spent hours on our knees, thinning the beets, row after row after row. The backs of my hands blistered. At dark we would literally fall into bed. I was never more physically exhausted.

That fall, 1935, Dad got a job in the sugar factory in Eaton and I got to start to college at Greeley.

Few freshmen were ever so ill prepared to enter college. I was seventeen years old, very immature, naïve, lacking in self-confidence, and had never even heard of goal setting for the future.

I made a request for what was called a "remission of fees". This amounted to only eighteen dollars a quarter, but was a huge amount of money to our family. The Dean told me that the last one had been issued for that quarter. "However," he said," if you keep a B average the first quarter, we will see that you get one for the next quarter." I kept a B+ average and went to his office. He had no remission of fees for me, nor any memory of his promise to me, and very condescendingly said, "If anyone ever tells you anything like that again, have them put it in writing." It never occurred to me that I might put up an argument, reminding him of other things said in that original conversation. I left his office like a whipped puppy.

I had always been a good student and loved school. With even a little guidance, I should have sailed straight through college and graduated with honors. I wish I could say that is what happened.

I lived at McClelland's "freshman house" on 8th Avenue and my roommate was a girl named Dorothy, whose parents owned a Cadillac agency in Kansas. She had arrived first and usurped all the closet space. Dorothy was very small, wore a "sample size" shoe and had made arrangements with the large department stores in Denver to buy their samples at the end of each season. The entire closet floor was covered with her shoes. I had never seen so many pairs of shoes. She was an only child, evidently very pampered, and immediately informed me, "You can't touch me with a ten foot pole." She flunked out the first quarter.

I worked at a variety of NYA jobs, plus anything else I could get to do in order to stay in school. How many of today's youth would be willing to paint porch furniture for ten cents an hour? Or baby sit several children for fifty cents a night with no "refrigerator privileges" and no ride home?

My main NYA job was in the library stacks, typing new cards for book pockets. It was boring and I hated doing it, as it meant spending long hours alone, down in the dungeon-like, musty basement of the library. I can smell it yet.

The head librarian, whose name I have forgotten, was on a city commission and had to write a lengthy report to be submitted to the city fathers. His handwriting was so atrocious that no one could read it. When he found that I could usually decipher his writing, he brought me up to his office. Thereafter, I spent most of my time transcribing and typing up his scribbled notes.

During my freshman year, I met, and fell head-over-heels for blonde, 6'3" Harold McBride (Mac), who looked like Gene Raymond. The Lord was with me. I didn't marry him.

During my sophomore year, I worked at McClelland's for my room. On Saturdays, I also worked downtown at the Kress store, a five and dime, where I had charge of the candy counter. The most expensive delicacy at my counter was cashew nuts, which were fifty cents a pound.

I usually walked the mile downtown, as it cost five cents to ride the bus. The "Blue Plate Special" was a quarter at the lunch counter. After getting off work at nine o'clock, I'd usually walk home again. My take-home pay for the day was ninety-five cents, and was what I had to eat on for the week.

During my sophomore year, my roommate was Marge Eberhart, a girl from Loveland. She was two years ahead of me in school, a mature, sensible girl, and the oldest of ten children. We became best friends.

Marge worked at J.C. Penny's downtown on Saturdays. She brought home about the same amount of money in her pay envelope that I did. We did "light housekeeping" in McClelland's basement, along with the other girls who lived there. Each girl had her own shelf space and cooked her own food. Marge and I "pooled" our resources. During the summers Marge worked at the canning factory in Loveland, where they canned a variety of vegetables—peas, beans, carrots, tomatoes, corn. Cans that missed getting labeled, or the labels didn't stick, were sold to them for a few cents a can. We never knew what we were going to be eating until we opened the can.

We bought day-old bread for half price. The "light housekeeping" was very light most of the time. But Marge and I have remained very special friends for over sixty years. We love each other like sisters.

During the first two years I was in college, the most money I spent during any one quarter was $92.00.

In January of 1937, during my sophomore year, our family moved to Ohio. Hoyt arranged for Dad to "share-crop" the Treece place, near Rushsylvania. Helen was teaching in LaSalle, just south of Greeley. The night before the family was to leave for Ohio, they stayed at a motel on Greeley's south side. Helen and I met them there. I remember Mother touching my arm, her lips quivering, as she said, "I may never see you again." Of course, she did. But it must have been a very sad time for her, leaving two young girls in Colorado, not knowing when, if ever, she would see us again.

Marvin, fifteen, drove the Studebaker with Mother, Jean, and Grandpa riding in it, and followed Dad, who was driving the farm truck loaded with everything they owned. Most "Okies" went to California. Our family, fortunately, went to Ohio.

1937 was the year of the "big flood" along the Ohio River and much of the Cincinnati area lay under water. Someone reported to Helen that our parents had drowned in the flood. Communications were poor at that time. Helen walked to the train depot in LaSalle to see if a telegram had come for her. When she found none, she wrote to Ohio, and waited, and waited, for a reply. Those were anxious days.

Our family reached central Ohio safely, of course, as they were nowhere near the flooding Ohio River. Marvin, who had driven the tractor and the farm truck for several years, was too young for a driver's license, so it was fortunate that no police stopped them during the trip east.

That summer, I found a room at Mrs. Lynn's on 9th Avenue near downtown Greeley, where I worked full-time at the candy counter at the Kress store. Mrs. Lynn was a petite lady, with snow-white hair, and a pixie sense of humor. Her daughter, Frances (probably thirty-five) had never married, had a good job in Mr. Kelly's law office, and lived at home. Frances played the piano well, and we all three loved to sing. My stay with them was very pleasant and we remained good friends for many years. In fact, more than twenty years later, when I was teaching in California, I turned from the chalkboard one day to see the two of them standing in my classroom, looking exactly as I had remembered them. It was a delightful surprise.

While living at the Lynn's, I was sleeping late one Saturday morning when a Mrs. Greenlee, whom I had never met, walked into my upstairs bedroom. While I was still lying in bed, she offered me a job as teacher of the East Sunnyside District's one-room school, located just east of Grover. I have no memory of how she even knew I existed. I had no money to continue college, so I took the job. I had completed my "methods" courses under Dr. Paul McKee and Dr. Annie McCowan (authors of many textbooks), and Dr. Helen Davis. I had done my observation in Maridel Rudd's first grade class at the College Training School. And I had spent spring quarter doing my student teaching at Big Bend School, just out of LaSalle, where I had thirty-two second graders, all children of Mexican beet workers. Therefore, I was eligible for a teacher's certificate in Colorado.

That first year of teaching, I had five students from two families—one in second grade, two in fourth grade, and two in fifth grade. I roomed/boarded with the Greenlee's and drove their two little girls, Shirley, a fifth grader and Roberta, a fourth grader, to school every morning in their Model A Ford.

Once Mrs. Greenlee asked Shirley, "How does Miss Mitchell drive?" Shirley's answer was, "About like me." They laughed, but Shirley was near the truth, for I had driven very few times before coming there.

The Greenlee's lived eighty miles northeast of Greeley, just about a mile north of the butte, which Michener wrote about in his book "Centennial". Many times, during that school year, I walked down to that butte for a few moments of privacy, as respite from the Greenlee youngsters who I was with both night and day.

I'm sure I would have died of loneliness in that isolated area had it not been for Gladys Popham Cameron, who taught in the adjoining district. She was newly married and her husband, Arthur, drove out to get her on alternate weekends. They would swing by Greenlee's and take me into Greeley with them. Arthur was an interesting fellow who raised tropical fish. He had a brother, Rex, who was a journeyman plumber, working toward his Master's license. The four of us had lots of good times together.

Before the year was out, Gladys became pregnant and had to stop teaching. Rex, bless him, continued to make that long drive on alternate weekends, coming to get me on Friday nights and taking me back on Sunday night. I usually stayed with Marge, at McClelland's, but sometimes I stayed with Gladys and Art over the weekend.

My salary was seventy-five dollars a month, which was the base salary paid by the State. I paid twenty dollars a month for my room, board, and laundry. Each weekend that I went in to Greeley, Mrs. Greenlee refunded two dollars. I shared a bed with her elderly mother.

By Christmas of 1937, I had saved enough money to make my first trip to Ohio. I rode the Flyer, one of the first streamlined trains, from Greeley to Chicago, and then caught a regular train on to Kenton. Dad and Marvin met me at the station. Marvin had grown from boy to man since I'd seen him, and Jean was five years old. It was good to be home.

It rained every day. This dry-lander, who had seldom seen rain—and had never seen fog—loved it. In northeastern Colorado, our ground had been covered with snow since early October, and it would not melt before late April or early May. In "beautiful Ohio", the lawns were still lush and green. I knew then I'd come back to Ohio.

June Peterson, a college friend who roomed at McClelland's, invited me to spend New Years with her at her home in Chicago, en route back to Colorado. That experience proved to be the highlight of my young life.

June's family lived well, and her mother very generously gave us twenty-five dollars to spend that weekend, a lot of money in 1937. On New Year's Eve, we ate pheasant under glass at a fancy restaurant in downtown Chicago, and then went to see Sonja Henie and her troupe of skaters, who put on a beautifully staged ice show at the Chicago Stadium.

It was the first time I had ever seen a large stadium, or such a huge crowd, or such an exciting and beautifully staged performance, and I literally wept with the thrill of it all. It was, for this country girl of very limited experiences, the first exposure to the many wonders awaiting me in the big, big world.

Chicago is aptly called the Windy City. When we left the Stadium after the ice show, we walked several blocks to meet a group of June's friends who planned to spend New Year's Eve together. I had on fur-lined leather gloves, a Christmas gift from Rex, yet my hands were nearly frozen by the time we reached our destination.

Toward morning, the whole group of us went to one of the large Catholic churches in the area, for early mass. (I'm not sure anyone in the group was Catholic.) As we were walking up the steps outside the church, someone said to the priest, "Well, Father O'Malley, did you get drunk last night?"

Father O'Malley laughed heartily and answered, in a heavy Irish accent, "No, airly this mornin'." I was shocked. Such talk at church.

No doubt the most valuable thing I did for the five students that first year of teaching, was to take them to the Museum of Natural History in Denver. None of them had been to Denver. The three McLaughlin children had never even seen a grocery store, except for the "pretend" one we made at school to liven up our arithmetic lessons.

Soon after Marge graduated from college that spring, she married Orville Hoffman, a high school friend who had gone to Boulder to college. Rex and I stood up with them, and we went with them to tell her parents.

Marge was very musical. She had a lovely true-toned soprano voice, played the piano well, and had applied for a position as music teacher in Denver. When she said, "Mother, we have some news to tell you," her mother excitedly said, "You got the job." Years later, Marge saw a letter her mother had written concerning that night, and only then we learned how perturbed her mother was at hearing her "news."

After my first term of teaching ended, I returned to Ohio via a Greyhound bus. A large choral group from the University of Michigan, if I remember correctly, was on that bus. During the long trip, we sang all the songs popular at that time, plus a lot of "oldies" and had a marvelous time. These students included me in all their activities as if I belonged to the group. It was the most enjoyable bus trip I ever had.

Ohio is beautiful in the spring. I had never seen anything like it—lilac bushes and dozens of other flowering shrubs in bloom, hundreds of beautiful hardwood trees, and lush, green lawns everywhere. I will never forget my first trip into the MacO'Chee Valley, just out of West Liberty, on our way to visit Aunt Alice. It was, without a doubt, the most beautiful panorama I had ever seen. After the flat, barren eastern Colorado prairies, Ohio seemed like a fairyland. It was the beginning of a love affair that would last a lifetime.

Aunt Alice, Dad's only sister, was two years older than he. She was a lovely, neat little lady, very prim and proper, and married to gentle Uncle Irvin Stuart. They had three children: Mildred Stuart Greene, Byron Stuart, and Mabel Stuart Foster. Mabel, my age and a

Parkinson's victim, died in 1981. Byron, too, is gone. Mildred, the oldest, passed away at ninety-three in 2002.

After a short visit at home, I returned to the Greeley campus to attend summer school, again living at McClelland's.

One Sunday, I was at Marge and Orville's in Loveland. We went swimming in their lake.

Too late, I realized I still had on my new Elgin wristwatch, my first major purchase. I'd saved money all year to buy it. It cost thirty-five dollars. Orville put it in gasoline to keep it from rusting. I took it to the jeweler the next day. It never again kept accurate time.

That fall, I taught seventh and eighth grades at Trilby School in Larimer County, just south of Ft. Collins. I rented an efficiency apartment in Ft. Collins, as I thought it would be great to have a place of my own. I hated it. I kept it one month, then moved in with a family whose daughter, Frances, taught the lower grades at Trilby. I paid twenty-five dollars a month for my board and room, and I also paid for the gas, as Frances drove us to school each day.

Vi, my fifth grade teacher, was teaching in Larimer County at a nearby school. Why the County Superintendent asked me to give a book review at the first county teacher's meeting, I do not remember. I was new in the area, younger than most of the teachers, and less experienced. However, I worked hard to prepare a good review. I have forgotten the name of the book, but it had to do with the emerging forces that destined Europe for WWII.

On the day of the meeting, Vi was not in the audience and I was relieved, as I felt I would be very nervous, speaking in front of her. I started well, my voice not shaking as it usually did when I spoke before a group. Then, I saw Vi come through the door and take a seat. Her presence did not bother me, however, and it was great to see her again after all those years.

When school was out that spring of 1939, I rode the bus to Ohio again, for a visit with my parents. The local Rushsylvania School needed a sixth grade teacher. I applied for the job and was hired. I returned to the Greeley campus for summer school, living on 11th Avenue with the Kelly's (the lawyer that Frances Lynn worked for.) Mrs. Kelly was one of the dearest ladies I have ever known. We became great friends and corresponded until her death many years later.

In back: Jean, Sarah, Helen, Marvin. In front: Dad and Mother.

The fall of 1939, for the first time in five years, I lived at home with my parents, on the Treece place, just out of Rushsylvania. Jean was a first grader. Marvin was a high school junior. Our parents were still "sharecroppers", but were beginning to recover financially.

The first year in Ohio, Mother nearly worked herself to death trying to preserve all the fruits and vegetables produced on their farm. After the meager living they'd eked out on the eastern Colorado plains, she could not believe that such abundance was going to be available to her every year in the rich farmlands of Ohio.

That fall, I bought my first car, a maroon Ford, which had been used as a demonstrator. It had two hundred miles on it, was in perfect condition, and cost me four hundred fifty dollars.

At Rushsylvania, I had forty-five sixth graders, most of whom were eleven years old. I was twenty-one. They loved me and I loved them. We had a large, pleasant classroom, and it was a most enjoyable year. My salary was one hundred dollars a month for nine months.

Years later, when I was sixty-five, I attended a wedding reception in Rushsylvania, the first time I'd been back there for many years. Jean said to me, "Do you recognize the gentleman in the light tan suit?" Of course I didn't. He was a white haired, middle-aged man. "That is Charles Stanford," she said—a member of that sixth grade class.

I walked over and sat down beside him. When he finished talking with his wife, I laid my hand on his knee and asked, "Do you have any idea who I am?" Of course, he didn't. "I was your sixth grade teacher," I said. He threw his arm around me, drew me over to his wife, and said, "Honey, I want you to meet the first lady I ever fell in love with." I have always felt that was a super compliment—the kind every teacher would like to hear.

Another couple from that class, Patsy Beck and Bob Lyons, married. The first trip they took, after Bob's retirement, was to come to Cincinnati to see me. Their visit was a highlight of my summer.

I had a head of thick, dark-brown, shoulder length hair, which (in Colorado) I had been wearing in a pile of curls on the top of my head. In 1939 in Ohio, none of the other teachers were wearing that style, so the first weekend after school began, I shampooed my hair, and left it shoulder length. On Monday morning as I went up the stairs to the Principal's office to sign in, the coach was coming toward me in the hallway. He stopped me, turned me around by the shoulders, and said, "I always wondered what you'd look like with your hair down." Those were the first words Paul Gettys ever spoke to me.

Sometime later, he said, "If you will drive your car, I'll take you to the football game at Ohio State on Saturday." Paul did not own a car at that time, as this was his first full year of teaching after college graduation. (He had worked for three years, after graduation from high school, in order to save money to start to college.) I agreed to drive. That was our first date—an Ohio State football game, October 21, 1939.

I had just purchased a new winter coat, a black Betty Rose with a gorgeous black fur collar. I paid forty dollars for it, a good price for a coat at that time. A drizzly rain fell all during the game, and as the fur got wet, it smelled just like our old farm dog. I was so embarrassed. I was sure Paul would never ask me out again. He did.

By Christmas we were going pretty "steady" and one night, after a date, I found a beautiful, mirrored silver-and-blue velvet boxed set of "Evening in Paris" in the back seat of my car. Not a word had been said about the gift.

During the early spring, after Paul had been to his home, just east of Columbus,

he showed me two fur stoles—a black fox and a red fox. Both were beautiful fur pieces as Paul's father was a fur dealer. "Choose the one you like best," he said.

I hesitated, as I knew this would be a real commitment, and I was not sure I was ready to make such a commitment. Finally, I took the red fox fur home. I stored it away in tissue in the cedar chest Rex had sent me, for several weeks before showing it to my parents.

Paul was living with Don and Hildred Chism in Rushsylvania. After a date, we'd park in front of their house and listen to "Moon River", a program that came on WLW at 11:00 P.M. We fell in love to the rich, melodious tones of Peter Grant's voice saying:

Moon River, a lazy stream of dreams,
Where vain desires forget themselves
In the loveliness of sleep.
Moon River, enchanted white ribbon,
Twined in the hair of night,
Where nothing is but sleep.
Dream on, sleep on,
Care will not seek for thee.
Float on, drift on, Moon River,
To the sea.

His program ended at 11:30 P.M., after which I still had to drive home. I never got enough sleep that spring.

Sarah, Marvin, Helen and Dad. Jean and Mother in front.
• Sarah's 1939–40 school picture

During the summer of 1940, I went back to Greeley for summer school, this time sharing a room in one of the new dormitories with Helen. I worked in the dining hall, serving tables, for my meals.

Luckily, I was asked to usher for a series of lectures on nutrition, led by a doctor from the Mayo Clinic, and held at one of the downtown hotels in Greeley. I have been grateful for this "extra-curricular" education many times, as it inspired me to make a continuing, life-long study of nutrition. As I have reached my eighty-fourth birthday in excellent health, I give much credit to the happy circumstance of ushering for that very informative lecture series.

I also credit two books, Adele Davis' *Let's Cook It Right* and Norman Vincent Peale's life-changing *The Power of Positive Thinking*, both given to me in 1940 by my sister, Helen.

Every day during that summer, I got a long letter from Paul, who was working on a private yacht in Grosse Point, Michigan, with his former brother-in-law, Chuck Yokum. I was the envy of all the girls in the dorm. The letters were an incongruity, however, for Paul proved to be a very quiet, very private, uncommunicative man. He always said he never had a chance to talk—he had four older sisters and then married me.

Paul moved to Marseilles the fall of 1940, where he taught high school English and coached basketball, baseball, and track. Our country had not yet recovered from the Depression. There were fifty-three applicants for that job, which paid $1200.00 a year. He was fortunate to get it. He roomed/boarded with Paul and Katherine Hughes, who lived across the street from the Marseilles school.

During that year (1940–41), I again taught a sixth grade class and lived at home, just out of Rushsylvania. One Wednesday night after school started, Paul and I met in Kenton and went to a movie. When we came out of the theater, my car had a flat tire. We called AAA and while they fixed the tire, we sat in Paul's car (he had bought a cute Plymouth coupe with yellow-spoked wheels) and planned to elope, which we did on October 5, 1940.

Paul Gettys. • Paul on the yacht.

We told my parents that we were going down to see Irene and Beulah, Paul's sisters who lived in Cincinnati. Instead, we went across the Ohio River, to Covington, Kentucky. Immediately, a man jumped on our running board, wanting to guide us to a Justice of the Peace. Covington was a haven for elopers from Ohio and was targeted by newsmen seeking information on marriage licenses issued to Ohio residents. I knew that I would be fired if anyone found out we were married, as the job market in 1940 was not open to married women. Therefore, we drove on to Burlington, Kentucky to purchase our license.

It was a Saturday afternoon and I still marvel that the Court House was open. The World Series game—Detroit vs. Cincinnati—was on the radio and we sat in front of the Burlington Court House and listened to the game. Eventually, we realized it was nearly 4:00 P.M. and time for the Court House to close. Luckily, we got our license. We drove on to Williamstown, Kentucky to be married, thinking we might escape the prying eyes of news hounds.

It was a very hot day, roads were poor, and I thought we'd never get to Williamstown. The fact that we'd told my parents a scenario that was not true weighed heavily on my mind and I began to get a miserable headache. We finally located Mr. Felix Struve, a retired Methodist minister, who married us in his home, with his wife and a neighbor man as witnesses. "It's a good thing you didn't come an hour earlier," Mr. Struve said, "as I was too sick to marry you." I knew exactly how he felt.

We drove back into Cincinnati and north on Route 42, a main artery at that time. Somewhere in the Reading area, we found a small restaurant and a place for the night. Holiday Inns were still a convenience of the future.

It had been a long day and we were both nervous about this first night together. We took long, hot showers. We perfumed and after-shaved. The prolonged preparation was the prologue to a night of tender intimacy. It was a habit that we continued for more than fifty years together.

During the following week, Paul wrote that he thought we should tell our parents that we were married. We did. Jean, only a second grader, never told a soul until after school was out and we could announce our marriage.

When that school year ended, Paul and I took a honeymoon trip to Niagara Falls. We stopped in Cleveland to see Bob Feller pitch for the Indians—my first major league baseball game.

Paul in 1939

When we got to Buffalo, we drove out to see Minta Keever Galbraith and her two little girls. Minta and I had not seen each other since we were about eight years old.

Niagara Falls, one of the world's most spectacular tourist attractions, is awe-inspiring. However, I would never risk taking any of the rides across the roaring, whirling waters.

On our return trip, we drove south through New York State, through the Pennsylvania mountains, West Virginia, and into Marietta, Ohio. It was a beautiful, if belated, honeymoon trip.

That summer, 1941, we moved our few belongings, in the back of Paul's little Plymouth coupe, to a house on East Lane Avenue in Columbus, where we lived rent-free for the summer quarter at OSU, in return for taking care of the house, the yard, and the student renter in one of the upstairs rooms. Paul began work on his Master's Degree. He did not complete it until 1947, due to the intervention of WWII.

The fall of 1941, we rented Frances Chandler's furnished house, on the outskirts of Marseilles, for eighteen dollars a month. We had a coal stove in the living room, an oil kitchen stove to cook on, a pitcher pump in the yard, and a two-holer out back. We were happy as larks.

During that year, our church undertook a rather ambitious production of a three-act play called "The Rock", about Peter, the disciple of Jesus. Paul played the part of Peter. I also had a major part. We put it on for the Presbyterian Church in Marseilles and also in Forest, as Pastor Duggan had charge of both churches. Many people thought we named our son after that play. We didn't. Paul chose the name, Rock, long before, from a Zane Grey book he'd read.

During the summer of 1942 Paul helped build the Marion Supply Depot for the war effort. He came home so exhausted at night that I even had to shave him. I knew that type of exhaustion, as I had experienced it the summer I worked in the beet fields in Colorado.

Paul on the yacht. • (After) Wedding picture.

Frances wanted to move back into her own home, therefore, we moved just across the road to old Doc Chandler's house.

Doc Chandler, the town's veterinarian, was dead, but his widow lived in one part of their house. In the side yard, a luxurious $4000.00 house-trailer drew a lot of attention from passers-by. It belonged to "Chief Black Horse" and his wife, Millicent, who lived in it. The "Chief" was really one of old Doc's sons, but he passed himself off as a full-blooded Indian. He looked like an Indian, with dyed black hair, which he wore in a long braid down his back. One day he told me, "The summer after I graduated from high school, I had a job digging ditches. I made up my mind right then I'd never work that hard again." He manufactured his own life story and had "legal papers" to prove every bit of it. He traveled to state and county fairs, selling elixirs of various kinds, and soaps, from the back of the trailer. He also did tricks with a big bull- whip. He could flick a cigarette from between his wife's teeth. He gave a well-rehearsed spiel about his Indian ancestry. He had "certificates" to prove his parents had lived to be 105. It reminded me of an "ad" Dad used to say in rhyme, about some magic potion "that was guaranteed to grow hair on bald heads, doorknobs......"

During that summer, Paul accepted a coaching job in Lexington, Ohio and we moved to Mansfield, as we could find nothing to rent in Lexington. We lived on Marion Avenue, on the southwest side of Mansfield, in a beautiful old home belonging to Mr. And Mrs. Dan Wolfe. They had divided the downstairs into two sets of living quarters. We had the south side, consisting of a living room with a huge fireplace, a bedroom, bath, kitchen, and a small back porch. They had a similar unit, the complete upstairs, and the large front porch, which wrapped around the front and their side of the house. The Wolfe's were very nice people. We became good friends and corresponded for many years.

Soon after we moved to Mansfield, I went to stay with Paul's sister Sara and husband, Freddie, in Columbus, awaiting the birth of our first baby. On Saturday, Paul and I attended the Ohio State football game, and then climbed clear to the top of the stadium, in order to look out over the city. The next night, Freddie drove me to the hospital. Our first child, and only son, Rock Mitchell, was born in Doctors' Hospital, Monday, October 12, 1942, and weighed in at six pounds three ounces. Paul had time to arrive before the baby was born.

Due to a long, difficult labor, the baby was not very strong and lost a pound in weight before he started eating well. However, he soon began to thrive and was a very good baby, sleeping twenty hours out of twenty four. Mother wrote, while I was in the hospital, "I hope you give him a good solid name." We did.

No one really appreciates, nor understands, the love of their parents until they have a child of their own. Rock was a much-loved baby and is today a fine, much-loved son.

In 1942, new mothers were kept in the hospital about two weeks. Paul's sister, Sara, delivered Zane ten days after Rock was born. She was put in my room, as Dr. Brehm was our doctor. Zane was a ten-pounder and looked like a football player compared to Rock. As adults, Rock is a much larger-built man than Zane.

The year Rock was a baby was a very lonesome year for me. We had only one car, which Paul drove to Lexington every day. He often stayed late at night for basketball practice, or a game. I knew no one in the city of Mansfield. Rock was my entire world.

Toward spring we got acquainted with the Peltons. Jim taught English at Lexington, where they lived in an upstairs apartment. Anna Jane was also a new mother. Their Joe was six weeks older than Rock. We became very fond of each other and through the years have had many good times together. We consider them among our dearest friends, even though we have seen them only once in the last forty years.

Jim Stull was one of Paul's basketball stars in Lexington. He visited us often while he was a student at Bowling Green State University and followed Paul's basketball teams with great enthusiasm. Later, Paul brought him to Guam to head up the Physical Education Department at George Washington High School, where his wife, Jeanne, also taught.

After leaving Guam, Jim got his PhD at Toledo University, under the tutelage of Dr. K. C. DeGood. He and Jeanne joined the staff at Eastern Kentucky in Richmond. They have been very special friends for more than fifty years.

Paul worked at the defense plant in Shelby during the summer of 1943, then we moved back to Marseilles, where he served as Principal of the school as well as coach and teacher, replacing Oscar Musgrave, who joined the Navy. We moved into Mr. Uncapher's house, where the Musgrave's had lived. Sixteen years later, they moved into our quonset when we left Guam. As I write this, Oscar is deceased. However, Maxine and I continue to be special friends through long, newsy letters. In the fall of 1993, we saw each other for the first time in fifty years at "Homecoming" at the Presbyterian church in Marseilles. It was as if we'd never been apart. That is real friendship.

Proud mother with Rock. • Rock at 5 months.

The Uncapher house was very nice. Upstairs were four bedrooms, a sun porch, and a full bath. Downstairs there was a large front porch, a large living room, small sitting room, dining room, half-bath, kitchen, and an enclosed back porch. There was also a good-sized basement.

Mr. Uncapher had owned the grocery store in Marseilles for years. After his wife died, he sold the store to the Stalder sisters. He kept an upstairs bedroom and sun porch, and ate his meals with us.

We bought our first furniture—a blue rug, a large blue recliner, and a rose cut-velvet davenport for the small sitting room. We also bought a bedroom set and an upright piano. The rest of the furnishings were Mr. Uncapher's. We lived there for five years and he was "grandpa" to our two older children. He spent hours teaching Rock new words, such as zipper, button, sweater. Once, he made a small birdhouse and hung it out near the garage. Rock, a toddler, saw a bird go inside it and said to Mr. Uncapher, "Birdie go in." Immediately, he added a sign to the birdhouse: "Birdie Go-Inn".

When Rock was about two years old, we bought him a cute little pair of blue felt bedroom slippers. One morning while I was busy making the beds, he locked himself in the upstairs bathroom. I don't remember whether he couldn't open the door, or wouldn't open it. I could hear him playing with water. Finally, Mr. Uncapher got the ladder, climbed up the outside of the house, and let himself in through the bathroom window. He found Rock, happy as a lark, pouring the toilet bowl water from one blue felt slipper to another.

Another time, when he was about five, he was playing hide-and-seek with Allen Hughes, whose back yard abutted ours. Allen's cousin, Vernon, and the little Martin boy were also playing with them. Vernon was "it". Suddenly, the other three little boys disappeared. We looked everywhere for them, but they had just dropped out of sight. Paul let the high school boys out of school to help look for them.

The Tymochtee Creek, at the edge of town, was running high and one lady said, "This reminds me of the time years ago when those three little boys drowned in Tymochtee Creek. We buried them all in one grave." I am always amazed at the comforting remarks some people make at such a time.

After a two-hour search, a black man who delivered eggs to the Cave grocery store brought the three little boys into town. He'd picked them up at the bridge a mile south. The little Martin boy had enticed the other two to hide over near his house. The creek ran

Rock at two years.

just back of his house. The town dump lay between the Martin house and the creek. The boys threw tin cans from the dump into the fast flowing waters of the Tymochtee, then had gleefully followed the cans as they floated downstream. They had no idea they'd generated a lot of gray hairs that day.

While living in Marseilles, we became good friends with Reva and Maurice Terry. She was a teacher, and they lived on a farm just west of Marseilles. We used to go there often for home-made ice cream. We named our youngest child after Reva. They have been special friends for over fifty years.

We also became good friends with Ellen and Dick Emptage. We found that we'd been married the same day. They also eloped and were married in Kentucky. Dick and I were probably related, as both our parents attended the Johnson-Ansley family reunions. Dick is gone now, but Ellen and I remain like "sisters".

Gladys Hartle, one of the most accomplished women I have ever known, was so good to me when I came to Marseilles as a young married woman. She was an expert seamstress and taught me to sew. We remained good friends, until her death at ninety-two years of age. One of my prized possessions is an oil-on-canvas painting of the Bavarian Alps, which she did as an elderly lady. I had it beautifully framed and display it proudly as the centerpiece of my "memory wall'" in our living room.

Because of her many accomplishments, through the years I urged her to write her life story. She eventually did so, writing in long-hand, and filling two hundred thirty-six notebook pages. Susan, one of her granddaughters, put it on the computer for her. I asked her how I could get it to read. She told me that Susan's brother, Mike, lived in nearby Loveland.

Susan, Mike, Andrew, and Cheryl are the children of Gladys' only son, Richard, a medical doctor (now retired) in Lancaster. Richard was a middle school and junior high student while we lived in Marseilles. It has been fun being in contact with him again, and learning to know his son, Mike, and his lovely wife, Anna. They have two delightful little girls, Jackie and Becky, and I love them dearly.

In a school as small as Marseilles, it was almost a miracle for a coach to field championship teams, year after year, in basketball, baseball, and track. Yet, that happened while Paul was coaching at Marseilles. Several teams "made history" during his years there. The Marseilles community has a core group of unusually fine families and none of them ever doubted Paul's dedication to their young folks. It is always a joy to go back to that community, which still feels like home, even though we left there many years ago.

Ronda was born March 26, 1945 at Grant Hospital in Columbus. She weighed eight pounds two ounces. In order to be near Dr. Brehm and the hospital, I stayed with Paul's sister, Irene, who lived a few blocks from Grant. One weekend Paul brought Rock, nearly two and one-half, to Columbus. On Sunday, March 25, we drove out Sunbury Road, where Irene was nursing a phlebitis patient. It was such an extremely hot day that I got sunburned.

Soon after Paul left for Marseilles that evening, I knew that our baby was on its way. Since he was en route home, he could not be reached. I asked a friend to call the hospital the next morning, find out what I'd delivered, and then call Paul at school. She did. Unfortunately, the hospital reported on the wrong birth. A Mrs. Geddes had delivered a boy the night before. I hadn't gone to the hospital until after midnight, thus my friend should have caught the mistake. However, in her excitement, she misinformed Paul. He wrote on the blackboard at school "ANOTHER BOY!"

During WWII, every hospital was short of nurses. Twenty-three babies were delivered at Grant that night and the few nurses on duty were swamped. I had not seen our baby, but I knew that Dr. Brehm had said, "You have a lovely baby girl."

When Paul arrived at the hospital, I asked, "Did they tell you we have a baby girl?"

"No," he said. "They told me we had a boy." He went to the nursery and asked to see the baby in Room 401. When he returned, I could tell by his expression that he was not pleased. "What does she look like?" I asked.

"Well, she'd got a shock of black hair," he said. I knew immediately that they'd shown him my roommate's baby. She was married to an Italian and her little girl, who was several days old, had a head of thick, straight blue-black hair. I had seen her when they brought her in at nursing time. Paul was so upset that the nurse let us have Ronda in our room all afternoon. There was no doubt that she was our baby. She looked exactly like Paul's mother.

It's a wonder Ronda ever grew up, she had so many things happen to her. She was a climber. She'd pull out the bottom drawer, crawl into it, pull out the next one, and would soon be up on top of the buffet, or the dresser. Once, she climbed up on Uncapher's front porch railing, lost her balance, and fell over the side. Her foot caught between the posts and there she hung upside

Dick & Ellen Emptage

down, several feet from the ground. We feared she'd pulled her hip out of its socket and rushed her to the doctor. There was no apparent harm.

Another time, five year old Rock shared a caramel with her, cellophane and all. Only the good Lord kept her from choking to death. Once, she slipped on the hardwood floor at the foot of the stairway and split her lip wide open on the newel post, a scar she carries to this day.

In spite of a big garden, which meant lots of fresh vegetables all summer, bushels of potatoes for winter, plus many quarts of canned goods, we needed more income. Paul made application for a job at Delaware, a college town and a good place, we felt, to raise our children. He was offered the job, but the salary was considerably less than he was getting at Marseilles. We could not afford to take it.

That summer, we drove to Naperville, Illinois, west of Chicago, to check on a coaching offer there. En route home, we stopped in Chicago to see Paul's sister, Anah. She and her husband, Harold Crawford, lived in a lovely apartment and insisted we spend the night with them, which we had not intended to do. Anah was such a gracious hostess, I will never forget it. Her breakfast table was covered with a lovely white tablecloth with matching napkins. Pretty stemmed glasses were filled with freshly squeezed juice. I scolded her for going to so much extra trouble for our little family. She said, "In a big city, you do not get to know many people. Long ago I asked myself, 'Who would I rather serve nicely than my own family?' We live like this every day." I never forgot that, and always tried to follow her example with my own family. I regret that I never had the opportunity to know Anah better. She was an RN and an elegant lady.

Paul finished his Master's Degree and, the fall of 1948, was hired as principal of the Holmes-Liberty School in Crawford Country. We rented the Johnson house, several miles out in the country, just for the school term. While we lived there, Ellen Emptage and her children came to see us. Ronnie and Rock, six years old, went out to the barn to gather eggs.

They put them in the pockets of their overalls while they climbed the fence between the barn and the house. You can imagine what happened. We still laugh about that, but they didn't think it was funny at the time.

During the early fall, twenty-two members of Paul's family came up pheasant hunting. We had them sleeping three in a bed. Sara, Freddie, Paul, and I slept on the floor in the living room. We didn't really sleep, as we couldn't stop giggling. Freddie, always the clown,

would come up with some bit of crazy humor whenever we would finally quiet down. Paul's mother, bedded down on the couch nearby, snored loudly through it all, but the next morning thought she hadn't slept a wink because of our giggling.

Amid the laughter, Freddie had to go to the bathroom, which was off the bedroom in which three of the men were sleeping. He found his way in, but couldn't find the door out of the bedroom, nor the switch to turn on the lights. We lay in the living room, wondering if he'd fallen in. We laughed about that night for many years.

In the spring, the young Johnson couple wanted to move into their own house. Therefore, we rented Harold Kocker's house on Temple Road, and moved just prior to Reva's birth.

Once, after the Johnson's had gotten settled in their own home, I went back there for some reason. I was struck by how "homey" their house looked, compared to the way it had looked while we lived there. Mrs. Johnson had nicely framed pictures on the walls, a lace tablecloth on the table, several pretty potted plants, and nic-nacs here and there, all of which made a remarkable difference. Would I ever be able to afford such touches of luxury?

Always trying to think of some ways to earn extra income, we invested in a flock of chickens, soon after we moved to the Kocker house. The brooder-house, we found out too late, was contaminated and we lost our investment. But not before an irate Rhode Island Red rooster backed lit-

Ronda • Left to Right; Rock, Sarah, Paul and Ronda

83

tle four year-old Ronda up against the building and pecked a hole clear through her upper lip. We had him for dinner the next day.

Reva was born on June 5, 1949 in the Bucyrus Hospital. She weighed seven pounds and one ounce and was a beautiful baby. We did not know then that we would take her literally around the world and bring her back a quarter-century later to marry a Bucyrus boy.

Annabelle Angene was Rock's first grade teacher. By the time Reva was born, we'd become good friends with Annabelle and Ellis and their four children—Lyle and Carol (twins Rock's age) Nancy (just older than Ronda), and Jane (just older than Reva). Annabelle was a wonderful teacher and the best mother I ever knew.

The Angene's lived in a large home a mile or so out of Bucyrus. At that time, they didn't use their upstairs bedrooms. Annabelle laid mattresses on the floor and made it a play area for the children. She'd go to church rummage sales and buy "dress up" clothes for the children to play with—hats, bags, scarves, old jewelry, and shoes. Our children had so much fun together. I can hear them yet, clomping around on the bare wood floors, and down the stairway, in those high-heeled shoes. The Angene's have been very special friends all these years.

Again, Paul had a beautiful garden. People used to come from miles around to see his garden. I remember the abundance well, as only a few days after returning from the hospital with Reva, a brand new baby, I picked, hulled, and put up a wash-tub full of lima beans. We picked two hundred quarts of strawberries off eight rows of vines that year. And we raised eighteen bushels of potatoes. At the school Fall Festival, I won one of the prizes—a bushel of potatoes.

In spite of a big garden that helped out on the cost of feeding a family of five, we needed more income. Paul applied for a job with Bluffton College. He was offered the position of Dean of Boys, with living quarters to be an apartment in one of the dorms. The salary was so low, we could not accept it.

Paul at Western Michigan the day they played Lou Gherig and the N.Y. Yankees! • Paul

The year Reva was a baby, we got the "itch." A child visitor from New York brought it to the Chrisler family in Rushsylvania. Before they were aware of the problem, the little Chrisler girl spent the night with Jean and shared it with her. Before Jean knew she had it, she brought it to us. We generously passed it on to Louise and Bob's children, who were at our house for a weekend.

They don't call it the seven-year-itch for nothing. I thought we'd never get rid of it. I boiled the children's bedding and underclothing every day for weeks. We finally determined that the scabies had been eradicated long before, but both Rock and Ronda were allergic to the medication, thus the rash continued. I just about lost my marbles that winter. It was a scourge I would not wish on anyone.

In October, I asked Rock what he'd like to have for his eighth birthday celebration. His answer will no doubt surprise you, as it did me: "A candle-light dinner with a white table cloth." Of course, he got his wish. Reva, only fifteen months old, had been fed earlier. We were seated at the table, just the four of us, candles glowing, when someone knocked on our back door. In those days, no one locked their doors, and we called, "Come in." It was Mr. Koons, our good neighbor up the road, who had a family of half-grown, rough-neck boys. I will never forget the look on his face as he came through our kitchen door and saw our little family seated at a pretty, candle-lit table.

The fall of 1950, I began work with Empire Crafts, a New York company that sold Oneida silver flatware on a club plan. I chose to work in the plated division, as it was less expensive than the sterling and I thought I could sell it more easily.

The Baumgartners, my managers, were former teachers from Orville, Ohio. Peg Andrews, a successful sales lady from Galion, trained me. She was excellent and I always credited my immediate success to her.

The first thing I had to have, in order to work, was a car. At that time, it was almost impossible to borrow money. We went to several banks and were turned down. We finally got a loan of four hundred dollars and bought a maroon Chevy that had been used as a demonstrator. It was my responsibility to repay the loan.

Every day, I took Reva and Ronda to Annabelle's at noon. Rock went home with the Angene children after school. Annabelle fed them their supper, then Paul picked them up after his school day and took them home. I usually worked from noon until seven or eight o'clock, as many of my appointments were after the working girls got off work.

We had three beautiful patterns in Nobility silver: Royal Rose (ornate), Caprice (modern), and Reverie (plain). Nobility, a quadruple plate, was excellent quality and I did well in sales. I soon repaid the car loan. I recruited several others into the business, including Gladys Hartle, and drew an over-ride on their sales, as well. No doubt, I would have stayed with Empire Crafts for many years had we not gone to Guam.

One day early in 1951, the phone rang. It was John Niederhouser, head of the Placement Service at Ohio State University. Paul was not at home. "Do you think Paul would be interested in going to Guam?" he asked.

"I don't know, but I would." I told him, and we arranged for Paul to return his call. Rock and I got a large map and spread it out on the dining room rug. It took us awhile to locate Guam, a tiny dot in the vast Pacific Ocean, east of Manila.

Guam was for many years under the auspices of the U. S. Navy. In 1951 Congress passed what was called The Organic Act for Guam, giving Guam a semi-autonomous government under our Department of Interior. The Honorable Carlton Skinner, Guam's first appointed Governor, selected Dr. Jose Palomo, a native Guamanian, as the first Director of Education.

Dr. Palomo, educated in the Philippines, received his Ph.D. from the Ohio State University and had, at one time, been professor of Romance Languages there. He, naturally, returned to Ohio State University for personnel to help rebuild the educational system on Guam, after WWII.

The Japanese bombed Guam the same day they bombed Pearl Harbor. During the Japanese occupation, schools did not operate. The Island was liberated by the Americans approximately three years later. Liberation Day, Guam's "Fourth of July", is celebrated each year with a gala parade along Marine Drive.

If you would like to learn more about the occupation of Guam by the Japanese, read "Robinson Crusoe of Guam", a true story of Tweed, a U. S. Marine, who hid out on the Island during the Japanese occupation. He tells how his life was saved time and again by Guamanian heroism, at the cost of many Guamanian lives.

As I remember it, our interview with Dr. Palomo, at the OSU Placement Office, was in February. He was looking for three assistants: a Supervisor for the Island's more than twenty elementary schools, a man to head the Vocational Department, and a Principal for George Washington High School. Paul was applying for the latter position.

At the close of the interview, Dr. Palomo said, "I will make no decision until I reach the west coast, as I have interviews set up at several other universities."

"That will be too late for us," I blurted out. "We have to move by the end of the school term." The Kockers wanted to live in the house we were renting from them.

Reva with a large Pandamus nut on Guam

Within a day or two, we got a call from Dr. Palomo, who was in St. Louis. He offered Paul the position as Principal of the George Washington HS (over two thousand students), a two-year contract, with a first year salary of $4700.00 and a second year salary of $5700.00. The Government of Guam would pay our travel expenses, via Pan Am, from Ohio to Guam and back to Ohio at the end of the contract. They would also ship our car and small household goods. Quonset housing would be furnished to us for fifty dollars a month, including utilities. We blindly agreed to embark upon this unusual adventure.

The next few weeks saw us making preparations for moving eight thousand miles from home. We had to get vaccinations, apply for passports, arrange for a public sale of our furniture, and notify our relatives. In many ways, telling our families was the most difficult thing we had to do.

One Sunday, we invited my parents over for dinner, thinking that it would be an appropriate time to tell them our plans. Rock's vaccination had really "taken" and his upper arm looked very angry. I was standing at the stove, stirring gravy, when Mother noticed his arm. "Rock," she said with a great deal of concern in her voice, "what did you do to your arm?"

"Oh, it's just a vaccination," he told her.

"Vaccination? Why would you be getting vaccinated?" she asked.

"We're going to Guam," he told her, matter-of-factly.

After the shock wore off, Mother was great about it. "I always envied Grace her experiences in Europe," she said. "For years I've wished I could do something like that." Her reaction was a real encouragement to us.

Clockwise from left: Sarah, Paul, Rock, Ronda & Reva
in Jim Stull's yard on Guam.

Dr. Palomo filled the other two positions with Ohio Staters, also—Dr. Robert Meran, of Columbus, for the Vocational position and Pearl Heidorn, of Pataskala, for Supervisor of the Elementary Schools.

We were ready to leave, but our passports didn't come. After our sale, we stayed several days with my folks, then a couple of days with Mose and Helen. Eventually, after several desperate phone calls to Washington D. C., the passports finally arrived.

Mose had coon dogs, which were alive with fleas. I had never had any experience with fleas and didn't realize how allergic I was to flea bites. On our way west, I worried that no country would let me out or in.

As we left Springfield, headed west in our little maroon Chevy, on old route 40, with the children in the back seat—Rock (eight), Ronda (six), and Reva (two)—I was suddenly overwhelmed with the feeling that we were all alone in the world. We were leaving all our friends and family behind, and going into the proverbial unknown. What lay ahead for us and for these three little ones? We had no way of knowing, then, that this move would provide many broadening, educational experiences, including world travel, a host of exceptional friends, and security in our retirement years.

En route west, we stopped in Norton, Kansas to see the Keevers, who I had not seen since I was about eight years old. Letha was the same dear lady that I'd remembered all through the years and she welcomed us with open arms. She still had the little wooden rocker we used to sit in as children, and I could still sit in it.

We drove west of Denver to the Red Rocks Park, then north to Loveland, where we had dinner with Marge and Orville Hoffman. We were late getting there, as we drove considerably out of our way getting out of Denver. Marge had gone all out to make a delicious dinner—fried chicken, mashed potatoes, and all the trimmings. It had been ready for an hour. Orville was starving to death. Two-year-old Reva spilled kool-aid on their new cream-colored carpeting. It's a wonder our friendship survived.

From Loveland, we drove up the Thompson Canyon to Estes Park, over Trail Ridge Road to Grand Lake, where the children all rode horses, and on to Steamboat Springs. In Salt Lake City we toured the Mormon Tabernacle grounds, then crossed the slat flats around the Great Salt Lake, and drove on to Sacramento, California's picturesque capital.

It was early August and our children had traveled across country dressed in shorts. When we reached San Francisco, we had to open suitcases and get out sweaters and long pants for them, as it was cold. Men had top-coats on with collars turned up to protect their ears.

When we took the Chevy to the dock for shipment to Guam, Paul mistakenly left his good camera in the trunk of the car. Of course, he never saw it again, so we lost all the pictures he'd taken as we traveled across country.

Pan Am got into Honolulu mid-day and we roasted in our too-warm clothes. We were on space available tickets and had not expected to get "bumped" there, so had no hotel reservations. The manager of the Edgewater Hotel was good enough to let us use a room to change into lighter-weight clothing, but they were booked solid and had no rooms for us. With three small children and very limited funds, we sought help from our government personnel stationed in Honolulu. (Remember, Hawaii did not become a state until 1959.)

I have forgotten his name, but a very nice government official came to our rescue. He even invited us to their home on the other side of the Island, across the Pali, for dinner. We ate on their lanai, surrounded by swaying palms, and thoroughly enjoyed the evening. I remember his wife saying that house cleaning was minimal in Hawaii, as the trade-winds came over water and brought no dust. That sounded good to me.

This nice gentleman helped us find a cottage right on Waikiki Beach for twelve dollars a day. Sadly, those cottages, which lay in a lovely little courtyard between the Edgewater Hotel and Waikiki Beach, have long since been torn down. It was a delightful place to stay. We were there nine days before we could get on a flight to Guam.

We used the time to get acquainted with the island of Oahu. While on an island tour, we saw miles and miles of the most beautiful fields of pineapple, with not a weed anywhere. However, the ripe pineapples were rotting in the fields as the workers were on strike. Our guide told the children to go out in the field and pick as many pineapples as they wanted. We had a constant supply during our stay in Hawaii. Fresh pineapple, ripened in the field, is a treat for the gods.

In 1951, the most beautiful and most outstanding hotel on Waikiki Beach was the Royal Hawaiian—the exterior a delicate pink stucco and the interior appointed in luxury. Today, you can barely see it among the many new, towering hotels that crowd Waikiki.

We spent a lot of time on the beach with the children, just soaking up the sun and frolicking in the waves, which lapped gently on the shore. One of two elderly ladies, sitting in the sand watching our little family swim and enjoy the beach, said to the other, "I wish we could have come here when our children were small. Now, all we can do is play bridge and we could do that at home."

Sarah, Reva, Ronda and Rock at the Hawaii Conservatory
on our first trip to Guam.

89

Hawaii is certainly one of God's loveliest creations. Graceful palms sway in the gentle trade-winds. Plumeria, hibiscus, bougainvilla, alamandas, and great masses of orchids bloom continually. Everything, everywhere is clean, and colorful, and beautiful.

So many good things happened to us that I'm sure it was more than a mere "stroke of luck." The Annual Hawaiian Hula Festival was held in Kapiolani Park while we were there. What a treat to watch all those graceful, dark-skinned beauties swaying to the gentle rhythms of their native hula dances.

At that time, Hawaii Sands, a lovely open-air restaurant right on Wai-kiki, served an evening buffet that was a delightful assortment of seafood, fresh pineapple, and a myriad of other delicacies—all you could eat for one dollar. The "Gettys Five" became very familiar faces at Hawaii Sands. Sadly, this lovely place, too, has long since been torn down to make way for "progress."

One of the truly tragic sights we saw, that first trip, was the Punch Bowl Cemetery, which lies in the bowl-shaped crater of an extinct volcano, overlooking the city of Honolulu. Ernie Pyle is buried there, along with thousands upon thousands of America's finest, killed in WWII.

The sight of those interminable white crosses, row after row after row, evoked a sadness that was absolutely overwhelming. I could not stem the tears. Evidently, it affected many others in the same way, for, in a short time, all of those crosses were removed and replaced with small white markers to identify the fallen soldiers. A solid green lawn, sloping off into the distance, does not present such a vivid picture of the horrible cost of war.

We fell in love with Hawaii and have enjoyed visiting there many times through the years, as we made trips back and forth from Guam. We hoped, after our first stop there, that Guam would be at least somewhat similar.

When we finally got aboard Pan Am again, we met Catherine Sherman and her daughter, Pricilla, who were also going to Guam for a tour of duty. Bill, and two older children, Linda and Buddy, could not get on that flight, but arrived in Guam on the next flight. We became very good friends with the Shermans. Buddy was Rock's age. Pricilla, Ronda's age, was in one of my first grade classes. When they left Guam, we inherited their cat, Tailspin, who

Rock and Ronda picking ripe pineapples on Oahu.

had gotten his tail caught in the proverbial screen door as a kitten, and the end of it jutted at an angle and twirled full-circle when he purred. Later, when we lived in Redlands, we visited them in their lovely home in Riverside, California. I regret that while we were living in South America, we lost touch with the Shermans.

In 1951, Pan Am and other air carriers, flew the old prop planes. Wake Island was the refueling stop between Hawaii and Guam. Wake is a small, flat piece of barren coral in the vast Pacific. It is a miracle that any plane ever locates it for landing. When we landed there for refueling, we hoped that Guam would not be like Wake. It wasn't.

Guam is a beautiful mountainous island, covered with thousands of palm trees and lush green tropical foliage. Myriads of flowers—plumeria, house-high poinsettias, Royal Poinciana trees (called "flame trees" by the natives), tulip trees, bougainvilla, and hosts of other varieties of lovely flowers bloom year-round.

Guam is thirty-two miles long and ranges from four to eight miles in width. It is shaped like a peanut in the shell. It lies thirteen degrees from the equator and the temperature ranges from seventy-five to eighty-five degrees year round. Guam is more sultry than Hawaii, but not as steamy as Manila for it lies in the path of the trade winds.

Guam's capital, Agana, had been decimated during the Japanese attack. Everything, including the beautiful Catholic Cathedral, was leveled. In 1951 when we arrived, it could hardly be called a town. However, a few places of business had sprung up along Marine Drive and on the main street, which led up to Agana Vista.

Chomorro, the native (unwritten) language, is spoken by the older Guamanians, but the young folks all speak English, as the U.S. Navy controlled Guam for many years. Guamanians, of course, are American citizens.

We were assigned to a housing area called Tutujan, pronounced Tutuhan, located on a bluff just above the village of Agana. A circular drive came into the area and our quonset was located on the inside of the circle. Quonsets are approximately thirty feet wide by sixty feet long, with screened windows and added porches.

Our quonset had two bedrooms on one end, one large master bedroom with closet and bathroom on the other end. In between was a large living-dining area, which was screened from about 3 feet above the floor to the ceiling and ran the full length of the room. A galley kitchen flanked the dining area and a large archway "pass-through" with a wide shelf opened between the two.

Basically, families of government personnel, including the Attorney General, the head of Public Works, the Chief of Police, and an assistant to Governor Skinner lived at Tutujan.

The "Governor's Mansion", as it was called, was very close to our area. Ronda and Franz Skinner were the same age, and were soon bosom buddies. They played together regularly, as I tutored Franz in reading one summer. Ronda was prone to leave her thongs (zoris) at the

Skinner's. The chauffeur-driven black limo with license plate number "1" was often seen in our circular driveway, returning Ronda's zoris.

For the first time in our lives, we were associated with "mixed marriages." One of our neighbors was an American married to a Korean lady. Several American men were married to Japanese-Hawaiian wives. All were lovely wives and homemakers. Eventually, I had several of their children in my classes and they were all beautiful, bright, well-behaved youngsters.

The Government of Guam lent us a jeep to use until our car arrived from the USA via ship. Our quonset was sparsely, but adequately furnished, except for kitchen equipment. After "camping" for six weeks, we were very happy when the Port Authority called us to say that our household goods and car had arrived on the island.

A typhoon hit Guam the first day after our arrival. Typhoons don't just sneak up on you. They are tracked for two or three days in advance. No doubt everyone on the island knew that there was a typhoon headed our way, but no one bothered to tell us. Paul and I had gone to the PX (Navy Post Exchange) to get our first supply of groceries. We left a teen-age neighbor girl with the children. She had lived on Guam for some time and seemed dependable. While we were doing the shopping it began to rain. By the time we got our groceries loaded in the jeep, the heavens opened. The rain came down in torrents and the wind howled like a banshee. Long before we got to our quonset, we were drenched and so were the groceries. The paper bags had turned to mush and each item had to be carried in separately in the downpour, after we arrived at our quonset.

Fortunately, the experienced teen knew enough to roll down the tarps to cover the screens, so that the rain did not blow in on the furniture and the grass mats, which covered the floors. However, she had not been able to "batten down the hatches" (secure the wooden poles at the bottoms of the tarps), and they banged against the metal quonset, making a loud, frightening din. The canvases smelled musty and allowed no air to circulate within the quonset. It was not an auspicious beginning.

I suppose I shouldn't say this, but on that first day I was ready to turn around and come home. However, when you are eight thousand miles away, that is easier thought than done. I hasten to add that our eight years on Guam provided us with many fine experiences, wonderful friends, and scores of fantastic memories, and we have always felt that our decision to go to Guam was one of the best decisions we ever made—but on that first day, I didn't know all that.

The first Sunday we were on the Island, we were invited to a fiesta. Guam is a Catholic island and each native village has its "patron saint." Each village sponsors a fiesta, sometime during the year, to honor its patron saint.

One of the chief island delicacies is fanihi, or fruit bat, which is cooked (fur and all) in chicken broth. Fanihi is expensive and is reserved for special guests. Since Paul, the new George Washington High School Principal, was the "guest of honor", they proudly served fanihi at this fiesta. We dared not refuse it.

Most of the foods served were not familiar to us. Two year old Reva was really hungry, as the food line was late getting started. I took some of what appeared to be ground shrimp and gave her a bite. She immediately spewed it out, all over the floor, in front of everyone.

When I tasted it, I could see why. It had lots of "aji" in it (pronounced ahee), which is an extremely hot pepper and nearly takes your breath away.

Liquor was always served at these fiestas, and Paul, of course, was offered a drink. When he declined, one of the government men who had observed this came up and put his arm around Paul's shoulders. "Mr. Gettys, you will have to accept a drink when one is offered to you, otherwise you will offend your host and will not last long on the island."

"Well, then I won't last long," Paul, a teetotaler, responded. We were there eight years.

Paul's first big job was making out the schedule for over two thousand students at the high school. Fortunately, before leaving Ohio, he'd spent some time with the Principal of the large Mansfield High School, where he got a quick education in the mechanics of using a "schedule board."

Assigning teachers was a nightmare. Many of the returning teachers were not at all qualified to teach the subjects they had taught the previous year.

Paul requested a special meeting with the Guam Legislature. He explained to this august body that his goal was to upgrade the qualifications of teachers at GWHS to meet the accreditation standards set by the North Central Association of Schools and Colleges. The men who made up the Guam Legislature were very receptive and it is certainly to their credit that they had vision enough to see what education could do for their people. They followed Paul's recommendations almost one hundred percent and agreed to supply emergency funding to bring over qualified teachers from the States. They also agreed to fund a teacher training program starting the summer of 1952, which eventually developed into a

fully-accredited University of Guam, and now serves that entire area of the Pacific. Paul taught some of those first college classes.

Dr. Jose Palomo persuaded The Ohio State University to sponsor this embryo college. They sent Dr. Eugene Lewis, former head of the graduate School at OSU, to provide the leadership. He was an outstanding educator and leader. He immediately brought over Dr. E. B. Sessions and Dr. William Carter to work in the college. Leonard O. Andrews, who had been head of Teacher Training at OSU, also came at that time. Dr. Spencer came the following year.

Paul immediately began the process of recruiting teachers for GWHS, long-distance, for the following year of 1952–53. He tried to select young couples, where both were quali-fied teachers. He was highly successful. Among the couples he brought to Guam were Jim and Jeanne Stull, Bernie and Fran Yokel, Kay and Bill Swan, Jesse and Jeanette Pinion, Alfred and Thelma Bell, K. C. and Freda DeGood, Joe and Ann Shaw, Lute and Maxine Troesch, George and Carol Bettle, George and Sammy Jump, and many others. During the summer of 1954, a chartered plane, which we met in Honolulu, brought over another large contingent of teach-ers. This influx of qualified, dedicated teachers changed forever the face of education in the Pacific. Paul Gettys proved to be a godsend to the Island of Guam.

Because of Paul's position, we were on "the list" and were invited to all the major social affairs held on the island, both those sponsored by the Government of Guam and those spon-

Paul's students in one of his 1st college classes.
• Rock, Ronda and Reva

sored by the Navy and the Air Force. Paul worked closely with the Governor, the Admiral in charge of the Naval Base, and the Colonel at Anderson Air Force Base, who was also a member of the School Board.

When we arrived on Guam, I had no intention of teaching, as Reva was only two years old. However, Ronda was a first grader and her class needed a teacher. Interestingly, the teacher assigned to that class was Emily Haas, a girl from Windsor, Colorado. She had developed a severe ear infection and her doctor would not release her to return to the tropics. Her older sister, Clara (a junior at Windsor the year I was a senior), served as a most efficient secretary to Paul all the years we were on Guam. Her husband, Victor Obermeier, the son of a Lutheran minister in Greeley, also taught at GWHS. It's a small world.

The fall of 1951, I enrolled Reva in Mrs. Brookhart's nursery in Agana Vista, a neighboring housing area, and took charge of one of the six first grade classes at Adelupe Point, a school housed in thirty-some quonsets. Most of Adelupe's students were children of navy personnel from the big navy base at Apra Harbor, or government personnel. There were few, if any, native Guamanian children in that school.

Our quonset classrooms were sixty feet long and thirty feet wide, with screens on either side, rather than windows. The Principal, Mr. Haley, was a Georgian whose wife was Paul's librarian at GWHS. If I remember correctly, we had thirty-two teachers at Adelupe that year.

The next year, all the Adelupe students were transferred to quonsets on the naval base, while a new concrete steel-reinforced school building was constructed on Adelupe Point.

Rock's teacher at the naval base was Alta McWilliams, a Greeley graduate and a very fine teacher. I remembered her from college days.

Guam was a wonderful place for the children. We could go swimming every day. Tumon Beach, one of the most beautiful anywhere in the world, was an ideal picnic spot, with clean white sand and graceful palms for shade. We went there often, usually with the Sherman's or some other family with children. We had lots of fun on Guam.

The USO Beach was also a favorite spot, especially as the children got older. Rock became an expert ping-pong player there, and during his teens could beat any service man on the Island.

Tarague Beach, on the Air Force Base, was one of the truly spectacular beaches on the Island. All the beaches had cookout facilities and we spent many hours with a variety of friends through the years, breakfasting, or picnicking at one of the many beaches.

Guam is surrounded by a coral reef, which makes all the beaches safe for swimming.

We had, however, three "close calls" during our years on Guam. The first time we went to Tumon Beach, the tide was out and the ocean floor was covered with sea slugs, commonly called "sea cucumbers", as they resemble huge, green cucumbers. We had not seen them before and Paul and I walked out several feet into the water, still less than knee deep, absorbed with the novelty of these unusual creatures.

Reva, two years old, was sitting on the sand at the edge of the water, which was only a few inches deep. She was directly in front of a life guard. Suddenly, we looked back toward the shore and saw a lifeguard working over her. She had tried to stand in the wet sand, had lost her balance, and had fallen face down into the shallow water. There were coconuts bobbing in the water all around her, and for an instant the lifeguard had not realized the child was there. Fortunately, she swallowed the salt water into her stomach, rather than breathing it into her lungs. She vomited all the way home and was a sick little girl for two days.

We had been on the island a very short time, when the Sinclair family invited us to go with them to Talafofo Beach, a black sand beach, where, we later learned, there was a very dangerous undertow. The surrounding coral reef lies a considerable distance out from the shore at Talafofo and the waves came in more forcefully than at the other beaches.

I was swimming some distance from shore when, suddenly, I was caught in a gripping undertow that took me down to the ocean floor and head-over-heeled me several times, grinding me into the sand, before it finally released me and I bobbed to the surface. I spent the rest of the afternoon recovering my equilibrium on the beach, and we never swam at Talafofo again.

When Rock was probably eleven or twelve, a group of us went to Merizo, at the southern end of the Island, rented a small boat and went over to Cocos Island, off shore perhaps a quarter of a mile. During the afternoon, Rock was stung by a sting-ray, or perhaps a jelly-fish. His foot swelled within minutes to the size of a football and was extremely painful for days.

Most of our beach experiences, however, are very enjoyable memories.

The summer of 1953, we made our first trip back to see our families in Ohio. We flew to Honolulu, then boarded the Lurline, a Matson luxury liner, for a four-day cruise into San Francisco Bay. Catherine Sherman, who had returned to Hawaii to live, came down to the dock to wish us "bon voyage." Paul got off the ship to take one more picture, just as the crew started to raise the gangplank. I frantically called to Catherine from the ship's rail and, fortunately, she was able to persuade them to put the gangplank back down so that Paul could re-board. Had she not been there, we almost certainly would have sailed without him.

Since we were a family of five, and needed two adjoining staterooms, they assigned us much more luxurious accommodations than our space-available tickets entitled us to. We had two

Paul in his office at GWHS.

"lanai suites", with windows from floor to ceiling, rather than the usual portholes. We could literally sit and watch the ocean go by.

Even in my childhood fantasies, I had never dreamed of traveling in such luxury. The menus had no prices on them. We could order anything and everything we wanted. After two years on Guam, where the supply of fresh produce did not nearly meet the demand, our children wanted to eat nothing but fresh sliced tomatoes. They made a hit with our waiters, who called Reva, "River".

We took hula lessons, purchased a ukulele, played shuffleboard, swam in the ship's pool, ate, and loved every minute of the trip.

After two years away from our homeland, our hearts pounded with anticipation as the Lurline approached San Francisco Bay. The graceful arches of the Golden Gate Bridge, the majestic views of the Bay, and the beautiful city of San Francisco were, to us, breathtaking vistas. There is no place like home.

We flew from San Francisco to Los Angeles to see Uncle Harry Crawford, who was living with his daughter, Bertha (Mrs. Glen Zink), and her family in the suburb of Downey. Bertha and Glen took us to Knott's Berry Farm for a day of fun and good food. We also drove out to the San Fernando Valley to see my cousin, Bradley Crawford, and his family.

On our flight from Los Angeles to Chicago, the plane developed a cabin pressure problem. The pilot announced that we would have to fly south, as he dared not fly at the altitude necessary to go over the Rockies. A summer storm raged over the Ozarks, making it necessary for the pilot to fly around it. Therefore, we were late getting into Chicago and missed our plane to Ohio. The airline gave us free meal tickets for Marshall Fields dining room, but, because of lack of cabin pressure, we were all too sick to eat.

Paul bought a car as soon as we arrived in Ohio,

At Tumon Beach in 1951.

in order to have transportation during our vacation. We visited a variety of relatives, as well as friends, and had a most enjoyable summer.

When it was time to start west, on our return trip to Guam, we drove a more northerly route through South Dakota, where we saw the Corn Palace, the Badlands, Rapid City and Mt. Rushmore. We took the children to a rodeo in Cody, Wyoming, and toured Yellowstone National Park. We were thrilled to see huge herds of buffalo in Custer State Park. We followed the beautiful Grand Tetons to Jackson Hole, where we spent the night. We remember, particularly, the archway made entirely of antlers. A power outage that evening had us searching the streets of Jackson Hole to find a place to eat our evening meal. Eventually, we found a restaurant and ate a lovely meal by candlelight.

From Jackson Hole, we drove through Provo and St. George, Utah and into Las Vegas. We spent a day at Hoover Dam, a magnificent structure built on the boundary of Nevada and Arizona, in the Black Canyon of the Colorado River. We rode the elevator the

equivalent of forty-four stories down into the dam and still did not reach the concrete base, which is six hundred sixty feet thick. Lake Mead, the dam's reservoir, is one of the largest man-made bodies of water in the world.

A few days later, we left our car with Glen Zink, who had kindly agreed to sell it for us, boarded Pan Am again to return to Guam via Hawaii.

The fall of 1953, we started school in the new building on Adelupe Point. It was a beautiful structure, but proved to be inadequate to house all the students, even that first year. Three quonsets had to be added on to my end of the building, as soon as school began.

Did you ever try to get thirty-eight first graders started, with good discipline and quiet study habits, while bulldozers and cement mixers prepare three additional classrooms right next door? It was almost too much for me.

Eventually, however, that year turned out to be a joy. Doug DeGood was one of those thirty-eight first graders. He was an outstanding student, a real perfectionist, and went on to graduate from Miami University with a major in Political Science. He served as Mayor of the city of Toledo, Ohio. I tell him he is my only claim to fame.

A little blonde boy named George was also in that class. He was blessed with perfect pitch. Often, when everyone was busy working on some project, George would start a song.

At Talafofo Beach.

All the children would then join in. The seven dwarfs whistled while they worked. That very special class sang while they worked. We had a delightful year together.

During that school year, we had to move from Tutujan, as the whole area was being torn down to make way for the new Naval Hospital. We were assigned a "Butler Barracks" unit in the old Guam Memorial Hospital compound, just south of Tamuning.

Butler buildings, built originally for the military, each had three units. Ours was an end unit. The center unit was occupied by a Japanese pharmacist, Danny Moriasu, and his wife. Two ladies lived in the other end unit, beyond which was a fenced "corral" where several mentally incompetent persons spent their days. They loved our two little girls, who often went down to visit with them through the link fence.

The fall of 1954, I transferred from Adelupe to the Wettengel School, where Jesse Pinion, originally one of Paul's teachers, was the principal. I was one of the six first grade teachers. Most of our students were children of Air Force personnel stationed at Anderson Air Base.

Jesse Pinion is one of the finest principals I ever taught under. We have remained great friends through the years. He served as administrator in the Los Angeles School system for many years and we saw each other several times while we lived in California. Now retired, he and Jeanette live in Cambria, California, where Jeanette works as a guide at Hearst Castle. Jesse jokingly says, "I keep Jeanette working part-time so we can continue to take many Elderhostel trips all over the world." And, bless them, they always remember to send me a card.

Near our Butler Barracks was a ball diamond, where the neighborhood kids liked to play. The older youngsters loved to jump from the bleachers, catch the iron bar that had at one time held a backstop, and swing on the bar like monkeys.

One late afternoon, Reva, not quite six, jumped and missed. She broke her arm in two places. Rock had just finished a first aid course and was a great help to me in getting her into the car, and arranging her arm comfortably on a pillow, while we drove her to the hospital.

Guam Memorial Hospital left much to be desired. I immediately told the doctor, a DP (displaced person) from Lithuania, that she had two breaks in her arm. She was X-rayed, put in a cast and brought out to me. Her cast only went to the elbow. I told the nurse that she had a break above the elbow. She went back and talked to the doctor. They both came out to the waiting room and assured me that X-rays had been taken and there was only one break.

I took her home and neither of us got any sleep that night, as she was in excruciating pain. Early the next morning, I took her back to the hospital and demanded to see the X-rays. The doctor protested greatly, but I persisted. When I was finally allowed to see them, I found that they had no picture of her arm above the elbow.

Fortunately, a bone specialist from Hawaii was on Guam, doing some intricate surgery on another patient at the hospital. He took over Reva's care. He cut off the cast, re-took X-rays, and re-set the wrist. The bone above the elbow was not only broken, but twisted in the joint. The Lord was surely with us, as the first doctor would have left Reva with a crippled arm.

At the same time, Reva lost eight teeth. So much calcium was needed for those permanent teeth that her wrist bone did not heal properly. A few days after the cast was removed, she attempted to crawl down from an upper bunk bed, while holding on to a box of crayons. She fell and re-broke her wrist in the very same place. It had to be in a cast again for several weeks. She wore a leather brace on that wrist for a year, but eventually it healed and has never caused her any problem. Her teeth, however, came in at odd angles, and in later years, required braces.

The only days of school I missed, during the years I taught on Guam, were the two days when Reva broke her arm. When I left Guam, I left seventy-five days of sick-leave unused.

During the spring of 1955, we moved from the old Guam Memorial Hospital compound to a nice housing area on the Naval Air Station, just above GWHS. Our quonset was furnished with new rattan furniture, a new electric stove, refrigerator, and deep freeze, all supplied by the Government of Guam. We also purchased a new GE washer. This was the nicest house we lived in during our eight years on Guam.

About the time we moved, I happened to be at the USO Club at Hoover Beach and noticed a studio piano, painted military gray, turned facing the wall. I asked about the piano and learned that it was scheduled for discard. They gladly gave it to me, if I would move it. I paid someone with a pick-up truck seventy five dolars to haul it from the USO Club to our quonset at NAS. We had it checked over by a Philippino piano tuner, and Paul painted it a lovely shade of green. This Gulbransen piano had a wonderful tone and was truly a gift from the hand of the Lord. Not only did our family use it, but two neighbor girls, Wanda Hassell and Mary Jane Hanna, came to our house to practice their piano lessons.

Tumon Beach in 1951

We had a wonderful group of neighbors at NAS and many warm, lasting friendships developed. We still keep in contact with many of them.

In 1956, Dr. Harm Harms and wife, Polly, came to work in the college. We will always feel very fortunate to have had the opportunity to know, and love, both Polly and Harms. They were responsible for bringing Dr. Reed Davis and wife, Mary, to Guam from West Virginia, where Reed was Dean at West Virginia Tech. About the same time, Drs. Bob and Jean Whiting came to work in the college. Also, George Perdew and his wife, Fran. We all became very close friends. When you are eight thousand miles away from your own families, you form unusually strong, long-lasting friendships with others. Through the years, these rich associations have added greatly to all our lives.

Most of the fifty-two families who lived at NAS were teachers, school administrators, or college professors. Our housing area was completely surrounded by a high, military fence. It was a worry-free environment for all the children.

Before we left for home leave, during the summer of 1955, Paul ordered a new Oldsmobile to be picked up in Lansing. It was shell beige, the first brand new car we ever owned, and one of the prettiest.

From Guam, it is nearly as close to fly to the USA through Asia and Europe, as it is to fly across the vast expanse of the Pacific Ocean. Our contract provided first class Pan Am tickets for a family of five. We traded them for tourist class, which took us a great deal farther for the same amount of money, and planned a round-the-world trip.

We flew to Manila, where we had about three hours sleep at the Manila Hotel before boarding a splendid Clipper for Hong Kong. On board with us were Marty, Esther, and Butch Williams, friends from Guam.

The Philippines, ceded by Spain to the USA in 1898, after the Spanish-American War, were governed by the United States for more than forty years, until being granted their independence in 1946.

As we flew above the city of Manila, we could see Dewey Boulevard following the coastline and lined with many beautiful buildings. Outside the city, hulls of warships

A typical Guam home.

were a grim reminder that some of the bloodiest battles of WWII were fought on Philippine soil.

Hong Kong is on Victoria Island, however the airport was on the mainland, or the Kowloon side. It is a very difficult airport to approach and our pilot circled a good many times before he could get us down safely. The first sight that greeted us was a shocker—women, dressed in black baggy pants, jackets, and "coolie" hats, mixing and carrying cement, enlarging the Pan Am terminal.

In 1955 Hong Kong's streets were crowded with refugees from Red China, many of whom were literally living on the streets. We saw a lady giving birth on the sidewalk, with only newspapers held up by friends to shield her from the passing throng. Women squatted on their haunches for hours at a time, holding embroidery hoops three or four feet in diameter, with yards of material tucked around them so as not to get it dirty on the sidewalk, as they worked intricate designs into beautiful table linens.

Porters trotted down the streets carrying long bamboo poles across their shoulders, square oil-tins of "food" hanging from each end of the pole. They poured this slop into army mess tins as dozens of hungry street-children flocked to eat the mixture. Many times, we crossed the street to get away from the sickening stench of it. It is certainly true that one half of the world does not know how the other half lives.

In the harbor at Aberdeen, thousands of junks serve as the only homes many Chinese ever know. Hordes of children live and die on the junks, without ever setting foot on land.

Our two blonde girls, Reva, six and Ronda, ten, with long curly hair hanging almost to their waists, were a novelty to the Chinese. Shy, demure mothers would pause to let their children stare and point and smile.

Indian merchants abound in Hong Kong and are very aggressive. They expect a buyer to barter and thus do not quote a reasonable price at first. We needed to purchase a suitcase. Eventually, we got a large, beautiful leather case, with solid brass fixtures, for only a few dollars.

While in Hong Kong we had the penthouse suite, including living room and dining room, at the Miramar Hotel for only sixteen dollars a day.

Guamanian students at GWHS.

From Hong Kong, we flew low over the Gulf of Tonkin, North Vietnam, and Laos—which looked from the air like a massive virgin jungle—to the city of Bangkok in Thailand, the Rice Bowl of Asia.

Bangkok, a city of over a million and a half people, lies on the Chao Phraya River about fifteen miles north of the Gulf of Siam. Bangkok, affectionately called the "Venice of Asia", was, at that time, a city of canals. Much of the city's business was done in small boats, which were poled or oared by women wearing "basket" or "lampshade" hats, as they vended their wares from floating vegetable and flower gardens. I understand that during the sixties, many of the canals were filled in to make boulevards.

The first evening, two young Thai fellows came up to Paul and asked him how they could get information about entering Ohio State. They asked the right man.

Thailand has more that 19,000 Buddhist temples, and several of the most beautiful are located in or near Bangkok. We visited the Temple of the Reclining Buddha and the White Marble Temple, both made from marble imported from Italy. We climbed the steep steps of the Temple of the Dawn, which is completely covered with decorative flower designs formed from broken bits of pottery imported from China by the ship-load, then filed into shapes of petals and leaves to decorate the exterior of this large Buddhist temple.

Thai foods are highly seasoned. We found a fine restaurant, the Oasis, which served wonderful filet mignons, grilled perfectly, with all the trimmings, for one dollar. We ate there each evening and enjoyed the floor show, beautifully staged by exotic classical Siamese dancers.

From Bangkok, we made stops at Rangoon, Burma and Calcutta, India. We landed at Calcutta airport about 8:00 P.M. The lights of the city seemed to go on forever. Calcutta is one of the largest cities in the world and is one of the world's busiest harbors. Paul bought me an unusual silk scarf, made from gold threads, beautifully embroidered, pretty enough to frame.

The beauty of Guam.

We wanted very much to fly to Agra to see the world-famous marble Taj Majal. However, we would have had to arrange for an Indian Airline flight, as Pan Am could not fly within India. That meant an extra three days, and extra expense. We decided not to include Agra, and therefore missed seeing one of the world's truly magnificent buildings.

After leaving Calcutta, we landed for refueling in Karachi, Pakistan in the middle of the night. The airport terminal "treated" us to warm mango juice. On Guam, mango trees grew in our backyard and we picked the ripe, succulent fruit from the trees many times. We wondered how mango juice could possibly taste so bad in Pakistan.

We flew over Baghdad and then Damascus, the oldest continually inhabited city in the world, and into the lovely city of Beirut, Lebanon. We were surprised at the huge terminal and the fact that every country's aircraft were there—France, Holland, Yugoslavia, Belgium, Egypt, etc. Even a U.S. Air Force plane.

Our reservations were at the St George Hotel, right on the shores of the beautiful, blue Mediterranean Sea. We arrived on a Sunday afternoon, tired after a long trip, and all of us got into our swim suits and spent the rest of the day enjoying the hotel's private beach and swimming in the clean, warm waters of the Mediterranean.

At that time, 1955, Beruit was a very beautiful city. As I write this, Beruit lies in ruins, the St. George Hotel is a skeleton, and thousands of beautiful black-eyed Lebanese children have known nothing but the horrible realities of war during their entire lives. Man's inhumanity to man is unbelievable. Years of building up are followed regularly by years of tearing down. Will it never stop?

On one of the guided tours we took through the city, we toured the campus of the American University, a lovely campus with double red hibiscus blooming everywhere. We seriously considered taking a job there. We have been grateful many times since, that we didn't.

From Beruit, our guide drove us, at break-neck speed in a 1955 Plymouth, through the lovely Bekaa Valley to Baalbek. It was like turning back the pages of history. Here, as in bible times, women were gleaning in the fields, donkeys walked the roadsides weighted down with "saddlebags" attached to either side, and camels strode lazily across the land with great loads of hay strapped to their backs.

The ruins of the Temple of Heliopolis at Baalbek present a dilemma. How did man, thousands of years ago, transport the huge granite columns from Egypt, and move the massive blocks of granite weighing several tons across the miles to Baalbek? These splendid columns stand today as proof that "where there is a will, there is a way."

From Baalbek, we drove to Damascus, Syria, where we saw our first condominiums—eight story buildings owned by eight families, each family owning one entire floor. In the early sixties, we saw the same type of condos in Lima, Peru, in South America.

In Damascus, we walked the "Street Called Straight", a covered, narrow street which runs straight through the city for one mile, and is lined on either side by tiny, dark, unventilated bazaars where intricate inlay work was being done with brass and silver and mother-of-pearl. One shop boasted of weaving the brocade used for Princess Elizabeth's wedding gown.

We saw the wall, where, reportedly, Saint Paul was lowered in a basket in order to escape death at the hands of the Jewish leaders, who were enraged that he, a highly educated and devout Pharisee, had become a zealot for the cause of a "dead Galilean".

On the way back to Beruit from Damascus, the guide drove us through a rural area where goat's cheese was made and sold. At a small shop he bought some unleavened bread, spread it with goat's cheese, and presented it to us as a treat. The children and Paul waited until the driver's eyes were on the road again, and disposed of theirs. I gamely ate mine, and rather enjoyed it, too.

From Beruit, we flew to Jerusalem, stopping en route at Damascus and at Amman, Jordan, where we saw King Hussein, then a very young and handsome man, at the airport. We flew directly over Jericho, where "the walls came tumblin' down."

Jerusalem, in 1955, was a divided city with a mile of "no man's land" between, and no one was permitted to cross the line as certain death awaited any trespasser. However, we were able to see a great deal of the city. We had nice hotel accommodations at the American Colony Hotel, where we had a lovely apartment with two bedrooms (five beds), a living room, huge bath, and three meals per day—all for twenty-one dollars.

Starting at St. Stephen's Gate, we walked the Via Dolorosa and saw all the Stations of the Cross. The guide pointed out the courtyard where Pilot, allegedly, brought Christ out and asked the crowd to release Him. We saw the stone on which He supposedly sat when they crowned Him with thorns; the spot where He sank beneath the weight of the cross and was assisted by Simon of Cyrene. We walked the Via Dolorosa to Golgotha, but the Church of the Holy Sepulchre, erected on the site where the crucifixion took place, was on the Israeli side and we could not see it. Many of the sites spoken of in the Bible are protected from visitors and cannot be seen.

We took a guided tour to The Garden of Gethsemane, which lies just east of Jerusalem, across the Kidron Valley, on the Mount of Olives. Friars of the Franciscan order have controlled the Garden since the 1600s. Because I was wearing a sleeveless dress, they were not going to let me in. I'd lived in the tropics for several years and had few things that were not sleeveless. On that particular day the temperature was 104 degrees. Finally, the guide let me borrow his coat to throw over my shoulders and I was allowed to enter.

Eight large olive trees, thought to have been there in Christ's time, still stand in the garden, among great masses of blooming bougainvilla. I picked a bougainvilla blossom to press and bring home to Mother as a souvenir. Paul kidded me about "stealing' flowers from the Garden of Gethsemane. The outer portico walls of the Garden's chapel are made up of forty-four huge wall panels, each beautifully decorated around the edges with intricate mosaics. On each of the forty-four panels, the Lord's Prayer is written in a different language. That scene remains a lovely picture on the screen of my mind, even today.

We hired a driver with a new Chrysler Windsor and made an all day trip to Bethlehem. Bethlehem is not "Oh, little town", but a city of 75,000. The myths and legends that have grown up around the Holy Land are myriad, many of which have no Biblical basis, and that was a disappointment to me.

Most of the people in that area are Muslim. Only twelve percent, they told us at that time, are Christian, and they are Catholic. When I related this to Mother, she almost scornfully said, "Well, Catholics aren't Christian." Later, Paul sized up the situation well when he said, "There are two things it would be hard to make your mother—one is a Catholic and the other is a Democrat."

From the Holy Land, we flew south over Petra and the Dead Sea, out of the "danger zone," on our way to Cairo, Egypt. The Sinai Peninsula looked absolutely desolate from the air. We saw many large ships in the Suez, waiting for permission to go through the canal. We flew over the lush Nile Valley, into Cairo, the largest city in Africa.

Cairo is a teeming city of over three million on the west bank of the Nile. In the old section of the city, little has changed through the years. Even in the new, more modern section, poverty abounds. And, of course, stifling heat. Our hotel, the Continental Savoy, was a first class hotel, yet the windows had no screens and flies were everywhere.

I picked up a "bug" in Jerusalem. By the time we got to our hotel in Cairo, I dared not leave the bathroom. Thus, I missed much of the sightseeing there. Paul took the children to the Egyptian Museum and thought that was one of the finest things he saw during the entire trip. I still regret that I missed seeing that, as it holds some of the world's great treasures, many taken from King Tut's tomb.

Every day the guide, a devout Muslim said a prayer for my quick recovery. And each evening, when he brought the family back to the hotel, he'd leave them with a wave of his hand and a "Good luck, long life, and happy times." We found that most people are very nice, wherever you go in the world.

I recovered in time to go through the City of the Dead and on to Giza, to see the Pyramids and the Sphinx. I had wanted to see them since studying about them in Vi's fifth grade geography class.

All three of the children rode camels up to the Pyramids. The girls were thrilled, but Rock called them "four-legged Osterizers."

It would have been nice to spend several days in Athens, but we had only a refueling stop there. Flying in and out of the city, we could see the Parthenon on the Acropolis. We thought, then, that sometime we would come back to that city steeped in history. (In recent years, I have made a return trip to Athens, and continued on with a cruise through the various Greek Islands, and visited the fascinating city of Istanbul, the only city that lies on two different continents.)

We spent nearly a week in Rome, the Eternal City. Pan Am had arranged a hotel for us, however, the cost (twenty-three dollars per day) was too expensive. While I sat with the children on our non-descript luggage, Paul went in search of accommodations that we could afford. As usual, he found a wonderful pension, Residensia Texas, where our family of five got nice rooms plus all meals for twenty-five dollars per day.

Rome caters to tourists. Our guide picked us up right after breakfast, brought us back to the pension for lunch, took us out again for the afternoon, and had us back in time for the evening meal. We really got to see Rome, a city of marble. It seemed especially beautiful to us, after several years of quonset huts.

The children had looked forward to Italian spaghetti, one of their favorite dishes. At the pension, spaghetti was served as a side dish with every meal and they didn't like it at all, because it wasn't like "mother used to make."

We visited St. Peter's square and saw the Pope, as he waved from an upper window and blessed the huge crowd, which had gathered in the Square below.

Our trip to the Borghese Museum was a highlight for me. I will never forget one elegant piece of sculpture, done by the artist Canova (1757–1822), "Pauline Borghese as Venus." The folds of her white marble skirt are draped so softly they look like satin.

From Rome we flew over the Alps to Zurich, Switzerland. What a beautiful country Switzerland is. We had a lovely drive through the countryside to Lucerne and Brunnen and marveled that even the barns had window boxes at every window, filled with colorful, flowering plants. At Lake Lucerne we saw the famous "Lion of Lucerne." The Alps are absolutely magnificent and every vista nurtures the soul.

In Switzerland, we lived in a lovely pension, the Florhof, where we enjoyed delicious family-style meals and slept on feather beds with down comforters and pillows. In our old Elson Readers, there was a story entitled "The Nuremburg Stove" which always intrigued me. I got to see a real Nuremburg stove in the museum in Zurich. (There is also one in the Toledo, Ohio museum.)

Zurich's Zoological gardens are among the finest in the world.

One of my favorite childhood books was *The Little Dutch Twins.* As a youngster, I had memorized "A Leak in the Dike" and read *Hans Brinker and the Silver Skates.* All my life I'd longed to visit Holland. That was our next stop.

We loved Amsterdam. It was cooler there and we bought bright red wool sweaters for the children. We stayed at the Shiller Hotel, where we had two nice rooms plus continental breakfast for $10.00 a day. We toured the city, via the canals, in beautiful glassed-in motor launches.

A hired driver took us to Vollendam, where we watched Edam cheese being made. We saw a Dutch home which included an inside milking parlor, neat as a pin. Even the tree trunks are whitewashed. We watched people standing in line to buy a "snack" from a truckload of roasted eels, a delicacy in Holland. Children in Vollendam raced about in their sabots (wooden shoes) as fast as our youngsters could run barefoot.

The Zuyder Zee, now a lake, is held back by a dike. The picturesque Dutch windmills reminded us that much of Holland is land reclaimed from the sea. To be able to visit there was a dream come true for me. I could have stayed in Holland.

From Amsterdam, we flew across the English Channel to London. We arrived there on a Saturday evening and registered at the Regent Palace Hotel, right in the heart of Picadilly Circus.

We immediately went to the front desk to arrange for guided tours of the city. We found little cooperation. It was a far cry from Rome, where everyone seemed proud to have us see the places of interest in their city.

Tired after a long day's travel, we all showered, dressed, and went down to the dining room for dinner. The waitresses, dour in low-heeled black oxfords, long-sleeved black dresses with hems at mid-calf, and small black bonnets on their heads, scowled their displeasure at having to serve us. Rock's remark was perfect, "From the looks of these waitresses, you'd think they were still mad about the Revolutionary War."

On Sunday, we took a bus tour of the city, and the driver, realizing we were seeing London for the first time, was kind enough to point out many interesting landmarks. We saw St. Paul's, Christopher Wren's beautiful Cathedral, which was miraculously spared when all the surrounding buildings fell to Nazi bombs.

We took a "tube train", as Londoners call their subway, to Hampstead Heath, where we spent a delightful afternoon watching a cricket match. The girls needed to use the bathroom and all the stations were locked. A matron opened one without charge because she "loved the beautiful sound of American voices."

We finally were able to arrange a guided tour through some of the art galleries, museums, St. James Cathedral, and Westminster Abbey.

At St. James, Rock (twelve) decided to sit on the steps at the front of the church and read, and meet us when we came out. Unfortunately, the guards would not let us return the way we entered. By the time we could get back to the front steps, Rock had simply disappeared. I was frantic. The rest of the afternoon, I could think of nothing except finding our son, lost in a strange city of millions.

When we finally got back to the Regent Palace, there sat Rock, hunched up and cold, waiting for us in the hallway, where an open window at one end produced a chilling "wind tunnel". He had decided we weren't coming back and had walked all the way to the hotel, through Trafalgar Square, and into Picadilly Circus. He was very glad to see us, but, believe me, not nearly as glad as I was to see him. As Paul's sister, Phyllis, says, "These gray hairs are service stripes."

We went through the National Museum, took a tour of the Tower of London, watched the changing of the guard at Buckingham Palace, and visited the Parliament building. In the House of Lords, I very casually sat down on one of the red leather seats, to rest a bit, as we'd been walking miles and I was tired. Immediately, one of the guards came and asked me to leave. "Only a Lord may sit in the House of Lords," he admonished. I may be the only American ever kicked out of the British House of Lords.

From London, we flew to Glasgow over miles and miles of gorgeous English country-side—endless miles of low stone fences, huge flocks of sheep, enormous country estates, and beautiful formal English gardens. I still hope to spend more time in England.

In Glasgow, Scotland we stayed at the St. Enoch Hotel, a railroad hotel, which looked drab from the outside, but proved to be a very nice hotel. We arranged a train trip to the Lake Kerin area, then went by motor coach to Loch Lomond where we boarded a loch steamer and sailed the entire length of Loch Lomond. A Scottish ladies' choral group was on board and they entertained us all afternoon with a delightful repertoire of Scottish songs. These women were beautiful, their faces glowing with health and happiness. One, a Mrs. Isa Ward, thought our girls were "wee bonnie lassies." We had high tea at the Loch Lomond Hotel, served on a patio overlooking the lake, then took the train back into Glasgow. We loved every minute of our time in Scotland.

Paul wanted to take an extra day and go to Edinburgh. We'd been on the road with three youngsters for nearly six weeks and everything we owned was dirty. I felt I had to get some laundry done before we headed to Ohio. I've always regretted that we didn't go to Edinburgh, as I'm sure I would have "burned the mid-night oil" and somehow managed to get the laundry done. Hind-sight is always so clear.

Traveling is not easy, especially with three children. In London I'd gotten on a scale which printed out my weight in stones. I paid little attention to it until we reached Ohio, where Dad kept remarking about how thin I was. I found the slip that registered stones to show him, and on the back, which I had failed to notice, it listed my weight as 116 pounds. I'd lost 14 pounds during our trip.

En route home, we flew from the Shannon Airport in Ireland to Gander, Newfoundland, where we stopped for refueling at daybreak. We could see little of the countryside, except for some scrub pine as we taxied in and out.

During a lay-over in New York, Paul and Rock went to see the United Nations Building. I stayed with the girls at the airport. We watched in horror as a little three-year-old girl got her hand caught in an escalator. I can still hear her blood-curdling screams and have often wondered what trauma resulted from that terrible accident. There are so many tragedies in the world, even for the completely innocent. I am very grateful that the Good Lord has had His umbrella of protection over our family all these years.

Our flight to Ohio landed in Pittsburgh. That landing is memorable only because it is the most painful I have experienced. My ears felt as if a cruel sadist had plunged a knife into them, then turned it continually. The pain was so severe that I went into the restroom, alone, and cried.

When we began our descent, flying low over Newark into Columbus, Ohio, we said to each other that nowhere in all our travels had we seen more beautiful scenery than right here in our own "Beautiful Ohio." Again, it was great to be home.

Paul went by bus to Lansing to pick up our new Olds. We spent a fun summer, visiting all the relatives. One evening, a bunch of us went over to Buckeye Lake Amusement Park—Irene and Beulah, Sara and Freddie, Helen and Carl, Mose and Helen, Louise and Bob, Jim and Judy, and Paul and I. There may have been a few others, I don't remember. Anyway, Paul and Jim, both baseball players, used their skills pitching at the milk bottles and were winning all the prizes. The "barkers" called Paul "The Big Rascal" whenever they saw him coming. We had a fun evening. About midnight, we all stopped at a diner on the Park grounds. The diner was ready to close, but when they saw such a large group of customers, the let us come in. We filled every booth in the place. When they found out we were all from one family, they really treated us royally.

Freddie Bever and Carl Smith were absolute clowns. With proper management, they could have made a fortune with their crazy humor. Two hours later, the waiters didn't want us to leave. We'd provided them with a lot of business, and more importantly at that hour, with a lot of laughs.

When it was time to head back to Guam, we drove through the Wisconsin dairy lands to Duluth, then west to Glacier National Park, where we were treated to some excellent entertainment by a group of native American Indians.

En route to Spokane, we drove through miles and miles of ready-to-harvest wheat fields, truly beautiful amber "waving fields of grain".

In Oregon, we stopped in Grants Pass to see Frank and Susie Lesher, neighbors during my childhood in Eastern Colorado.

Highway 101 took us to Eureka, California, where we watched the fishing boats come in and unload their day's catch. We marveled at the giant sequoias, one of which we could drive our car through, and again shipped our car from San Francisco to Guam.

We spent a few delightful days in Honolulu, as we usually did on our return trips, staying this time at Don the Beachcomber's. When we arrived back in Guam, we had been, literally, around the world.

Time on Guam passed very swiftly. It was a great place to raise a family. All the beaches had grills and picnic tables nestled among the palms, so we had lots of cook-outs and swim parties at the various beaches. Since our quonsets had screens instead of windows, often some neighbor would call, "We're going to grill out tonight. Bring your food and come eat with us." We adults would eat and visit, sitting under the swaying palms. The youngsters shot baskets, rode bikes in the area, or played their favorite game of "Yak", a lingo all its own which no adult could understand.

One evening each week, after school, I stuck a meat loaf in the oven, with some baking potatoes, and took a load of kids to the USO Beach at Hoover Park. I always had as much fun as they did. Many years later, when we celebrated our fiftieth wedding anniversary, that was one of our kids' cherished childhood memories.

Dr. Harms was an avid bowler, and he and Polly were renowned for their long morning walks. However, he had never played golf. Paul and Reed Davis, both avid golfers, enticed him to come with them to Windward Hills on Saturdays, just for the walk. Casually, they offered him a club and a ball. He began to hit a few down the fairway. Soon he had the "bug". He and Polly, Reed and Mary Davis, and Bob and Jean Whiting joined us for golf every Wednesday evening. We made up two foursomes and played together week after week. We each took turns "hosting" the group for the evening meal, after the game. We developed very close-knit friendships that have brought us all a great deal of joy through the years.

Television came to Guam in the mid fifties and we bought a TV set. We had programming for only four hours, 6:00 P.M. to 10:00 P.M., if I remember correctly. We golfers always watched Maverick together after we ate.

When it came time for our trip home during the summer of 1957, we made arrangements to go via Japan and Alaska. We flew to Manila and were given a tour of the city by a Philippino friend we'd learned to know on Guam.

He took us to a block square open meat market, the aisles running corner to corner. Carcasses of meat hung from two-by-fours on both sides of the aisles, with vendors supplying customers, and an assortment of flies fighting for their share. Before I got even midway, I had to make a quick exit into fresh air.

I have never forgotten a group of small children searching for food in the hotel's garbage cans.

We were scheduled to stop in Naha, Okinawa, but for some reason, which I have forgotten, we flew directly to Tokyo. The beautiful Imperial Palace Hotel, designed by Frank Lloyd Wright, was our home while we toured the city of Tokyo and the surrounding area. We took a day's trip by train to Nikko, past the endless rice paddies, where women were stooped over, calf-deep in water, planting the rice shoots. They were still in that position many hours later when we returned. It made me appreciate the fact that I was born in the good old USA.

Nikko, a lush, green mountainous area, had thousands of gorgeous azalea bushes in full bloom. That picture, on the screen of my mind, still gives me pleasure. The train was a super-modern, fast electric train, clean as a whistle. We Americans could learn many things from our various neighbors around the world.

One of the most memorable parts of our time in Japan was a trip we made to Mt. Fuji. Jesse Pinion, my favorite principal on Guam, had been an interpreter in Japan for three years during WWII. He had never seen Mt. Fuji, during those years, as it is usually shrouded in mist. The day we drove there, Mt Fuji was clearly visible, a perfect cone from every angle.

En route, we stopped for lunch at a lovely mountain café. There we saw trucks loaded with old newspapers. I asked what the paper was used for and learned that it is the basis for the lovely Japanese Imari ware. Paper is mixed with layers and layers of lacquer, then made into trays, bowls, or coasters, and painted with the delicate scenes that Japanese artists do so skillfully. It is an important industry in Japan.

When we reached Hakone Lake, we were amazed at the busyness of the marinas around the lake. Lots of folks had preceded us. The view of Mt. Fuji, perfectly symmetrical, was truly awe-inspiring. We were grateful that the Good Lord had removed the cloud cover for at least that one day.

Japanese cooks are famous for sukiyaki, a delicious mixture of lightly sautéed vegetables served over hot rice. Therefore, we treated ourselves to a sukiyaki meal in the dining room of the Imperial Palace. We all sat on the floor and ate from the low table in typically Japanese style. We thoroughly enjoyed the sukiyaki, but came to the conclusion that long-legged Americans don't eat as comfortably in that position as the petite Japanese do.

Continuing our flight toward Alaska, we crossed the Aleutian Island chain at early daybreak. Those small islands looked very forlorn and alone in the vast expanse of the Pacific. My brother, Marvin, was there during WWII. Fortunately, he was evacuated to

Agaña Cathedral, Guam

Salt Lake City's Bushnell hospital, due to an injury resulting from horseplay aboard ship, prior to the Japanese taking those islands in a bloody battle during that war. Nearly all his buddies were killed there.

Anchorage, Alaska looked like a familiar town to this Westerner. I liked it. We rented a car and toured the area, along with Agnes Hassell and Wanda, who also happened to be in Anchorage at that time. We saw the Portage Glacier, drove through the beautiful Matanuska Valley to Palmer, and enjoyed seeing that part of our forty-ninth state.

After a few days in Anchorage, we flew to Fairbanks, over miles and miles of wilderness marshland, cut through with rivers too numerous to count. No wonder everyone flies small pontoon planes in Alaska.

On that early morning flight, I saw one of the most beautiful sights I will ever see—Mt. McKinley, snow-covered, sparkling like a million diamonds as the early morning sun literally set it ablaze in the sky.

We walked down to the river that first evening in Fairbanks, to arrange for a Tanana River tour the following day. Mosquitoes were so thick that Rock pulled his jacket completely over his head, leaving only a peek-hole just the size of his glasses to look through as he walked. They were extra large mosquitoes, nearly the size of small grasshoppers it seemed to us, and in unbelievable masses. Needless to say, we soon went back to the hotel.

We did take a river tour the next day. On board, were two large, beautiful huskies, which took a liking to our girls and added a great deal of enjoyment to their day. We stopped at an Indian Village and watched as wolf hides were stretched during the tanning process.

Merizo at the south end of Guam. • Merizo showing an
"outhouse" over the water. • Asan, along Marine Drive on Guam.

113

We saw fish traps used by the native Indians and visited a Greek Orthodox cemetery, with interesting little burial "houses" above the ground.

When we left Fairbanks, the airplane had engine problems and we had to return to Fairbanks for repairs. Several hours later, we flew over the Yukon Territory to Skagway, Whitehorse, and Juneau. Our aircraft flew just above the rugged mountain peaks, and we felt that we could almost reach out the window and grab a handful of snow. It was a beautiful flight. We saw several glaciers, giant snow-paved roads, inching their way down the mountain-tops. Juneau, Alaska's capital, sits at the base of the Mendenhall Glacier, a spectacular setting.

After two years away from our own country, flying into the beautiful city of Seattle, on the eastern shore of Puget Sound, with Mt. Rainier towering in the distance, was one of the most beautiful sights we had ever seen.

From Seattle, we took a streamlined train, the Zephyr, gliding smoothly through the Columbia River Valley and on east to Chicago. Two very comfortable "sleeperettes" provided accommodations for the family. During the days, we thoroughly enjoyed sitting in the glass-domed upper deck, relaxing, and "watching the world go by."

In Chicago, we caught a small commuter plane, which landed in Dayton and then Columbus. Again, it was good to be home.

As I look back on these "homecomings", I'm sure that our relatives were not as glad to see us come as we were to get home. Generally, we stayed a few days with each of our parents, then a day or two with several different ones of the family. We always had a fun month before heading back to Guam. Paul's elderly father was no longer driving and was good enough to let us use his beloved Packard during our time in Ohio that summer.

Paul's long-term goal—the accreditation for the George Washington High School by the North Central Association of Schools and Colleges—came through in April. However,

The Gettys' Quonset at NAS (Naval Air Station) with a huge banana plant in the background.

we had already signed another two-year contract. We felt sure that this contract would be our last commitment to Guam.

On our return trip, we investigated the state of Florida as a place to live when we left Guam permanently. We flew into Jacksonville, rented a car, and drove across the central part of the state, visiting Marineland, Daytona Beach, Cypress Gardens, Bok Tower, Silver Springs, Orlando, Winter Haven, and Tampa.

At the Tampa airport, when we turned in the rental car, I realized for the first time that I was missing the cashmere coat I'd had made two years before, in Hong Kong. I'd left it in the luggage rack on our Delta flight into Jacksonville.

I called the Delta office in Tampa. While I was on the line, they contacted the Delta office in Miami. Soon the coat was located and arrangements made for me to pick it up at the Los Angeles airport, before leaving via Pan Am for Hawaii and Guam. Later, I wrote a thank you letter to Delta, saying, "Not only my coat, but also my hat is off to Delta Airlines."

Our years on Guam were busy, happy years. Our last two-year "tour of duty" sped by on wings. By the spring of 1959, Rock (sixteen) was finishing his junior year in high school. Ronda (twelve) was graduating from the eighth grade. Reva (nearly ten) was finishing fourth grade. When we left Ohio, in 1951, we had three small children. Now, we were preparing to return with three very mature youngsters who had seen a great deal of the world.

None of us really wanted to leave Guam after eight years of unusual experiences, delightful opportunities for travel, and the development of many close relationships with friends, yet all of us felt it was time to return to mainland USA.

We arrived at the Los Angeles airport after dark. We rented a car and drove east, looking for a motel. We found nothing. It was getting late. We were all tired after a long flight and needed to get settled for the night. Finally, we came upon a very modest motel, surrounded by a massive black-top parking lot. A brilliant neon sign flashed VACANCY. We stopped.

"We don't rent to anyone with children," the owner informed us belligerently. Our three youngsters, who had stayed at the St. George on the Mediterranean, the Regent Palace in London, and the Edgewater Beach on Waikiki, were not welcome in his dump. We were glad to drive on.

The Gettys "Five".

After checking out a job offer in Phoenix, Paul accepted a job as Principal of the High School at Twentynine Palms, California, a desert town north and east of Palm Springs, and home to a large Marine Base. In order to qualify for California certification, he needed two additional courses, even though he already had a Master's degree in School Administration, as well as more than fifteen years administrative experience.

We rented a house in Redlands for the summer and Paul enrolled at Redlands University. The house we rented had a back yard full of beautiful roses and two lovely crepe myrtle trees in front. We were close to Bill and Catherine Sherman who lived in Riverside, and we enjoyed several visits with them during the summer. Also, Uncle Harry and Bradley came out to see us while we lived there.

One day Paul came home from class with a great quantity of material that he wanted put on stencils and ready for the following day's class. I typed eighteen stencils that afternoon without one mistake. I wonder if that is a record.

We bought a brand new three bedroom, two bath home, with attached garage, in Twentynine Palms for fifteen thousand dollars. The yard was desert sand. Paul dug a ditch completely around the yard and planted oleander bushes. He could turn the hose in the ditch and water the plants easily. They thrived and soon became a local attraction.

I taught one of four first grade sections at the Oasis Elementary School just up our street, where Mr. McCune was the principal. California, at that time, had more money for schools than they knew what to do with and we lacked for nothing in the way of supplies. Teaching there was a pleasure, after having to "make do" for so many years on Guam.

One of the highlights of our first year in California was getting to know Frances Singletary, one of the most delightful, joyous personalities I have ever known. She was a high

In the living room at NAS (Naval Air Station).

school junior and became a close friend of Ronda's. For two years, she was at our house more than she was at her own home, I think, and we all learned to adore her. She and Rock were known to be the brightest students at the high school.

During Christmas vacation, 1959, we flew back to Ohio to see our families. A severe snowstorm struck central Ohio and we were unable to do much visiting of family members. Paul's elderly father had broken his hip and was bedfast, therefore, we spent most of our vacation with them at Bruno. I will always remember that Lois Anne brought some of her friends in to sing Christmas carols for us. It was not an easy thing for them to do in such weather, as telephone lines were down and many roads were closed. We appreciated her thoughtfulness.

Rock graduated from high school the spring of 1960 and was valedictorian of his class, as well as a National Honor Society Member. He wanted very much to attend Berkeley and was admitted there. However, at that time, the Berkeley campus was a hotbed of radicalism, and Paul insisted that Rock go, instead, to the University of Arizona in Tucson. He and Rock made the trip to Tucson to look over the campus, which Paul thought was beautiful. Rock was never enthusiastic about the University of Arizona. He always said the only thing he learned there was how to spit-shine his shoes, in required ROTC.

During the summer of 1960 we again rented a house in Redlands and both Paul and I attended summer school. Redlands University, at that time, was a very superior institution of higher learning.

Wayne and Martha Goddard, who we knew on Guam, and their youngsters were visiting us over the 4th of July, when we got a telegram that Paul's mother had passed away. The children and I stayed in Redlands while Paul flew home for the funeral. I attended his classes, as well as my own, and took notes for him, in an effort to keep him up with his work.

That fall, Rock started college at Tucson. It was a long six weeks before we had even a postcard from him. I missed him terribly, for we often had long talks far into the night. I not only missed him, but also his friends who had spent a lot of time in our home.

The school year of 1960–61 was the easiest teaching I ever did. Expansion at the Marine Base outside of town necessitated double sessions in our first grade classrooms. I fortunately drew the morning session. My classes ran from 8:00 A.M. to noon, when another teacher and her class took over my room. I used another workroom area until 2:00 P.M. then was free to leave.

Joshua Tree in California.

During the spring of that year, The International School Services contacted Paul and asked him to make a trip to Lima, Peru, South America to consider the position of Director of The American School in Lima. This was a private school, which served the children of American businessmen in Lima, American Embassy personnel, and wealthy Peruvians who could afford to send their offspring there.

Paul had always wanted to see South America. He flew to Lima and agreed to take the position even though it meant a considerable demotion in salary. Again, we rented a house in Redlands for the summer and both Paul and I attended summer school. Frances, bless her, continued to practically live with us and brought a great deal of joy into our household.

At the end of the summer, we packed all our household goods for shipment to Lima,

Peru via Bekins, an overseas shipper. Paul headed for Ohio in the Oldsmobile, taking Rock and Reva with him. Ronda and I stayed to supervise the packing of the furniture. Later, we cleaned up the house and left the key with the realtor, as the house had not yet sold.

We'd been back and forth, during our two years in California, with George and Sammy Jump, who we'd known on Guam. They lived in Palm Springs and took us to their home. The next morning, George drove Ronda and me to the Los Angeles airport to meet our plane for Columbus, Ohio. The smog was so thick that George had to keep his window open and guide the car just inside the white line down the middle of the road, from Banning clear in to the airport. What a friend.

Desert Blooms. • Organ Pipe cactus.

Ronda and I flew to Columbus and arrived even before the rest of the family. We had only a few days to say good-bye before leaving for Lima to fulfill a three-year contract. Rock, a sophomore, transferred to The Ohio State University, in order to be closer to family.

It grieved me greatly to leave Frances, as I loved her dearly and knew that I might never see her again. I never have. Leaving Rock was even more heart-wrenching. No one ever knew the tears I shed that summer. The last thing in the world I wanted to do was go to South America. (Years later Paul admitted that taking that job was an unwise decision.)

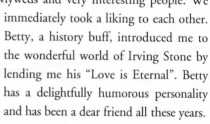

When we arrived in Lima, the house, which was to be ours, was not ready for occupancy, therefore we spent six weeks in a pension operated by an English lady. We had "high tea" every afternoon at 4:00 P.M. and it was always a treat, as the other meals were all generic brands of cauliflower casseroles.

At the pension, we met Betty and Chuck Simandl. Chuck, a retired naval officer, was the new head of the Port of Callao. He and Betty, our ages, were newlyweds and very interesting people. We

immediately took a liking to each other. Betty, a history buff, introduced me to the wonderful world of Irving Stone by lending me his "Love is Eternal". Betty has a delightfully humorous personality and has been a dear friend all these years.

For The American School to get a charter to operate, fifty percent of its student body had to be native Peruvians. Families registered their children at birth,

Yucca plant. • Rock's High School Graduation ,1960.
• More desert colors.

in order to be assured admittance to The American School. Therefore, Paul supervised a dual curriculum.

School rules would not allow the Director's wife to teach. I did, however, teach an English class during one summer session while in Lima.

Betty and Chuck eventually rented a house owned by a Mr. Delaney. She laughingly said, "En route to Peru we discussed whether to furnish our home with Early American or French Provincial. After seeing the prices, we've decided on early Delaney." They requested, and were delivered, an extra chest of drawers from one of Mr. Delaney's warehouses. When she opened the top drawer, it was alive with cockroaches. Betty loved to say, "They stood up on their hind legs and stared at me. They'd never seen a Gringo before."

By the time our house was finally available to us, the things we'd shipped from California had arrived and we moved to San Isidro, a very nice suburban area, adjacent to Miraflores. Some of the most beautiful, and unusual homes we've ever seen were in those two exclusive suburbs.

Ours was a large two-story stucco house, which fronted on Franklin Delano Roosevelt Park. There were three bedrooms and a large bath upstairs, as well as an extra wide hallway that overlooked a walled-in garden. Also, on that level, but outside the main house, was a small utility room, where I had my dryer and ironing board. A back stairway led from the utility room, down to the ground level laundry room and maid's quarters, just off the kitchen.

On the ground floor were a large living room, dining room, a full bath, an office—where I had the desk, bookcases, and piano—and a nice kitchen. There was also an attached garage.

The two floors were connected by an extra wide stairway, with a landing halfway up. On the landing, I had a large framed world map, and framed pictures lining the stairway. Once, an earthquake hit hard enough to make every picture askew at all angles. Betty and her mother were there. We first stood under the

Desert landscape. • Joshua Tree National Monument. • Southwest sunset.

archway between the dining-living rooms. When the quake continued, we vacated the house and stood out in the park until the shaking stopped.

Ours was a beautiful house. French doors opened from the living room onto a small patio, which led to the lovely walled-in garden. Marcus, a wizened little middle-aged man without teeth, took care of the yard and we always had masses of climbing geraniums in a variety of colors, tuberous begonias, carnations, alamandas, and dozens of roses and other lovely flowers blooming year round.

American families were expected to hire at least one maid. Many families had several. I eventually had to hire Julia, as everything came to the door—eggs, fresh vegetables, brooms, baskets, mail. All doors were kept locked, therefore, a maid was almost essential. Julia and Marcus each earned approximately sixteen dollars a month.

The tops of the high stucco walls around our yard were embedded with broken coke bottles to discourage thieves. Since rain seldom falls in Lima (some years never), roofs are flat and cat burglars operate with ease. During the three years we lived there, we experienced neither thievery nor toting (stealing from kitchen supplies). We believe the reason for our immunity was that we treated both Marcus and Julia with respect and, in fact, became very fond of them. I'm sure they passed the word along that we were not to be robbed.

Lima (pronounced Lee'mah), a city of approximately 1,500,000 people, lies on the Rimac River, about eight miles inland from the Pacific Ocean. The port city of Callao is a very busy harbor. Lima lies thirteen degrees from the equator, as does Guam, therefore, we expected a similar climate. Instead, we found a San Francisco or London-like climate caused by the Humboldt Current which flows about seventy miles off-shore and brings Antarctica's frigid temperatures with it. The massive Andes Mountains rise to spectacular heights just beyond the city and form a barrier, which holds the cold, moist air coming in from the Pacific in a thick cloud bank over the city. On weekends, everyone drives "up to the sun." Literally, a few miles outside of Lima, the road takes you above the cloud cover and into bright sunshine. After living in Lima for three years, we understand why the native Incas worshiped the sun god.

The seasons in Lima are reversed from ours, of course, and the direction-finder is the Southern Cross rather than the North Star.

In order to function in a Spanish speaking country, I had to learn some Spanish. I learned enough to get by. Across the park from us, a little five year old made me feel very inept. She spoke three languages fluently. Her father, an American with GM, spoke English. Her mother, who he'd married in Venezuela, spoke both French and Spanish. Their two maids, both Indians, spoke Quechua and Spanish. I'm sure this little five year old thought each person spoke a different language.

Ronda, always a fine student, soon learned to speak Spanish fluently. Many of her friends at school had lived in Lima for years, as their fathers were with General Motors, International Petroleum, Cerro de Pasco, Sears & Roebuck, or other American companies doing business there.

Reva's best friend was Lee Henderson, whose father was the Attache at the American Embassy.

Because of Paul's position, we were "on the list" and were invited to all the social functions held at the various Embassies. Usually, these functions were catered by the Lima Country Club, ranked first class in food-service artistry. I still wonder how a large turkey or ham can be carved so skillfully that one-inch squares can be lifted out with a toothpick, without disturbing the rest of the entrée.

While in Lima, we attended the large Union Church, a Protestant church, which served the North American Community. Mr. Kenyon, an English gentleman with a fine baritone, was our choir leader. Betty Simandl and I both sang alto in the choir. We also sang in a fine ladies' choral group, directed originally by Paul's music teacher, and later by an expert choral director.

On November 22, 1963, Betty and I had gone early to lay out the music for practice, which began at 1:30 P.M. The first choir member arrived about 1:20 P.M. with the news that President John F. Kennedy had been shot. Tragic news travels fast.

At the American School everyone wore uniforms. The girls' uniforms were gray wool skirts, white blouses, red ties, and navy blazers. Boys wore gray wool trousers, white shirts, red ties, and navy blazers. All wore white socks with black and white saddle oxfords. Mothers loved the uniforms and the students took great pride in their appearance.

In the late 1960s, after we were in business in Cincinnati, the Mariemont High School students traipsed by our office during their lunch period, en route to Angelo's Pizza. Scroungy dress was the "in thing" during those years, and as we watched those teenagers kicking each other in the rump, slouching along in poor posture and rumpled Levis, we could not but compare the behavior of the two student bodies, and wonder to what extent dress played a part.

Soon after arriving in Lima, we were invited to spend a weekend at a cotton plantation some distance from the city. The owner, a Mr. Campbell, was originally from Texas. He had married a wealthy French Peruvian lady, the sister of his college roommate at Case Institute in Cleveland. The Campbell children attended The American School.

Their hacienda resembled the White House. Huge stately pillars supported a massive front porch. At the back of the house, beautiful marble steps led us down to a very large swimming pool, surrounded by yards of blue tile, and invited us to relax and enjoy. A seven-car tandem garage occupied the full length of one side of the house.

Their dining room table, which easily seated twenty-four, was beautifully appointed and the elegantly carved, high-backed chairs were upholstered in rich brocade. Pearl S. Buck had been their guest the weekend prior to our arrival.

Before it began to get dark, Mr. Campbell drove us in his pick-up truck, out to the fields to show us the irrigation system, which provided ample water for his crops.

I was wearing a full-skirted dress. As I leaned over an irrigation ditch to observe the intricate valves, which he turned to increase or decrease the flow of water, I felt a stinging sensation on my upper legs and thought immediately of mosquitoes. Within an instant I was in real misery. Sand fleas, commonly called "no-seeums", had riddled my thighs and legs with a thousand stings. By the time we reached the hacienda, my legs were swelling and itching like fire. When we got home the following day, each place I had been stung was the size of a saucer (some places were as large as a dinner plate), raised a quarter to a half inch above the skin, red as fire, and hard as a rock.

A druggist recommended Kenecort-A, a cortisone cream available in Peru without a prescription. It helped, but it was weeks before all the poison was out of my system. I want to see no more "no-seeums".

While in Lima I did volunteer work at the hospital as a Pink Lady. I also studied Spanish. One day, as a challenge to myself, I thought I'd see if I could pass the test, given only in Spanish, for a Peruvian driver's license. I had an International license, so a Peuvian license was unnecessary.

During the test, I learned I had glaucoma, our nation's leading cause of blindness. Glaucoma results from a build-up of aqueous humor within the eyeball, due to clogging of the drainage membranes. Extra pressure is put on the vitreous humor, the jelly-like fluid that fills the eyeball behind the lens. Pressure of the vitreous humor on the retina causes the collapse of the tiny blood vessels that nourish the retina and the optic nerve, which play a vital part in vision. Surely, it was the hand of the Lord, and not just happenstance, that I challenged myself to take that test. The doctor quickly controlled my pressure with drops, which I used for many years. I continue to use a more updated medication.

Ronda's class chose to go to Huancayo for their senior class trip. We took Reva and a friend of hers with us. The Central Railway of Peru, built by the British, is the highest standard-gauge railway in the world. As I remember it, the trip took us through some sixty tunnels and nineteen switchbacks, as we climbed to 15,865 feet. Oxygen tanks were available for anyone suffering from "siroche", or altitude sickness. Seven of Peru's Andean peaks rise above 19,000 feet. Hauscaran, the highest peak, rises to 22,205 feet.

Huancayo is a city of approximately sixty-five thousand and lies due east of Lima. Each Saturday throughout the year, the native Indians hold a "farmers' market" there. The open square in the center of the city is lined with merchandise of all kinds, from tin cups, to mattresses, to beautifully embroidered wool skirts, to live pigs and chickens. The market is open all day on Saturday. By nightfall not a scrap of paper is left on the square. Each "bazaar" is taken down, stowed on the back of pack animals (usually llamas), and the Indians trudge home on foot, across the difficult mountain terrain. I can still see one barefoot Indian toting a live pig slung across his back, the pig squirming and grunting in the confinement of a coarsely-woven shawl. The smoothness of the setting up and the dismantling of this weekly market is a fine lesson in efficiency. It is like the tide coming in and going out and leaving on the beach not one speck of debris.

The most interesting trip we took while in Peru, was to Cusco, 11,440 feet above sea level, and the capital of the ancient Inca Empire. Here stood the Temple of the Sun, guarded by a huge fortress called Sacsahuaman, whose massive stones are laid together without mortar, yet nowhere can a knife blade be inserted between the stones.

We flew to Cusco with a group of students from Western Women's College, now a part of Miami University in Ohio. A narrow-gauge train took us from Cusco to the ancient ruins of Machu Picchu, which lie about fifty miles northwest, along the Ica River. This ancient, terraced city of stones stands majestically on a mountain eight thousand feet high and is believed to be the last bastion of the Incas. It was "lost" for over four hundred years, before explorer Hiram Bingham came upon the ruins by accident in 1911.

When we left the train station along the river, we had to board a rickety bus, the only transportation up the steep mountainside to the site of a modern lodge and the ancient ruins. If I remember correctly, we navigated twenty-one hairpin curves going up. Each new turn gave us a more panoramic view than the last and it was literally breathtaking. So was the thought of having to come down the mountain later in the day on this same rickety bus. Would the brakes hold? Or would tomorrow's *La Prensa* carry the usual headlines "Un Choque", this time referring to us?

Paul had a very interesting trip up into the mountains to Cerro de Pasco, a major mining center of approximately 25,000 population, which boasts the highest post office in the world. He served as a consultant for the new school being built there by the Cerro de Pasco Mining Corporation. He got to see the entire mining process, which separates a variety of metals, one at a time, from the same ore. And he was also shown a large room full of silver ingots, piled from floor to ceiling.

Peru has vast mineral wealth. We were told that thirty-five elite Peruvian families control all the wealth in Peru. They have no desire to see the emergence of a middle class, which the American companies doing business there were trying to develop. They prefer to keep the old feudal system, which provides them with plenty of "cholos" for slave labor.

Polly and Harms in Peru.

Not many years after we left, the leadership of the government of Peru changed and all industry was nationalized. American companies, forced to leave Peru, had no choice but to leave behind millions of dollars worth of equipment, which had no future except deterioration through years of non-use.

Another highlight of our time in Peru was a visit from Polly and Harms, our dear friends from Guam days. They were on an extended trip through South America, prior to returning to Guam for another tour of duty. Harms, an expert photographer, took dozens of color slides, which he planned to use in a series of lectures on South America.

Shortly after their return to Guam, Typhoon Karen hit the Island with winds of over two hundred miles per hour, the worst typhoon ever recorded in Pacific history. All measuring instruments broke, so no one will ever know just how much more savage the winds actually were. Nine people were killed. Harms said it could just as easily have been nine hundred.

The little family across the street brought their three small children and came to weather the storm with Polly and Harms, in their quonset. Eventually, as the typhoon worsened, all of them holed up in the bathroom. They put the children in the tub, with a mattress over their heads for protection. When morning finally came, and the eye of the storm had passed, the only part of Harms' quonset still standing was the bathroom—held together, evidently, by the weight of the tub, the water pipes in the walls, and seven very frightened people who had spent the night there.

Weeks later, Harms found one of his treasured slides of Iguassu Falls, down on the beach at Talafofo Bay. "Somehow it was not very important," Harms wrote us. "We are just glad to be alive."

When some catastrophe happens in the United States, help comes from many areas immediately. However, when you are on a small island in the middle of the Pacific Ocean, help is not immediately available. First, runways had to be cleared of debris before Red Cross planes could land. The navy base soon had reserve generators operating, but the rest of the island was without electricity for approximately six months.

During our years on Guam, Paul had worked diligently to upgrade the George Washington High School—not only the curriculum but the physical facilities, as well—to meet accreditation standards. He had, for example, supervised the installation of a stainless steel cafeteria and a modern science lab. GWHS was completely destroyed by Typhoon Karen. Years later, in Hawaii, we visited with Alvin Ratslaff, who had been head of the science department at GWHS. He told us that after Karen, nothing in the lab, of which he'd been so proud, was even worth salvaging.

Mother Nature, usually trustworthy and serene, can be unpredictably vicious.

Ronda was voted the most outstanding senior girl at The American School in Lima. Carlos Antione, whose father was the Ambassador from Costa Rica, was voted outstanding senior boy. I had never met Carlos, but had often heard Ronda speak of him.

It was the custom at The American School for the high school students to go to parties and other social affairs as a group, rather than as dating couples. One evening Ronda was waiting for her ride to a party. The doorbell rang. I answered the door. There stood a most handsome young fellow, about 6'3" and two hundred ten pounds, with a row of teeth like piano keys, and the biggest, most winning smile you ever saw—and black as the ace of spades. This was Carlos Antione, the driver of a station-wagon load of teens.

Ronda had lots of fun in Lima. For her seventeenth birthday, we had a party at our house and ninety-two of her young friends came. We rolled up the carpets, pushed the furniture all back against the walls, and everybody danced. We made up hundreds of finger sandwiches, bought dozens of frosted "donut holes" from the bakery, and had tubs of ice filled with bottles of soft drinks out in the walled-in garden. Everyone had a great time and there was not an untoward incident of any kind. This was a very special group of young folks, all from good homes, most of them college bound in the States after graduation.

Ronda graduated in December of 1962. Rock came to Lima for Christmas vacation that year. As the plane unloaded at the airport, I hardly recognized my own son, he had changed so much during the year and a half since I'd seen him. It was a very happy Christmas.

After graduation, and after the holidays, Ronda came back to the USA with Rock, and entered Ohio State University as a freshman, January 1963. It was poor judgment on our part, letting her enter such a large university at mid-year. It was even poorer judgment on the part of the OSU staff to place her in Spanish 5, simply because she could rattle the language off like a native. She had little background in Spanish, as far as grammar was concerned.

Ronda had not lived in Ohio since she was six years old. She was happy to be able to go ice-skating with her cousins and do all the usual teen-age fun things. I warned her, "Don't neglect your studies. It is important to set a precedent that first quarter." Peru's mail service was very inefficient. Often letters did not even get through. Phone service from Lima to Columbus was, for all practical purposes, non-existent, unless a call was arranged via short-wave, and for that you had to "know somebody." Before we knew what happened, Ronda was out of the university.

OSU was overloaded with freshmen students that winter quarter of 1963 and she was only a number on a page. When she failed Spanish 5, which she had no background for and should never have been assigned to in the first place, they ousted her without even contacting her. She'd gone to her grandparents' home for the weekend. When she came back to her dorm on Sunday evening, she had no room.

Ronda had always been a fine student and a very mature, dependable girl. What a crushing blow that experience was for her, and her parents were thousands of miles away. I will regret that to my dying day.

That summer, Paul made a recruiting trip to the states. He went to see the OSU officials who had been responsible for such an unfortunate event in a young girl's life. They agreed that it was, indeed, unfortunate, even tragic; that it was entirely unnecessary, and very unfair to Ronda, but it had happened. It was years before Ronda could even talk about it. And all these years later, I still feel a terrible sense of guilt.

She went to live with my sister, Jean, in Marion and graduated from the Marion Beauty School. It was in Marion that she met Fred Vest, whom she later married. Fred has been a much-loved son. The "mills of the gods grind slowly......"

Rock, a junior at OSU worked at the Delta Gamma Sorority House as a "salad boy". One of the girls who lived at the sorority house was Sue Radabaugh, from Toledo, Ohio. They started dating in the spring and married in the fall of their junior year, just prior to their twenty-first birthdays.

Linda, Sue's older sister, was newly married to David McCabe, whose father owned a large apartment building on East Towne Street. Fortunately, he arranged for Rock and Sue to have a nice apartment there. They served as Managers of the building while Rock continued his education. We will always have a soft spot in our hearts for David McCabe.

Mark, our first grandchild, was born the following summer. Rock, on the Dean's list, graduated from OSU with a major in math, and was immediately hired by IBM. He had also learned to play Sue's guitar.

We returned from Lima the summer of 1964, arriving in Columbus the first week of July. En route home, our first stop was Panama. I was fascinated with the Canal, as I'd longed to see it since studying about the Gatun Locks in fifth grade geography, when Vi Campbell was my teacher.

From Panama we flew to Costa Rica, where we had only a short stop-over as the air was nearly black with debris from an erupting volcano. I stayed on the plane while Paul got out to get some pictures. The pictures are mostly of soot.

We spent several days in Guatemala City and had a beautiful tour of that country before going on to the Yucatan Peninsula, and then to Mexico City. At Merida,

Mark at 1 year old.

127

in Yucatan, we were amazed at the number of windmills, the source of the city's water supply. We took a day's tour to the ruins at Chitzen Itza and visited several other remnants of the ancient Mayan civilization.

In one pyramid, while we were climbing an enclosed stairway, claustrophobia caused me to panic and I had to turn around and come back down the narrow stairway, "contra-traffico." I've been in my last cave and my last pyramid.

In Mexico City, we took a guided tour of the city, including the University of Mex-ico, where many colorful murals decorate buildings throughout the campus. We visited a glass factory, where artisans were creating decorative objects out of molten coke bottles. They presented me with two glass flowers, which I enjoy having in my home today. We also drove to some of the surrounding areas to see the pyramids, remnants of the ancient Aztec civilization. The largest pyramid in the world is in Mexico, not Egypt.

From Mexico City we flew to El Paso, Texas and then took a bus through the White Sands of New Mexico, shrouded in government secrecy for so many years. We found there was little to see except interminable miles of desolation.

Albuquerque was one hundred degrees in the shade, with a strong wind blowing the dust everywhere. We stopped in a small restaurant for a bite to eat. An unkempt waitress slapped a wet dish-towel across our table, then threw it over her arm as she waited to take our order. After three years in a very formal Lima, Peru, where the waiters (always men) wore impeccable white gloves, and had a neatly folded white towel over an arm, we had to adjust quickly to "culture shock."

Dr. James Cooper, who lived across the street from us on Guam, was associated with the University of New Mexico, and was good enough to lend us his station wagon for a few days, enabling us to see some of the area around Albuquerque. In the years since I'd been there as a youngster, one thing had not changed—the constant dry wind. I still dislike it.

When our plane landed in Columbus, many of the family members were there to greet us. Mark, a few weeks old, looked like Rock had as a baby, and soon wrapped his little fingers around our hearts. It was good to be home. We had been away three very long years.

Paul and I had plans to meet Polly and Harms at Reed and Mary Davis' in Montgomery, West Virginia. When Ronda and Fred told us they were going to be married on the eighteenth, less than two weeks away, we could not very well change our plans. We gave Ronda money to get some things she needed and we went on to Montgomery.

Reed, Dean at W. Va. Tech., wanted Paul to head up the student-teacher training program for the college. Paul, without discussing it with me, agreed to take the job.

Montgomery is a small town which lies in a narrow valley between two fairly steep mountain ridges. Railroad tracks run along one side; on the other, the Kanawa River. At that time, between Charleston and Montgomery, Union Carbide had a big chemical plant, belching black smoke into the atmosphere twenty-four hours a day. Mary's house, and everything in it, was covered with soot, no matter how much she cleaned. The whole town was shrouded in a choking cloud until the sun finally burned it off sometime after ten o'clock each morning. I knew I could never live there.

We slept in one of the college dorms that weekend. I simply could not sleep. I knew that my tendency toward claustrophobia would never allow me to live peacefully in that tightly hemmed-in town, no matter how friendly the people, nor how rewarding the job. And besides, it was too far from our children. Finally, I got Paul awake about three o'clock and told him my feelings. Paul would not make the call, but I called Reed at that ungodly hour and told him Paul would not take the job. It worked out well, as Reed had a stand-by applicant for the position who was eager to come to West Virginia.

We went back to Columbus and rented an efficiency apartment from Rock. We all went up to Marion for Ronda's and Fred's wedding at the Epworth Methodist Church. Jean graciously had the reception at her house, after the ceremony.

We had been out of Ohio for thirteen years. It was late July and we had no jobs, nor any prospects. Reva, who had one semester of her freshman year before leaving Lima, would be starting over as a freshman and we needed to get her settled somewhere.

The OSU Placement Service told Paul about an administrative vacancy in Portage County, an area strange to us. Paul became Principal of Rootstown High School near Ravenna. We rented a two bedroom house from one George Steinburger, about half-way between Kent and Ravenna and Reva started the year at Ravenna High.

After three years in South America, where uniforms were standard school attire, Reva needed school clothes. In a nice shop in Kent we found several things she liked. I wrote a sizeable check. "I'm sure you want to see my driver's license," I said, as I handed the check to the clerk.

"No," she replied with a warm smile. "Your face and the face of your daughter are the only references I need." That was one of the finest compliments I have ever received.

Reva, blessed with a lovely soprano voice, immediately made herself known in music circles at Ravenna HS. She was in the Girls' Chorus, the Glee Club, and a special Trio.

I had not planned to teach. However, a fifth grade teacher who'd had a colostomy during the summer, was not able to return to her classroom. I took over for her temporarily.

Eventually, she was unable to return until after Christmas. By that time, my principal, Mrs. Dunton, didn't want to lose me as part of her teaching staff. Therefore, the school board created a position for me—that of remedial reading teacher.

There was great need at this school for a special reading teacher, but no room was available. Eventually, a storage closet was cleaned out and my classes were held there, a windowless room that was perhaps six feet square.

We had a low round table with five small chairs around it and bookcases along two walls. I made the room attractive with posters and charts, and the children loved coming there. The Ravenna Library cooperated with me whole-heartedly and I got the children excited about reading.

I worked, basically, with youngsters in the elementary grades, however one senior boy came regularly for help. Some came in small groups and some singly. A whole new world opened up to those youngsters, when they found they could enjoy the printed page. Every week, I brought dozens of library books for them and they got so they devoured them.

During the summer of 1965, I attended Kent State University, which is known for its fine reading lab.

During the years we were on Guam, we bought and paid for a modest home at Buckeye Lake, on the premise that home-ownership would allow our kids to attend college in Ohio without paying out-of-state tuition. (This did not prove to be true.) Early in the spring of 1966, we sold that home. School salaries were still pitifully low, and Paul was looking for something else that we might do to make a better income.

He had me type a letter of inquiry in answer to an ad in the Akron Beacon Journal. Later a gentleman called and Paul made an appointment for an interview in nearby Cuyahoga Falls. Reva and I went with him—our introduction to Fashion Two Twenty.

Fashion Two Twenty, a cosmetic company, was then four years old. I was not a cosmetic user, except for a little lipstick, and could not imagine being interested. Both Reva and I were made up that evening in the studio at Cuyahoga Falls, while Paul was taken into the business office where the marketing plan was explained to him. He was interested enough to make a second appointment.

Our second appointment was with V. G. Gochneaur, at the company headquarters in Aurora, Ohio. Mr. G. had started the company with partner Aubrey McDonald, who for years had been a power-house in direct sales with Stanley Home Products, along with an associate,

Mary Kay. Aubrey proved to be one of the dearest ladies I have ever known. Her sister, Polly, lives in Cincinnati, and has been one of my dearest friends all these years.

FTT was a franchise company. We were shown the company books. The Feigenbaums, who owned the whole state of Massachusetts, were doing fantastic business as were the Roseberrys, who owned the state of Indiana. Paul and I decided to take the money from the sale of our house in Harbor Hills and invest in a franchise with FTT. We wanted the Columbus area, but it had already been sold.

We bought three counties in southwest Ohio— Hamilton, Clermont and Butler. We later added Warren County and two counties across the river in Kentucky.

Reva in Peru.

Family members thought we were absolutely crazy to leave an established profession and embark upon another unknown. We were middle aged, and undoubtedly, our decision was a risky one. However, Paul's responsibility in the business was recruiting people and taking care of the inventory. He'd been very successfully recruiting teachers for years and in complete charge of thousands of dollars worth of school supplies—everything from textbooks to chemicals for the science lab.

My responsibility was training (teaching), which I had done for many years, and selling. I had done well in direct sales with Empire Crafts before going to Guam, and had also recruited several others into the business and trained them.

When we made our first trip to Cincinnati to look for a place of business and a home, our Oldsmobile was nearly totaled. Fortunately, we had just left the car and were in a realtor's office. Some young kid driving his Dad's car without permission, swung around a corner too fast and plowed into the back of our car, which was parked at the curb. We had to buy a new car, which we surely had not planned to do at that time.

We rented a business place on Grace Avenue in Madison Place, and bought a nice brick home at 7200 Euclid Avenue in Madeira.

Back at Ravenna, Mr. Smith, our school superintendent arranged a farewell luncheon for us. During the luncheon he said to me, "We are very sorry to hear that you are leaving the teaching profession. You have a gift in the way you work with children. They love you."

I well remember my answer to him—"We have spent twenty-five years giving community service. During the next ten years, we hope to make some money for retirement." We did.

When moving time came, Ronda and Fred brought their friend, Johnnie, with them to help drive one of the two U-Hauls. It was a three-hour drive to Ravenna, and they came after the boys got off work. It was well past midnight before the trucks were loaded and we were ready to leave for Cincinnati. Fred and Johnnie drove the U-Hauls. Paul drove our car, taking Reva with him. I rode with Ronda and took care of little Lia, our second grandchild. It was an all-night trip. We arrived in Cincinnati mid-morning, July 15, 1966, all of us ready for a good night's sleep. The trucks still had to be unloaded.

Because we had a piano to unload, the boys went looking for a dolly. The Barnett Piano & Organ Company, in Silverton, lent them a dolly without charge. That was a kindness we later repaid by purchasing a Gulbransen organ from them.

We had mistakenly purchased our eight thousand beginning inventory of FTT products from the Home Office in Aurora, before we moved, thinking it would save us shipping charges. It may have saved a few dollars, but we handled that merchandise five times—first moving it from Aurora to Ravenna, where we stored it in our basement; then up the stairs and into the U-Hauls. We then unloaded it at 7200 Euclid Avenue, reloaded it to move it to the warehouse in Madison Place when it was finally ready. It still had to be unloaded and put on shelves in our place of business. Live and learn.

The business building, which we rented, had to have a new floor and partitions to fit our needs. We were scheduled to open on August 1. The night before, men were still laying floor tiles at midnight, so we had not been able to move in any of our newly purchased office equipment.

Meldean Simanek, an experienced field trainer from the Home Office, was in Cincinnati to help us get our business started.

On August 1, Paul and I drove to the office, picking up Meldean at the Mariemont Hotel. The first thing she noticed was that I had no make-up on. We had tons of cosmetics on the stockroom shelves and in cases in the storeroom, but none on me. "Let's get you made up before the phones start ringing," she said. We hurried. It was the second time I'd ever had make-up on, and I was not at all sure I liked it.

We had placed a "help wanted" ad in several newspapers. Promptly at nine o'clock, the phone, sitting on a window ledge as no furniture had been delivered, started ringing. Meldean took the first call and did the phone interview, with both of us listening intently in order to learn how. When she went to give directions for the applicant to come for a personal interview, she realized she did not know the city and said, "One moment, please. I'll let my secretary give you directions to our office," and handed the phone to me. I knew little more about giving directions than she did, but we bluffed our way through.

The Good Lord was surely with us as we soon had a number of ladies of real quality signed up to work with us. We taught a two-hour class in skin care, correct make-up application techniques, and color coordination. It was interesting to both the demonstrators and to the clients, and proved to be a profitable business venture for us and for our organization. Success in direct sales depends upon sales people who are honest, well trained, and willing to work.

The first lady we trained was Martha Landise, a Smith College lady who had grown up in Indian Hill. Martha was President of the Junior League and knew all of Cincinnati's upper crust. We will always give her a great deal of credit for helping us get the business rolling. She recruited several of her friends, became our first manager, our first car-winner, and later our first branch-office manager. She even got Irma Lazarus using Fashion Two Twenty cosmetics.

The fall of 1966 was the season of the "Strangler" in Cincinnati. It seemed that every morning's paper headlined another death by some unknown, masked man who strangled his victims. I was out every night doing presentations all over the city and was scared to death. My only consolation was that I was going a different place every night, so there was no way he could track me. It was, however, a wonderful relief when he was finally caught and put in prison.

Reva, a junior at Madeira High School, had not had time to make friends in a new school. Paul and I were working eighteen hour days, trying to get our business off the ground. Therefore, she depended upon Coco, her cocoa-colored cat, for companionship. Within weeks, she found Coco dead in the yard. She was broken-hearted. We had no proof, but felt certain she had found poison put out by our next-door neighbor. Several other neighbors had the same experience with their pets.

Fortunately, about Christmas time, Reva was invited to join Sing Out, a large, active music group. She made a lot of nice friends and participated in a great variety of Sing Out activities, including entertaining at the Ohio State Fair.

We had been in business less than six months, when I had an accident that could have put us out of business. It happened on January 9, 1967. I held a training class for Pat Schermbeck, one of our new recruits, at her home in Silverton. She lived in an upper unit of a four-family apartment building on Ohio Avenue. It was still daylight when I arrived and, as I parked behind the building, I noticed a foreign car in the large tandem garage, underneath the building.

After the training class was finished, at about ten o'clock, I walked toward the parking lot, carrying my showcase in one hand and my suitcase filled with hostess gifts in the other. The parking lot was dark except for the lights from Pat's apartment, which shone on the roof of my car. My eyes were focused on my car and, as I turned the corner of the building, I walked off into thin air, dropping about five feet down on to the cement driveway of the tandem garage. I landed with the hard plastic showcase just under my left breast. The pearl in the ring I was wearing was ground flat on one side, my watch crystal was gone, my hose were in shreds, and immediately my right foot swelled like an inflated football.

My body went into such shock that I did not realize how badly I was hurt. I insisted I could drive home, as it was only about five miles. I did, but by the time I got out on Montgomery Road, I was literally shaking like a leaf. I crept home at about five miles an hour and was not sure that I would make it.

Our one-car garage was narrow and attached to the house by a breezeway. I somehow got the car in the garage and got myself in the house. When Paul saw me, he immediately thought I'd wrecked the car, and, without a word, went out to survey the damage.

Reva's high school graduation picture.

I hung my coat in the hall closet, painfully got undressed, and filled the bathtub with hot water. I never hurt so badly in my life. Later, I found that I had three very badly broken ribs. It was a miracle I didn't have three broken legs and arms as well.

The next morning, when the alarm rang, I jumped like I had been shot from a cannon. I was literally wracked with pain. Eventually, I got to the hospital, but doctors can do little for broken ribs. They bound me tightly and for six weeks I suffered as I worked. Paul had to drive me to my classes, as I couldn't turn my head.

Paul's birthday was January 10, the day after my accident, and I had invited Rock's family over for sukiyaki. I simply was not up to preparing it, so we took them to the Hot Shoppe, a cafeteria in the Shillito Mall. To this day, sukiyaki reminds me of that pain-filled night.

The last weekend of February, we had a Directors' Seminar at the Home Office. I was beginning to feel somewhat back to normal and had taken off the heavy binder for this occasion. Marv Roseberry, the gregarious Director from Indiana, came up behind me, put his arms around my rib cage and gave me a big squeeze in greeting. It didn't help much that he was very sorry when he realized how badly he'd hurt me.

Statistics show that most small businesses operate in the red for the first five years. When we opened for business, we took two thousand dollars out of savings to have some money to operate on, but we never operated in the red. We had no other source of income, we were investing one hundred dollars each month in an IOS fund, which we'd started in Peru (Vesco later absconded with those funds! However, through the years, we recouped most of that investment, receiving the last payment during 2001!), we had a car payment to make (due to the accident mentioned earlier), house payment to make, business rent to pay, in addition to two sets of utilities. We also had a teen-age daughter in high school. To say we worked hard is putting it mildly. And that first year, we didn't buy a new pair of socks.

One Friday, toward spring, I noticed a marble-sized lump in my left breast. By Monday it was fiery red and the size of a tennis ball. I could not stand to wear a bra. I went to see a Dr. Shilling. He told me that it had to come out immediately, that it might be malignant, and if so, they would have to remove the breast. He made arrangements for me to be admitted to Christ Hospital within the next few days.

I did not mention the possibility of malignancy to Paul. Janet Zumwalt, Joanne Steele, and Phoebe Morse agreed to help in the office during the days I was hospitalized. I will never forget their kindness at that time and those three ladies hold a very special place in my heart to this day.

A caring pastor came in to my room, prior to the surgery and prayed for me. I had said plenty of prayers for myself for days. As it turned out, the cyst, which no doubt formed as a result of my fall, was not malignant and I was back at work in a few days. The Lord answers prayers!

During the second year in business, an ad brought Paul an interview with Jean Rieder. She had just had a new baby and did not want to go back to work full time. She proved to be one of the most delightful personalities and brought us many other young energetic ladies who wanted to make money and have fun doing it. She was enthusiastic, creative, and fell in love with the business of sales. She and her husband set up our second branch office and were a major part of our success in Fashion Two Twenty for many years.

The most expensive items we had to sell, were moisturizer and night cream, each retailing for $4.95. Cleanser was $2.95, freshener $1.95, powder $2.50. Our complete glamour case, including 10 very fine cosmetic items, retailed for $32.50. Yet our third full year in business we moved well over $800,000 in merchandise, and were always one of the top producers in our company. During those first years, we put in many eighteen hour days. I worked so hard that I hated to see Monday morning come. On Sundays, I could barely get out of bed and did not often get to church. Even so, I will always say that our success in business was the result of many answered prayers.

At the end of 1969, FTT held its annual convention in Honolulu. They chartered ten planes, which took off from various locations in the USA. We met the plane that left from the Cleveland airport. It was a great trip, especially since we won the trip by exceeding the quotas set by the Home Office. We took Paul's sister, Irene, with us,—a "thank you" for the care she had given to Mother and Dad and Beulah. She found a compatible roommate/friend in Natalie Marshall, one of our managers. Irene always said that trip was the highlight of her entire life.

Reva graduated from Madeira High School in 1968, and from the Larry Moore Beauty College in 1969. She worked at the McAlpin's Salon and also at a salon in Hyde Park. She also worked with the advertising department of the Enquirer downtown. Later, she managed an office for a doctor in Erlanger, Kentucky, across the River.

She had been sharing an apartment in The Forum with a girl from Kentucky. Car problems necessitated a move back to Kentucky, and Reva was left with a two bedroom apartment she could not afford.

Paul found her a nice apartment in the Oakley area. We had Elaine, our cleaning lady, go in and thoroughly clean the apartment. We decorated the dining alcove with bright wallpaper, bought her a new refrigerator, a new carpet for the living room, and hung new curtains throughout. It was a very pretty apartment, a lower unit in a four-family building.

She had not lived there long when Ronda and Fred called her about a job opening up at Whirlpool, in Marion. She hesitated to even apply for it, thinking that we would object to her leaving the apartment that we'd just refurbished. When we found out about the job offer, we encouraged her to apply. She got the job and moved to Marion.

During the short time Reva lived at that apartment, I met the young couple, who moved in to the apartment across the hall. They seemed to have very little and the young girl was obviously pregnant. I told the landlady that if she would allow that couple to move across the hall into Reva's newly-decorated apartment, we would never feel badly about the money we had spent refurbishing it. She agreed to let them move. I have often wondered if she kept her word.

After Reva's first day at Whirlpool, Ronda asked her, "Of all the men you saw today, how many of them would you like to date?"

Reva's answer was, "Just one."

"What do you mean, just one?" Ronda kidded. "With all those guys, surely you saw more than one you'd like to date."

"No, just one," Reva said again. That one was John Hord. John has been a much-loved son all these years.

Paul's mother was diabetic during her last years. I knew that one symptom of diabetes is tremendous thirst. In the late sixties, Paul seemed to be consistently thirsty. I insisted he go to Dr. Hudson for a check-up. He actually had the opposite condition, hypoglycemia, or low blood sugar.

We learned to control that condition with diet and a long period of vitamin therapy. However, Paul's health continued to be a concern. Dr. Hudson diagnosed the early stages of Parkinson's, a degenerative disease of the nervous system. Eventually, a long series of neurological tests confirmed Dr. Hudson's diagnosis.

In the spring of 1970, we realized that the two-bedroom home at 7200 Euclid Avenue was no longer adequate for our growing family. When young folks marry and leave home, you think you'll need less room, but, in fact, you need more. Reva, of course, still lived at home. We often had Ronda and Fred and their little Lia and Valerie over a weekend. By this time, Rock's family included two little boys, Mark and Gary. They lived close and came often. We needed a larger home to accommodate everyone.

One day, while driving through various areas, we saw a "For Sale" sign in the yard at 10431 Buxton Lane in Montgomery. The house had just been put on the market and was not yet in the multiple listings. We bought it and then put our Euclid Avenue home on the market. We closed on the sale of that house one Friday and on the Montgomery house the following Friday. Again, the Lord was with us as we have made a lovely, comfortable home here.

Wes, Paul's nephew, was living with us the summer of 1970, while he finished his MA at Xavier University. He gamely went through the throes of moving and has been a very special member of our family during all the years since.

In October of 1970, we also moved to a larger place of business, having completely out-grown our facilities on Grace Avenue.

We rented one of three sections of a large, brick business building, owned by Mr. Joe Ketterer, in the Neyer Industrial Park in Fairfax. Before we moved in, Mr.

Ketterer partitioned it to fit our needs—a nice entrance lobby, two offices plus a workroom, a manager's room, a small store room, an attractive training room, and a large warehouse area.

Through the years, we had branch offices in Cheviot, Middletown, and Chillicothe, in addition to Martha's and Rieder's', plus one in Lexington and one in Bowling Green, KY.

We had fifteen manager/car-winners. We were one of the top Directors, if not number one, every year after our first year in business.

One of the perks was driving a company Cadillac all those years. We also earned a two-week trip to Hawaii, and two trips on our company's yacht, as well as many, many other prizes. The grandmother clock in our dining room was a prize for recruiting during the spring of 1973.

That was the spring Mother died. This is an item I wrote at the time of her death:

My mother passed away last Saturday morning, March 17, 1973, at 3:30 A.M. She went easily.

Friday had been a normal day. She had worked all day, baking ginger-bread men, and decorating them, for Janet's sixth birthday on Saturday. Janet was her youngest grandchild.

She woke about 2:00 A.M. and called to my father in the room across the hall. He was a restless sleeper. Mother was a light sleeper, easily awakened. They had slept in separate rooms the last few years.

10431 Buxton Lane. • Mark & Gary.

Mother was having a problem breathing. She took a nitro-glycerine tablet. She wanted to lie down, but could not get her breath. She sat up; then tried to lie down again.

My father got a rocker for her from the living room, but she did not want him to help her into it. She only wanted to lie down. Yet, she could not breathe lying down.

My father sat down on her bed, lifted her shoulders and let her rest against him. She tried to speak, but her tongue was thick and he could not understand her. He knew this was different from anything she had experienced before.

He felt that she knew she was slipping away. She patted his hand several times. That was Mother's way of showing deep affection when her emotions would not let her speak.

She leaned back against my father and was gone.

A call in the night that my mother had passed away should have been neither a surprise nor a shock, as she was eighty-three. But it was both.

I went as soon as I could, to be with my father. My only brother and younger sister, who lived closer, reached him first. My older sister, who had farther to come, arrived later in the day. A severe storm had made roads nearly impassable.

It was a miserable day—St. Patrick's Day, 1973. Snow fell steadily and a strong wind swirled it into drifts. It was an unusual day for central Ohio and by nightfall many roads were closed.

My brother, my father, and I went to the funeral home to select the casket. The funeral Director greeted us at the door, his countenance that of sincere compassion.

We all sat down, he at his desk and we facing him. He wanted to go over the fixed expenses. Cemetery fees vary, he told us. Where Mother

The colors of fall on our corner. • The front flower bed.

was to be buried, the fee for opening and closing the grave was sixty-five dollars. Then there was the fee for the two ministers who would have charge of the memorial service—a young man who pastored the church where Mother and Dad were active members, and an older minister, a long-time family friend. This stipend usually ranged from ten to twenty dollars, he suggested. My father said to give each minister twenty dollars.

The funeral Director's fee, including all services, was then added to the cost of the vault. These were the fixed expenses, which we could expect, in addition to the cost of the casket chosen. He would talk to us later about the flowers.

We went into a large room filled with caskets. I was amazed. This was a small town, yet here were more than a dozen caskets to choose from. They ranged from one thousand seven hundred ninety-five dollars down to two, which a family could put their own price on. The Director told us that during the past year, he had performed four funerals without any charge whatsoever. "That isn't a lot," he said, "but for a small town, it is quite a few."

We chose a casket lined with pink-toned satin, rather than the gray-blues, as Mother loved happy colors.

By evening all the family had gathered—my brother, two sisters and I, and our spouses. We reminisced about Mother's life and the many ways we would miss her.

Today is August 4, 2000. As I recopy these notes, written on St. Patrick's Day in 1973, I can say that even though more than twenty-six years have fleetingly passed since these notes were written, yet Mother lives on—in each one of us, her offspring. Each of us has her dark brown eyes. Our father's eyes were blue. Three of us have her dark, almost swarthy skin. Each time I see myself in a mirror, I know that I look more and more like Mother. We all have her keen mind and her desire to keep learning. We all have her strong work ethic. Our younger sister has her music ability. Our brother teaches a Sunday School class, as Mother did many years of her life.

Who can put a value upon a fine Mother? And who can say that Mothers are ever really gone?

In early January of 1974, at our annual convention before several thousand of our peers, Paul and I were presented with a special award which had never been given before—a Sterling silver punch bowl, engraved "Semper Exemplum", which means "Always an example." It was quite an honor. I was glad I could share it with Dad, who was in the hospital in Marion, slowly recovering from the amputation of his leg.

Dad had lived alone, after Mother's death. The last day of October, he'd spaded up his small garden plot, getting it ready for spring planting. About 3:00 A.M., he was awakened by a terrible pain in his leg. Not wanting to disturb Marvin at that hour, he suffered through until morning. He later said that in all his eighty-seven years, he'd never suffered as he did that night.

When Marvin got him to the hospital, soon after daylight, they learned that the "pain" was a blood clot, gangrene had set in, and Dad's leg had to be amputated. At first, the doctors amputated below the knee, hoping to save the knee joint. When that didn't heal, they amputated above the knee. When that didn't heal, they amputated clear up to the thigh. He was in the hospital five long months.

After he was finally released, and after weeks of recovery at Jean's and at Marvin's, Jean took him to Columbus to be measured for a prosthesis. "Will I be able to mow my lawn with this prosthesis?" Dad asked the doctor.

"Well, Victor," he replied, "nobody else would, but you probably will." He didn't. Before the prosthesis could be started, Dad had a stroke at Marvin's on a Wednesday night. Again, he was back in the Marion Hospital.

When I arrived, the nurse sadly said, "I wish I could give you better news about your father, but he is comatose." I walked with leaden feet down the long hallway to his room. My dear, dear Daddy. I held his hand and tried to talk to him, but my voice was choked with tears. He kept pressing my hand. I will always believe that he knew I was there and heard the things I said to him.

Vernon Hensel played basketball for Paul at Marseilles and, later, served as Superintendent of the Elgin School District, where Lia and Valerie graduated from high school. He once said to Paul, "I know exactly where I was sitting, in the seventh grade, when I made up my mind I wanted to be a school administrator just like you." Vernon's wife was Dad's nurse.

When she came in to feed him, he tried so hard to do the things she asked him to do. "Open your mouth, Mr. Mitchell," she'd say, and he would try desperately to do so. I have read that even comatose patients can often hear; that hearing is the last sense we lose.

Dad died on Monday morning, July 1, 1974. Death, in his case, as in many others, was a blessing, but I still miss him.

Both Dad and Mother are buried in the cemetery at Rushsylvania, along with mother's father, J. F. Garrett, who died in his sleep in December, 1939, soon after Paul and I started dating. He would have been ninety-two in March.

Once in the early 1970s, Mickey and Al Craig, Paul and I, and Norma and Bill Royer from York, PA, met at Oglebay Park for a weekend. Oglebay is a city park, about eight miles up in the mountains above Wheeling, WV. We were very impressed with the facilities there and started taking our whole family there for a week's vacation each summer. We'd rent a four-bedroom cabin, secured for us each year by Inez Rakoskie, who lives in Wheeling. The men played golf, the girls swam in the Olympic-sized pool, the grandchildren played on the playground equipment, fished in the lake, and petted the animals in the zoo. Ogelbay holds very special memories for us all.

One day all the young crowd and I were downtown in Wheeling, at the Wheeling City Park. The youngsters enticed me to go down the water slide. I would not have been so daring had I known how fast and dangerous it was. On the way down, I prayed that I wouldn't be crippled for the rest of my life from a whiplash. Little did I know that, instead, I would nearly drown. The buoyant cushion I had been sitting on somehow got under my feet as I left the slide, and for several seconds (it seemed like minutes) my head was under water while the cushion held my feet up. I thought for sure my time had come. The kids still laugh about the time Grandma almost drowned. They never realized how unfunny it was to me!

Once, our dear friends Mickey and Al Craig from Piqua, Gordon and Helen Barnes from Detroit, Lucy and Doy Jones from Charleston, and Paul and I met at Greenbrier for a weekend. What a beautiful spot. We had a lovely four bedroom cottage, each room with its private bath. The dinner menus had no prices, as the food was included in the price of the rooms for the weekend. The four men played golf. We women roamed the shops and enjoyed the beauty and peace of this luxury hotel.

When we went to leave, I stood in line to pay the bill. Within minutes, the manager leaned across the counter toward me and said, "Mrs. Gettys, you don't need to wait. We will send you a bill." We left without having paid one cent for a lovely weekend. I still wonder how the manager even knew who I was. We did, of course, receive the bill eventually. Everyone should go to Greenbrier. It is a delightful experience.

In September of 1974, Paul and I went on a three-week tour, sponsored by The Ohio State University, to Tahiti, New Zealand, Australia, Fiji, and Hawaii. We left Diane Sweeney in charge at the office.

Tahiti is very much like Guam, we thought, except that French is spoken there.

One evening, we were eating dinner on the lanai in a local restaurant. Somewhere behind us, a music combo started to play and sing, and soon we knew they were headed our way. I had my head down, looking at the food on my plate, when out of the corner of my eye, I could see the musicians' bare feet approaching, then stopping at our table. I nearly choked on my food as the last pair of feet appeared. They were also bare, and the left little toe stood absolutely straight up. For some reason it struck me as funny. I dared not lift my head for fear they'd see me laughing. I'm sure it wasn't funny to this young musician when he attempted to buy a pair of shoes.

We loved New Zealand and got to see much of the North Island, including Aukland and Rotorura, where Paul played a round of golf, losing some balls in the boiling "mush pots" on the course. Millions of sheep graze the lush greenlands of New Zealand and wool is a major export. In the hotels, milk is dispensed free of charge from "coke" machines. Regretfully, we did not get to the South Island, and hoped to do so at a later date. We have never been back.

In Sydney, we attended a performance of "The Mikado" at the famous opera house, which lies in Sydney Harbor. We also had a boat tour of the harbor area one delightfully sunny afternoon. We took a train trip up into the Blue Mountains, where forests of eucalyptus trees emit an oily vapor into the atmosphere, leaving a bluish haze over the mountains, thus the name. The koalas feed upon the eucalyptus trees.

We had the good fortune to visit a museum where an educational documentary film, showing Australia's Outback, was running continuously. What a unique part of our world.

Our next stop was Fiji, where we spent a delightful few days. Jim Stull had been on Fiji

during WWII and always said it was his favorite island. I could see why. We loved our time there, even though I got badly sunburned.

From Fiji we took a one-day tour, by motor launch, to a small outlying island, where we ate a picnic lunch and swam in the incredibly clear blue waters that lapped on a pure white coral shore. On the launch, was a young couple with a delightful ten year-old lad who had grown up in Borneo. He and I had such an interesting visit during the trip that day, that I have never forgotten him. I regret that I didn't get his address so that I could keep in contact with him.

The next stop on our tour was Hawaii. Paul and I flew on home, as we had seen the Hawaiian Islands many times and felt that our business needed us. Upon arrival, we found things had gone very well in Diane Sweeney's care and she has remained a very special friend all these years.

At that time, I knew little about the neurological disorder known as Parkinson's. When I told our Pastor's wife, June Lowery, that Paul had Parkinson's, she hugged me with great tears welling up in her eyes. "Oh," she said, almost sobbing. "I'm so sorry for you. My father died of Parkinson's at age forty-nine."

That spring, Paul and Ralph Radabaugh made the first of several trips to Florida to watch the Reds during spring training. Ralph had a nephew playing for the Phillies, so they also scouted several of the other teams. While Paul was in Florida, Dr. Hudson asked

Sarah and Paul.

142

me to come in for a long consultation about what to expect as time went by and Paul's condition worsened.

Beginning at that time, I read everything I could find on the subject of Parkinson's. It is a cruel, debilitating disorder of the nervous system and slowly but surely wreaks its havoc.

Even though Paul's health had noticeably deteriorated by 1976, we arranged for a month's tour of Europe, leaving Peggy Robinson in charge of our office. We flew to London, where we met the rest of the group. Most of them were Australian, but three were young female lawyers from Chicago.

We first toured the London area, including the museums, West Minister Abbey, Buckingham Palace, and Windsor Castle. Our tour bus then headed for the "white cliffs of Dover" on the English Channel. En route we stopped at Ely, the "mother of time zones", and also at the Canterbury Cathedral, which lies southeast of London in the county of Kent, and is the religious center of the Church of England. This beautiful Gothic cathedral was built between 1000s and 1400s and was the destination of the pilgrims in Chaucer's famous *Canterbury Tales.*

We crossed the English Channel by ferry, landing at Odessa. When the tour bus was driven off the ferry, we all boarded again and drove through the Belgian countryside to Bruges—"City of Bridges", one of the most picturesque villages in Belgium. We arrived there in the late afternoon and found most of the villagers sitting at outdoor cafes, on the square, having coffee and discussing the day's events. I would love to go back there someday.

From Bruges, we drove to Brussels, a beautiful city of over a million people, center of art and learning, and government. Brussels is called "Little Paris" because its beautifully carved buildings and wide boulevards attract tourists from all over the world.

From Brussels, we drove to Amsterdam, where we found a great many changes had taken place since our last visit there. In 1955, Amsterdam was a clean, open city, which welcomed tourists. Now, many formerly beautiful areas of the city had been taken over by ill-kempt dope addicts and prostitutes. Large signs, posted in conspicuous places, warned tourists not to enter those areas.

After a trip to the market area, one of the young women lawyers from Chicago found that her over-the-shoulder purse had been slashed, her passport, traveler's checks, and money stolen. It was late at night and she could do nothing until morning, at which time she contacted the American Embassy and asked for their assistance.

Our tour bus was scheduled to leave for Hamburg at 9:00 A.M. I felt absolutely miserable, leaving that lovely young lady there alone, in a strange city, to wrangle a new passport and cash enough to get back to Chicago. What if she were one of my daughters? (This same thing happened to our granddaughter, Lia, years later when she was an exchange student in Madrid.)

There was nothing I could do, however, but say prayers for her safety, and go on with the tour group. It was a great relief when I learned that the Embassy personnel had met her needs and had helped her catch a train to Hamburg. She reached the hotel where our group was staying at about 4:00 A.M., the answer, I'm sure, to many prayers in her behalf. In spite of the Embassy's assistance, before the trip ended she ran out of money. Paul lent her twenty-five dollars, which she repaid as soon as she reached Chicago.

Hamburg, located on the Elbe River about sixty miles from the North Sea, is West Germany's second largest city and the largest seaport on the European continent. It is a very important, highly industrialized city.

From Hamburg, we drove north to Denmark. We had to take quite a long ferry ride before arriving on the main island of Sjaelland. Just before the ferry was due to land, I dashed to the bathroom. When I returned, they'd closed off the exit that we had intended to use. We tried several other exits. Each exit was closed. There was no one to give us directions. By the time we found a way to get off the ferry, its motors were revving for the return trip. We were near panic, feeling trapped and unable to find an exit. Our touring companions were very happy to see us when we finally boarded the bus.

Copenhagen, occupied by German troops from 1940–1945, is Denmark's capital and a very beautiful city. More than a fourth of Denmark's population live in Copenhagen, which lies on two islands. Old parts of the city lie on the eastern coast of Sjaelland; suburbs occupy part of the island of Amager to the east.

Copenhagen has many parks, statues, fountains, and beautiful buildings. Four palaces, including the King's Palace, are set around a large open square. Nearby, is Marble Church, whose dome is nearly as large as the dome of St. Paul's in London. The University of Copenhagen is one of the oldest in Europe, dating back to 1479.

We enjoyed touring one of the beautiful palaces, and we walked down to the sea to view the statue of The Little Mermaid, made famous by Hans Christian Andersen.

From Denmark we drove south through East Germany, through hundreds of miles of gray desolation. Vast acres of flat farmland lay fallow, out of production, with various pieces of gray machinery sitting idle in the fields. Not a home could be seen anywhere on the land, yet a few aging barns still stood, forlornly surveying a desolate countryside.

Later, in East Berlin, we saw row after row after row of drab gray high-rises (tenement housing), where these good farm families, forced from their land by the ruling communists, were living.

In order to enter West Berlin, we had to go through "Check Point Charlie". Berlin, of course, is a very large city, and at that time, a very expensive city to live in. I paid $1.75 for a cup of coffee with my dinner.

One of the Australian gentlemen, whose luggage had been stolen in Amsterdam, had hoped to replace his clothing in Berlin. However, the prices were so exorbitant that he continued to borrow socks and underwear from some of the other men in our group.

The Berlin Wall, drab, gray, and forbidding, divided the city into East and West Berlin. Guards, mounted in stations atop The Wall, every few feet, kept their guns at ready. Our guide arranged for a tour into East Berlin.

The Wall itself was impenetrable, but in addition, a barbed wire fence and a "no-man's-land" formed an area where our tour bus was stopped and searched before it was allowed to pass. We all had to get off the bus while each piece of luggage was searched. This happened both going in to East Berlin and, again, coming back into West Berlin. It was scary.

During the few hours we were in East Berlin, we never saw a playground or a child at play.

From Berlin we went to the charming city of Rotenberg, a walled city little changed from medieval times. We stayed the night there and saw some of the truly magnificent altar sculptures done by Riemenschneider, one of Germany's famous artisans. I shall never forget those beautiful pieces of sculpture nor that quaint walled city.

Our next stop was the infamous Dachau, one of the first Nazi concentration camps, established in 1933 about twenty miles north of Munich. Dachau was built as an extermination camp for Jews and political prisoners. Brutal medical experiments were performed on many of the prisoners, most of whom died as a result. Thousands of Jews and political prisoners were executed. When the American Armed Forces arrived there on April 29, 1945, they liberated approximately thirty-two thousand prisoners. Dachau stands today as a tragic memorial to man's inhumanity to his fellow man.

Near the border of Germany and Austria, we boarded a ship for a cruise up the Danube to Vienna. It was a most delightful cruise, through beautiful countryside. We passed several castles in picturesque settings and took a tour through one of the castles. It was musty and dank and dark. Undoubtedly, it was in just such a castle that my Aunt Grace lived, as a young lady, while serving as tutor to two little German princes.

Vienna, "Queen of the Danube", is the capital of Austria and an important trading center, located at the head of a fertile plain between the Carpathian Mountains and the Alps. The Danube Canal flows through the city and is crossed by many beautiful bridges. Vienna has long been famous for its cultural heritage and boasts many fine museums and art galleries. It is one of Europe's most popular tourist attractions.

From Vienna, we went by bus to picturesque Salzburg, the birthplace of Wolfgang Amadeus Mozart and famous for its annual music festivals.

From Salzburg, our tour bus took us south, through miles and miles of spectacularly beautiful mountain scenery. I asked the bus driver for his mike and "read" into it a poem I wrote in the Colorado Rockies during my college years. It had been years since I'd even thought of this poem, yet there it was—proof again that we should be very careful what we put into our memory banks, for it is always there, waiting to be called forth:

I do not need a building
Fashioned of stone by man,
For my place of worship has been here
Ever since the world began.
The floor's a mosaic of browns and greens,
Its dome, the blue sky above;
And the chant of its choir
Is the clear running brook
Singing softly of peace
And of love.
And oft, as I pause
To utter a prayer,
As down Life's pathway I trod,
I give thanks for the beauty
That each day I see
In the temple created by God.

Perhaps it was not great poetry, but it was very fitting and was appreciated by the fellow travelers.

When we reached the border of Yugoslavia, our bus was stopped by security police. All of us had to leave the bus while guards searched every piece of luggage on board. We watched them shake out each article of clothing. Eventually, after more than an hour, we were allowed to re-board and enter the country of Yugoslavia. We spent the night at Ljubljana (pronounced Lyublyana), where we had the poorest hotel accommodations on our entire trip.

From Ljubljana we drove around the north shore of the Adriatic Sea, to Venice, Italy, often referred to as the Queen City of the Adriatic.

Venice is unique, built on a cluster of some one hundred twenty small mud islands, which lie between the mouths of the Piave and the Po rivers on Italy's northeast Adriatic shore. More than one hundred forty canals form the "streets" and hundreds of gondolas serve as "taxicabs". The Grand Canal meanders through the length of the city in an S-shaped curve, dividing Venice into two major groups of islands. Hundreds of picturesque stone bridges arch the canals throughout the city.

The buildings which line the curving canals of Venice are built on piles, or posts, sunk deep into the mud. Many of the buildings are richly decorated palaces representing Byzantine, Gothic, and Renaissance architecture, with mural paintings and collections of the works of great artists.

Some of the city's most beautiful buildings are located in the Piazza of Saint Mark, in the heart of Venice. Thousands of tourists visit this square each year to see the beautiful Cathedral of Saint Mark, the Doge's Palace, the Campanile or bell tower, and to feed the huge flocks of pigeons, which make their home in the square.

From Venice, we drove south to Florence, aptly called the "City of Flowers". Florence, the capital of Tuscany, lies on the Arno River and is the world's major center of Renaissance art, including Michelangelo's David. The Ponte Vecchio, "Old Bridge", lined with tiny gift shops along its walls, was built by the Romans. It is the only bridge across the Arno River in Florence that the Germans did not destroy during WWII.

Our next stop was Sorrento, a quaint village built into a rocky promontory south of Naples, and jutting out into the Mediterranean Sea. As we entered the narrow streets of the city's center, a group of dark, swarthy men stopped our bus by forming a human blockade across the street. The driver could not proceed, they told him, until all of us went through the "tourist trap" gift shops, which lined both sides of the street. These men were members of Italy's Mafia, and our guide advised us to cooperate. We did, but I am not sure that any of our group purchased anything. I know that we didn't.

The next morning, we went by hydroplane to the Isle of Capri, where we spent the entire day. Crowds of tourists jammed every place of interest on the island. We braved the crowds to go to the famous Blue Grotto, but much of the day we sat in a sidewalk café on the picturesque square and visited with other tourists who were doing the same.

In late afternoon, word spread that a storm was brewing in the Mediterranean. Our guide insisted that we leave for the mainland earlier than scheduled. As it happened, our hydroplane was the last load of tourists to get off the Island. I have always wondered how such a large crowd of tourists were accommodated that night on the tiny, storm-battered Isle of Capri.

Our passage across the Bay of Naples, a distance of approximately twenty miles, was a most frightening experience. Had we been in any other type of ship, we would surely have inherited a watery grave. However, our hydroplane skimmed over the wildly churning sea at exceedingly high speeds, cutting through the giant waves that threatened to engulf us. We could see nothing through the windows of the hydroplane, but we could hear the demon-like force of the angry sea crashing around us. Reaching shore safely was an answered prayer. It made the story of St. Paul's Mediterranean shipwreck experience, as related in the New Testament, very real indeed.

Naples, a city of over a million people, lies in the shadow of Mt. Vesuvius, which erupted in A.D. 79 and completely destroyed several smaller cities, including Pompeii. Pompeii was destroyed, not by lava, but by showers of hot, wet ashes and cinders, as well as poisonous gasses that covered the city, killing more than two thousand people instantly. Ruins of the city lay undisturbed for 1700 years, before excavation was begun.

Today, more than half of the buried city has been uncovered. The Italian government decided not to remove the treasures, but to keep them intact as found, and restore the buildings, as much as possible, to their original condition. Walking through the ruins of Pompeii is an experience in living history. For example, a loaf of bread still sits on a breakfast table. The disaster occurred during a local election campaign and election slogans can still be seen on the walls. It is an eerie trip back in time.

Naples, Italy's third largest city, is highly industrialized. One of the most interesting places we visited was a "factory" where exquisite cameos are carved by patient artisans. These gems, usually carved from onyx, sardonyx, or agate of various colors, are done in bas relief and are very beautiful.

From Naples, we went to Rome. In 1955, our family spent several days in Rome and we had been very impressed with this magnificent city of marble. Now, more than twenty years later, the ruling communist party had allowed such tragic deterioration that it showed, not only in the physical condition of formerly majestic buildings, and in the dirty streets of the city, but also in the sad faces of its people. We left Rome feeling sadly depressed.

One remarkable experience, however, made us glad we'd come back to Rome. In 1955, we had not been able to see the Sistine Chapel, as it was closed off from the public while being refurbished. This time, we had a long, leisurely, guided tour. To actually see the magnificent frescoes on the Chapel's ceiling meant a great deal to me. I had read Irving Stone's *The Agony and the Ecstasy*, a fabulous biographical novel detailing the life of Michelangelo. I could almost see him there, lying on is back on the rough scaffolding, squinting his eyes to keep the plaster rubbings out. The Chapel's ceiling is a masterpiece of devotion, exemplified by an abused artisan who literally spilled his life's blood and his eyesight into his work.

We also visited the Catacombs, where many of the early Christians met in secret in order to avoid persecution.

From Rome we went to Pisa, birthplace of Galileo. Pisa lies on the Arno, on the northwest coast of Italy. Here the old bell tower, known as the Leaning Tower of Pisa, made this ancient city look familiar to us all. We had a very interesting tour of the city before going on the Genoa, a bustling Italian seaport, and birthplace of Christopher Columbus.

Our next stop was Nice, on the French Riviera. We made a side trip to the principality of Monaco and walked the streets so familiar to Grace Kelly. We also visited the area of Grasse, near Nice, famous for its fine perfumes. We were allowed inside one of the perfumeries and watched a popular fragrance being developed.

We saw our first topless sunbathers on the beach in Nice and experienced our first anti-American prejudices.

The trip from Nice to Bern, Switzerland took us through some of the most spectacular mountain scenery of the entire trip. The Jura Mountains and the Alps cover much of Switzerland. Bern, the capital, lies on the plateau between the two ranges, where more than half of the Swiss people make their homes.

From Bern we drove to Paris, where we spent an afternoon on the Seine, rode the Metro, saw the Eiffel Tower, the Arc de Triomphe, walked the Champs-Elysees, visited the Louvre, and toured the Cathedral of Notre Dame. We have always regretted that we didn't go on the side-trip to Versailles, to see the historic palace built by King Louis XIV, however we chose to see the Louvre instead, as we did not have time to do both.

Paul and I flew home from Paris, while the rest of the tour group went back to London, where the tour had started. We had been gone a month and felt our business needed us. We were very glad to get home.

Peggy Robinson had done a fine job during our absence and our business was running smoothly. In fact, she so enjoyed being in charge of our office that she soon opened a branch office for us in Cheviot, on the west side of Cincinnati.

I was asked to speak at our National Convention, held in the Cleveland Auditorium, the first week of January. Mr. Gochneaur was so impressed with the practical, helpful talk I gave, that he asked me to repeat it at the Western Division Conference in Reno the following week. The company paid our way, put us up in the penthouse suite at one of Reno's best hotels, and treated us royally.

The following summer, I spoke at the Summer Seminar in Chicago, and again, at the annual convention the following year, held the first week of January in Las Vegas. Years later, after I was doing some writing, some of that material was published in *Income Opportunities*, a business magazine.

During the Gerald Ford administration, you may remember, government health officials urged everyone to take the Swine Flu shot. Paul had that shot the last of November and nearly died at our convention in Las Vegas the first of January, 1977. He never knew a well day after that.

Several older men were left paralyzed from that shot, two of them in Milford, not far from us. They attempted a lawsuit, but found the government accepts no responsibility for their condition, and they remain wheel-chair bound and bitter.

In Las Vegas, Paul began to get very ill during the final night's Honors Banquet We rushed him to the hospital when he began to hyperventilate. Frank Rieder and Jean Crane stayed with me at the hospital all night, missing all the important end-of-convention festivities honoring the top producers, of which they were both a part. I will never forget their loyalty.

The doctors finally allowed us to bring Paul back to the hotel the next day. There he remained, too sick to be moved.

We were in a gaudy room with a large, plush, round bed, heavy red velvet bedspread and draperies, and a large mirrored ceiling. The hotel management wanted the room available for other guests, but were good enough to let us remain there until Paul could travel. By that time, a week later, I was nearly sick from boredom, sick-room odors, worry, and the depression of that gaudy room. I brought Paul home in a wheel chair.

When we arrived at the Cincinnati airport, it was covered with one of the heaviest snowfalls we have in this area. Rock met us at the plane, shoveled our driveway when we got home, and helped me get Paul into bed. That was the beginning of a slow, steady deterioration of his health.

On January 22, 1977, Paul's oldest brother, Forrest, died. Because of the unusually severe weather, none of us could get to the funeral.

At this time, our parent company, Fashion Two Twenty, began a rapid deterioration, due to a conflict, which developed between the two founding families. We did not take sides. When the Chairman of the Board called and urged us to, I told him (with Paul listening on the other phone) "As far as we are concerned, the Home Office is General Motors and we are a local car dealer. As long as you supply us with product, we will carry on our business as usual."

The Home Office situation began to go drastically downhill, with firing of personnel, lawsuits over misappropriated funds, investigations by the SEC, all of which ended with fines of several hundred thousand dollars levied against the Chairman of the Board. Eventually, perhaps in order to pay the fines and the lawyers' fees, the company was sold to a Saudi Arabian.

In Saudi, women are considered chattel and direct-selling, as a marketing device, is unknown. This Saudi knew absolutely nothing about running a business such as ours, yet he asked for no assistance or advice. Things went from bad to worse.

During the sales meeting on Monday, November 2, 1981, we received a telegram from him that all prices were doubled as of November 1. I immediately went to the phone and called Lucy Jones, who owned the business in Charleston, W. V. She had not yet received the telegram. What to do was the question.

We asked our Managers to stay after the meeting and shared the news with them. We urged them not to tell their Consultants, but give us a few days to decide how to cope with the situation the Saudi had thrust upon us. We promised to fill the current week's orders at the old prices.

By mid-afternoon, however, everyone in the city knew about it. Our competitors had heard the news and spread it rapidly.

We had a warehouse full of products, anticipating the increased business our people always did during the holiday season. We had thought our supply would last through the Christmas season. By Friday evening, our warehouse was nearly bare. Customers who usually ordered a few items, were stocking up while they could get it at the old prices.

Eventually, we placed three huge orders with the Home Office, paying the new prices and selling to our sales people at the old prices, in order to keep them making money during the big Christmas season. It cost us about four thousand dollars, but was a wise investment in our organization. They appreciated it.

During the first week, we contacted Maury and Dottie Feigenbaum, finally reaching them in Canada, where they were conducting a Seminar for their Canadian organization. They were the largest producers in Fashion Two Twenty when we joined in 1966. They owned the Massachusetts franchise, but a problem with the Chairman of the Board had caused them to leave the company and form a company of their own. At that time, the chemist, who created the FTT products, joined Maury and Dottie, and changed the products just enough to avoid lawsuits. Their company, Finelle, was headquartered in Boston. We knew our people could transfer to Finelle, get essentially the same products at modest prices, and their customers would never realize the change had been made.

Dottie came on November 17, if I remember correctly, and held a meeting with our people. We had one hundred twenty-seven present. They voted unanimously to join Finelle.

Not only our organization, but ninety-eight percent of all the FTT organizations from Maine to California, transferred to Finelle. It was a real boost for Dottie and Maury.

Feigenbaums did not operate their business in the same manner that FTT did. All products were shipped directly from Boston to Car-Winner Managers in the field. They had no position in their program that corresponded to the position we held in FTT, that of Director. Therefore, Paul and I gradually depleted our inventory of merchandise, sold off our office equipment, gave some of it to the Christian School in Madisonville, and closed our studio in April, 1982.

Dottie invited us to come to Boston at their expense, which we did. They offered us a position as Field Executives and put us in charge of a large central-states area, where we held recruiting, training, and motivational meetings during the next three years. Eventually, it got entirely too much for Paul and we retired from that position. However, for several months longer, I worked with their managers across the country via telephone.

The first year we were with Finelle, we joined their Executive Car-Winning Managers on a trip to Puerta Vallarta, on the west coast of Mexico. We played golf with Keith and Sylvia

Gochneaur one afternoon on a very rough course. Our dear friends, Lucy and Doy Jones and Bob and Loucille Burch were also on that trip. One morning while in Puerto Vallarte, I ate breakfast with Dottie's mother, Mrs. Lampert, a lovely, lovely lady in her mid-eighties. It was the first time I'd met Mrs. Lampert, but I knew that Dottie was her daughter and that she had a son, Alan, who was a lawyer.

To make conversation over breakfast, I asked, "Mrs. Lampert, do you have just the two children?"

"Ooh, no," she replied earnestly. "I have four children, Dottie and Maury and Alan and Connie." What a sweet comment. Wouldn't it be wonderful if every mother thought of her children's mates as her own children? I will never forget lovely Mrs. Lampert, who has since passed on to her reward.

The following year, 1984, we joined that same group on a Caribbean cruise. Doy and Lucy Jones were along, and as always, we enjoyed being together and found a lot of fun things to do.

Some of the finest people we ever knew were with Fashion Two Twenty and later with Finelle. We have treasured those friendships during the years and still keep in touch with a great many of them.

For several years, Paul had tried to get us on a Canadian Rockies trip. Each time the trip was sold out. Finally, he told the travel agent to keep his deposit and apply it to the next year's bookings.

The summer of 1984, we went on a wonderful trip through the Canadian Rockies. We flew to Seattle to meet our Westour chartered bus. We were unbelievably fortunate as there were only nineteen passengers aboard for this trip; therefore we got well acquainted and had many privileges that could not have been offered a larger group.

We drove north, where, about fifteen miles beyond the United States border, we came to Vancouver, Canada's leading Pacific Coast port and one of Canada's most beautiful cities. It lies in a magnificent setting of mountains, evergreen forests, and the Pacific Ocean.

Vancouver covers about forty-five square miles on the southern shore of the Burrard Inlet. Its ice-free, land-locked harbor has a shoreline ninety-eight miles long and ranks as Vancouver's greatest asset.

From there, we headed east, through vast fruit-growing lands, to a quaint little village called Kimberly. We thought we were in the Swiss Alps, as Kimberly's streets were lined with colorful chalets boasting flower-filled window boxes at every window, replicas of the chalets that dot the Swiss countryside. The picturesque mountain villages of Banff and Lake Louise were our next stops. What spectacular scenery.

While sitting in the lobby of the Lake Louise Hotel visiting with our favorite tour companions, a couple from California, a gentleman approached us about posing for a picture. "We're in the process of making up a new brochure and red photographs well," he remarked.

All four of us were wearing red sweaters. We posed and, as promised, he sent us a copy of the hotel's new brochure, featuring the four of us on its cover.

From Banff, we drove north on the Glacier Highway to Jasper. I loved Jasper as it reminded me of towns in the Colorado piedmont.

From Jasper, we headed west to St. George and then Prince Rupert on the west coast. Our hotel served the most lavish evening smorgasbord of fresh fish delicacies that you can imagine. Truly, it was a feast.

The next day, we boarded a ferry for an over-night trip to Vancouver Island, where we saw the beautiful city of Victoria with hanging baskets of lovely flowers decorating every light pole. We stayed in the Princess Hotel and had high tea at 4:00 P.M. ala English custom. From Victoria we had an all-day trip to the famous Butchart Gardens, a world-renowned showplace of exquisite beauty, created from an old stone quarry. Everyone should see the Butchart Gardens.

Another ferry ride brought us back to the mainland and into Seattle, where we saw our first Omnimax film, "The Great Barrier Reef." We did not know then that we would have such a theater in Cincinnati within a few years, thanks to the generosity of the Carl Lindner family.

En route back to Ohio, we stopped in Denver, where Marge and Orville Hoffman, my friends from college days, met us at the airport. It was the first time we'd seen each other since 1951, but it was as if we'd never been apart. That is real friendship.

Marge and Orville built a beautiful mountain-lodge home, about seventeen miles above Ft. Collins in Poudre Canyon. When they retired, their son, Robert, took over their Loveland acreage and they moved to their picturesque location along the Poudre River. There is quiet, soul-restoring magic in both the mountains and the sea.

Later that summer, we had a Finelle convention in Williamsburg. In spite of one hundred five degree weather, Paul and I toured the restored city, as well as nearby Jamestown, steeped in history.

Sarah and Paul.

Once, during the years that we traveled for Finelle, we held a meeting in Lima, Ohio. We contacted our friends, Jim and Anna Jane Pelton (friends from Mansfield days) who lived not too far from Lima. They came to the hotel to have breakfast with us. We had not seen each other for thirty-five years, yet sat there and visited for a good three hours. Again, it was as though we'd never been apart. And again, that is real friendship.

Earlier, I mentioned migraines. For many years I suffered from migraine headaches. Doctors do not really understand what triggers a migraine, but most agree that they tend to run in families and are probably stress-related.

The first time I ever had an attack was in the mid-forties. Bob Swinehart brought a friend of his to Marseilles to hunt pheasants. They stayed with us. Before they left, I was terribly sick. If you have never had a migraine or known someone afflicted with them, you have no way of knowing how debilitating an attack can be. My head would simply explode constantly from deep inside with a searing, piercing pain. I could not stand to look out of my eyes. I vomited, wretchingly, every few minutes for hours, and sometimes even for days.

I do not remember this gentleman's name, but he sent us a subscription to the *Reader's Digest* as a "thank you' for our hospitality. We appreciated his thoughtfulness, added his subscription to our already existing one, and have enjoyed the Reader's Digest all these years.

I don't recall having another migraine until the spring of 1954 on Guam. I had been in charge of a last-day-of-school picnic. The next day, I woke up with a migraine. I lay in bed, in the Butler barracks unit, at the old Guam Memorial Hospital compound, and vomited every few minutes for three straight days. I was sure I would die. Paul finally found a doctor who could stop my vomiting.

During our years on Guam, I had so many attacks that Dr. Smart, a Seventh Day Adventist doctor, would come into my bedroom and say, "Same room, same girl, same bed, same bucket." When I was vomiting continually, every few minutes, I had to resort to a bucket beside the bed, as I was literally too sick to get out of bed.

Dr. Smart would give me two shots, something to stop the vomiting and Demerol to put me to sleep. I would sleep around the clock, then it would take me three days to recover.

John and Allison.

In later years, doctors ceased, for awhile, using Demerol, as it is addictive. Then, I had to use a medication in the form of a suppository, as I could keep nothing on my stomach. This medication was not nearly as efficient and took longer to act. However, I always carried the suppositories with me, as I was vulnerable to be hit with a migraine at any time.

Paul, who never had a headache in his life, had no understanding of how sick I was during those attacks.

As the grandchildren grew up, they wanted to go to the beach instead of always going back to Oglebay Park for a week each summer. Therefore, in the early 1980s we started going to Myrtle Beach. We rented two three-bedroom condos right on the beach and enjoyed every minute of our weeks there. Sometimes, Wes and Harriette joined us with their family, and, through the years, they have become a much-loved part of our family.

Allison, our youngest grandchild, was born December 29, 1985, several weeks prematurely. She was one of Ohio's first successful "in vitro" babies, who often arrive a few weeks early. She weighed five pounds, twelve ounces, was hale and hearty, and much loved from the very first.

Our family vacation that summer, was spent on Longboat Key, near Bradenton on the Gulf Coast of Florida. We rented a four-bedroom condo and had a wonderful time, in spite of unusually hot weather. We swam, played tennis, and golfed.

The following year, and for several years after, we returned to Myrtle Beach. However, eventually that trip became too much for Paul and we had to stop those looked-forward-to family vacations.

Paul's health was showing marked deterioration. I knew that it was very important to keep him active for as long as possible. Therefore, the winter of 1987 we spent three months at Del Tura, a retirement area with golf course and other amenities, just north of North Fort Myers, Florida. While there, we visited Gladys Hartle, who lived in Lehigh Acres. She was suffering from shingles in her scalp and looked very miserable. I was terribly worried about her. Later, after she had finally recovered, she sent me a picture in which she looked like her usual lovely self. I literally wept tears of joy when I received it.

The following winter, we spent four months at Country Meadows, just out of Plant City, where the Reds were completing their new spring-training facility. We made friends with three couples there, Franz and Ginny Taylor, Lloyd and Jane Meadows, and Sam and Jan Craft, who we still keep in touch with. Sadly, Sam has died of cancer.

The third winter, 1989, we spent five months at Timber Pines in Spring Hill, Florida. At each of these places we played golf and met a lot of very nice people. However, the long trips

Allison at one year old.

became too much for Paul, who could no longer play golf, and we had to give up that nice "winter-break".

Paul played a very limited amount of golf during our winter at Timber Pines. After we returned home, Fred wanted him to go golfing. Paul said, "Fred, I just can't do it any more."

Fred replied, "Paul, you taught me to play golf. We have had some of our very best times together out on the golf course. I'm not ready to give that up."

Paul went with him for 9 holes. He shot a 45, in spite of losing his balance each time he tried to swing the club. That was the last time he attempted to play, a sad ending for an avid golfer.

Complete retirement was a wrench for me. The first thing I did was gain ten pounds, as I couldn't sleep and simply ate night and day. I had worked hard all my life. To NOT work made me feel guilty.

I enrolled in a creative writing course. When I was ten, I was paid ten dollars for a poem I wrote for Mother's Day, which was published in a Sunday School journal. I have always dabbled in writing, but never seriously. Now, I had the time to study techniques and learn the craft.

I still have a great many things to learn, but I have had a good many articles published in a variety of magazines and newspapers. This poem, written when Rock was a toddler, was published as the Editor's favorite "Poem of the Month", in the August 1987 edition of *Sunshine Magazine*:

Left to Right: Valerie, Lia, Gary and Mark.

Treasures

All through the warm afternoon he had played.
A train from a long string of spools he had made
And his little red truck had sped up and down
Every street in his sandbox town.
Throwing his ball, he had raced here and there,
The sun in his smile, the wind in his hair.
And, being a boy, he had ridden, of course,
All over the yard on his broom-stick horse.
When the sun bent low toward the end of the day
A tired little boy came in from his play.
He crawled on my lap, too weary to speak,
And I kissed the small scratch that he had on his cheek.
He showed me a marble he'd found in the sand
And the feather he clutched in his little-boy hand.
He leaned his head back, in my arms nestled deep
And I knew that my tired little boy was asleep.
I pressed my lips close to cheeks glowing with health
And I wondered if ever a king had such wealth!

Since I intended to work seriously at writing, I invested in a computer, which has been a god-send. Once I learned how to use it, it saved me hours of time. I was brought up in an era when personal letters were NOT to be written on a typewriter. However, I correspond with a large number of people and find that they welcome a letter from me, hand-written or written on the computer.

In the fall of 1985, I received a letter that impressed me in its clarity and its sincerity. It was from a Dr. Klaus Guder, a new dentist, announcing that he was setting up his practice in our area. Soon after receiving that letter, I had the shell of a wisdom tooth break off around an old filling. I went to Dr. Guder to have it repaired. It was a fortunate decision.

Since twelve years of age, when my molars erupted, my front teeth had continually moved out. The malocclusion had caused me to be a victim of bruxism, tooth-grinding. As I got older, the bottom front teeth, having nothing to bite against, had become very much out of line. Dr. Guder said, "Mrs. Gettys, you are a very attractive lady, but your teeth are spoiling your appearance. I'd like to help you."

What welcome words. I had gone to several dentists through the years, seeking help, but none had any answers to my problem. Of course, I should have had braces as a child, but in those days, orthodontics were a rarity. Later, even specialists told me I was too old, that there was nothing they could do.

Dr. Guder said he would make two permanent bridges, one to replace the upper front, protruding teeth, the other to replace the lower crooked ones. First he made a mold of my teeth, as they were. Then he made another mold, showing how they would look when the work was completed. I took the molds home to show Paul and ask his advice, as it was going to cost over three thousand dollars.

"They're your teeth, and you'll have to go through the misery," Paul said. "You'll have to decide."

Dr. Guder waited until after Thanksgiving to start. He did the first procedure on December 2 and finished on April 9. I have never been sorry that I went through with it and credit Dr. Guder with saving my teeth.

The summer of 1986, Marvin and Flo Jean took a trip west. Somewhere in the foothills of the Rockies, they rented a car and drove east to Kit Carson County, where we grew up. Marvin was only a seventh grader when we left that area in 1934, and did not remember just how to get out to our homestead. He stopped in Bethune to ask directions. The man he asked could not direct him, but said, "See that man painting the house down the block? He can help you. He used to live out in that area."

Marvin drove on to where the man was painting. After they had talked awhile, the painter asked, "Did you have a sister named Sarah?" The painter was Vaughn Taylor, my buddy in fifth grade, the one who always had candy in my desk on Monday morning and the victim of the casually tossed bull snake.

Vaughn and his wife, Aletha, drove Marvin and Flo out to our old homestead, through various areas of the community, and on to where the Taylor's sod house still stands just west of the old First Central School site.

Marvin's chance meeting with Vaughn proved a fortunate one for us Mitchell "kids". Through the years, we had lost contact with our old friends, and no one in that community knew where any of us lived or how to contact us.

Several months later, I received a note from Loraine Iseman Wood, telling me that they were starting a "First Central Reunion", to be held the last Saturday of July, in the Broomfield Park, northwest of Denver. Could we come? We could.

Reva agreed to come and stay with Paul. Little Allison was less than two years old, and Paul enjoyed having them with him, while I was away. Helen and I flew to Denver for this initial get-together with our old neighbors and friends, who we had not seen for fifty-three years. I recognized many of them because they looked much like their parents had looked when I had last seen them. It was a very rewarding experience, even though we felt like total strangers.

We rented a car and, after the picnic on Saturday, drove east to Burlington. That distance, in our childhood, seemed endless. Now, with good cars and super highways, it was a pleasant three-hour ride. We arrived in Burlington just in time to get the last available motel room for the night.

The next day, Sunday, we went to see our dear teacher, Thelma Nielson Armstrong Lowe, and her husband, Arthur, who were living at the Manor Nursing Home. Their daughter, Ladeen (Helen took care of her when she was born), came and took her parents over to their home, a few blocks away. We spent an hour or two with them, reminiscing. Thelma had been a much-loved teacher, both in grade school and again in high school. I was glad that she had lived to read and enjoy the "Blizzard" story I wrote, which was published in *Colorado Homes & Lifestyles Magazine*.

After leaving them, we drove to Bethune, then south to our old homestead. This article, written about that trip, was published in *Colorado Homes & Lifestyles*, Jan/Feb issue, 1989:

Bittersweet Homecoming

Despite what Thomas Wolfe believed, you can go home again, even when "home" does not exist. Home is memories.

Last summer I went home. After 53 years, I returned to Kit Carson County in eastern Colorado, where I grew up. I left there in 1934 at the height of the Great Depression, the drought, and the dust bowl, immortalized in Steinbeck's gripping novel *The Grapes of Wrath*.

When Lylah Ayers Ness advised me to watch the odometer because exactly ten miles south of Bethune was the road that led to her old home, I took little note of it. I knew every mile of that road and knew that the Charlie Perkin's home sat on that corner. However, as I crossed the railroad tracks in Bethune, I made a mental note of the mileage on the rental car I was driving. It was lucky I did, for as the miles went by, with great clouds of dust billowing out behind the car on that graded road, there was little but a vast expanse of flat, plowed land, as far as eye could see. Nothing looked familiar. Even the deep gully in the road, where it crossed a dry creek-bed at that corner, and which I had counted on as a recognizable landmark, had been leveled. I turned off the motor and sat "looking" at the old Perkins' place—the long, low sod house, (now cemented on the outside), the well house, the barn. All were there in my mind, just as they had been a half-century before. A little beyond, a lone wind mill stood, abandoned by time.

Allison.

I recalled vividly one evening during the dark days of the depression, when all the neighbors gathered at the Perkins' for a "hard times" party. Cornbread and beans were served as refreshments. I could still see Miranda at the old black kitchen stove, serving up great slabs of delicious cornbread, then ladling on hearty helpings of beans from one of the several pots brought in by neighbors. I even recalled the songs we sang and the games we played. That long-ago party gave me pleasure, still, in memory.

I remembered a picnic held there one Sunday afternoon. The men were down near the barn pitching horseshoes. Nina Dunlap and I ran to the barn to ask Dad's permission for me to go home with her until evening church service. Careless in our childish excitement, we ran directly into the line-of-fire and I caught a horseshoe on the back of my head. I did go home with Nina, but we sat in their big porch swing—a swing on a frame with two seats facing—because my head hurt too much to run and play. Memories.

I started the motor and continued south another mile, past the corner where the old Midway School stood. Now, there was only a vast plowed field. But I could "see" the school-house and the coal house out back, flanked on either side by the outdoor toilets, one marked GIRLS and the other BOYS. I could see the swings and the merry-go-round. I recalled, as if it were yesterday, the time twenty-eight of us youngsters were marooned there overnight when a fierce blizzard savaged the prairie. The schoolyard came alive with youngsters playing Dare-Base, Run-Sheep-Run, Last-Couple-Out, and during the long months of snow, Fox-and-Geese. Time may destroy things physical, but mental images remain forever young.

From that corner, looking west one-half mile, I could see a sloping row of cottonwood trees marking the old Keever place. The trees nearest the well got more water and so grew taller. The others graduated down to mere shrubs. The only porcupine I ever saw was there amid those cottonwoods, more than a half-century ago.

At the Correction Line, there was no trace of the old Snelling place. A short distance to the west, a small pile of rubble showed where the Rich place once stood. I remembered the little white milk-glass hen Mrs. Rich always kept on her parlor table. I wondered if she ever sensed how much I longed for it, as a child. And did she guess my terror when I had to pass her flock of noisy geese?

At the old Nazarene Church site on the corner, only the windmill stands, a silent reminder of a time long passed. The road that led one mile south of the church, to our home, is now part of a huge plowed field. I turned off the motor and began to walk that last mile. The fine soil under my feet was powder dry. The hot wind blew relentlessly, whipping the red tie at the neck of my blouse and stinging my face. I thought sadly of the dust bowl of the 1930's and considered how much worse the next one would surely be. At that time, many sections of virgin grassland provided not only open range for grazing cattle, but also a buffer against wind-erosion. Now, every inch was plowed, disked fine, and lying fallow, ready to blow.

About a half-mile from the car, I topped a small rise in the terrain and could see, for the first time in fifty-three years, our old home site. Nothing remained but a vast expanse of space. No house, no outbuildings, no fences, not even the windmill. Memories flooded over me. It was as if a long-closed door had silently opened to let me see my childhood home again.

There was the tree-patch, bordering the north side of the yard. Our parents had planted a variety of trees, hoping to grow a brake against the relentless Colorado wind. How many buckets of well water, I wondered, had I carried to water those trees through the years? Chinese elm, box-elder, locust, willow. Now only two small locusts, less than head high still struggle to survive.

On the west side of the yard, a bedraggled clump of tamarisk leaned against the wind. Once, tamarisk and currant bushes provided a large privacy screen for our outdoor privy. A plain wooden casket, built by Mr. McArthur, our neighbor to the south, lies beneath those bushes. It holds the body of our little brother, still-born on a Halloween night some sixty years ago.

I remember that night as if it were yesterday. Mother's bed was in the "living room" of our sod house. She wept softly as she turned her face into her pillow. I sat down at the piano and began to play a childish version of "The Eastern Gate", a hymn we often sang at church. The words, "I will meet you in the morning over there," even though unsung, caused Mother to ask me to stop playing. From that day to this, I have never played that hymn.

Our well was over two hundred feet deep and brought up delicious soft water, nearly ice cold. Our largest tree was a willow, whose roots had grown around the well-casing and, therefore, got a constant supply of moisture. I could "see" the harvest crew, and later the threshing crew, washing up under the shade of that willow, with water pumped fresh and cold from the well. Now, neither the tree nor the well exists. Only the memories.

And memories can play tricks. I had remembered the hill one mile west, between our place and Dunham's, as a big hill. I chuckled to myself because it is actually little more than rolling prairie land. How many times, I wondered, had we picked a header-barge load of dried cow-chips from the open range there, to be used as a quick-start when building a fire in the coal stove?

I could "see" the refrigerator Dad built for us, before the days of rural electri-fication. It was a pit, approximately four feet square and four feet deep. In the bottom of the pit was a foot or more of sand. Above the ground, a wooden collar rimmed the pit and it was covered with a hinged lid. Each morning we carried two buckets of cold water from the well and wet down the sand. This made a very efficient cooler for perishable foodstuffs, such as milk, meat, eggs, butter, and cream. I was an agile youngster and it usually fell my lot to jump down in the cooler and set out, or put away, food before and after meals.

The refrigerator lid also served as a convenient tabletop when we churned butter there in the shade, on the north side of our sod house, using the old crockery churn and the long-handled dasher, then the wooden butter-paddle to collect the butter particles from the buttermilk when the churning was done.

I recalled one evening when we stood in our yard and watched as the northeast sky became a brilliant red. Only later, we learned that Snelling's barn had been struck by lightning. During that same storm, lightning struck two of our best horses, dropping them side by side at the pasture's edge. I remembered, too, seeing the entire northern sky ablaze with color as the Aurora Borealis played out its fantastic ballet with giant streamers of reflected light.

My father, Victor Mitchell, home-steaded a half-section of land. Our home sat on the north section line, at mid-point. The road coming in from the east was bordered on the south by our fence and on the north by Rich's fence. It was narrow and we always called it the "lane". The lane no longer exists. It is part of the vast expanse of plowed-up prairie. However, I could easily see where the fences had been. During the years of the dust bowl, Russian thistles,  commonly called tumbleweeds, piled up against all fences, collecting the fine topsoil, which blew across the prairie in great choking clouds. Through the intervening years, fence posts rotted and barbed-wire rusted, but the soil ridges remain, marking clearly where the lane had been.

Ted Knodel, our mail carrier, came down that lane, bringing our only contact with the outside world. How we looked forward to his coming. We pored over the Montgomery Ward catalogs and the colorful seed catalogs he brought. We vied for "first rights" to *The Saturday Evening Post*, in order to savor the next installment of Pearl S. Buck's "China Sky" or Zane Grey's "Riders of the Purple Sage."

Most of all, we looked forward to the Round Robin, a large pack of letters that Mother and eleven of her friends from college days exchanged regularly. They started the Robin as a way to keep in touch after graduation, when marriage or

1990, fiftieth wedding anniversary.

careers separated them by many miles. Each agreed to keep the Robin no longer than two weeks. Therefore, twice each year, the Robin arrived, containing letters, and sometimes pictures, from each of the Robin "girls". How we loved getting news from Steamboat Springs or Pueblo or Leadville or Denver.

During the two weeks that Mother had the Robin, she would read and re-read each letter. Then she would discard the one she had penned six months earlier and spend days composing a new one to include before sending the Robin on. Sometimes, one of the Robin "girls" would come to visit. Basically, however, our only contact with them was by letter.

One morning in 1933, Ted Knodel brought, as a part of our mail, a suitcase. It was a good, sturdy suitcase, costing probably $2.95 at that time. In it were a variety of practical things that a young girl going off to college would need—undies, slips, nighties, a robe, blouses, a sweater, and a skirt. In the "pocket" in the lid, was a $100 bill. At a time when grown men worked for $1 a day and were glad to find any kind of work to do, this was real money. That gift from the Robin "girls" to my older sister, Helen, enabled her to start to college at Greeley. Later, after she was teaching, she helped me go to college. It was a gift that changed all our lives.

Memories.

Yes, you can go home again. In fact, we can never really leave home. Home is indigenous to our very being. It is home that births us, nurtures us, guides, trains, provides for, and challenges us. Home is the root system from which we grow. Any virtues, which I may possess, had their foundation in that lowly home on the eastern Colorado prairie.

Henry Ward Beecher said, "Home should be an oratorio of the memory, singing to all our after life melodies and harmonies of oft-remembered joy." Going home, after fifty-three years, was indeed, a bittersweet oratorio of memory for me.

Paul and I celebrated our fiftieth wedding anniversary in October, 1990. On Saturday evening, before the big day, we took the family, Wes and Harriette, and Reva and Maurice Terry out for dinner at Florenz. When we had finished eating, we all came back to our living room.

Ronda got everyone in a circle and started the ball rolling by saying, "The thing I remember most vividly about my growing up years is that, even though Mother taught school, she was always the mother who would take a bunch of us kids to the beach, or let us have a slumber party. When we girls would start planning something like that, the other girls would always say, 'Ronda, you ask your mother. She'll let us.'" And she went on to comment that her daddy had always set such high standards for their behavior, that even though the neighborhood kids might do something wrong, she wouldn't, because he was principal of the high school and it would reflect badly on him.

Reva said, "The thing I remember most vividly about my childhood is the great number of books Mother read out loud to the family."

Rock added, "We tend to think of our parents as very conservative, but how conservative were they to strike out for Guam in 1951 with three small children? Or leave an established profession at middle age and move to Cincinnati to start a new business?"

Each person in the room, then, began to add memories. John commented that he'd never known anyone who received the number of Christmas cards that we do. We'd fallen in love to Peter Grant's program, *Moon River*, and they'd found that music, along with some other songs popular at that time. Jean and Reva sang as Flo Jean played the piano. It was a super evening.

The next day, Sunday, some sixty invited guests came to share a very special time with us. Fifty years together is a milestone worth noting. At least two dozen couples, among our close friends, have celebrated fifty years of marriage. Our dear friends, Doy and Lucy Jones, celebrated sixty-two years together. I wonder how many present-day marriages will survive fifty years?

In 1991, Helen and I again flew to Denver for the fifth annual reunion of our old Colorado neighbors. This time, we did not feel such strangers and had a wonderful time.

While I was gone, each of our young folks spent two days with Paul, sharing the responsibility for his care.

When we arrived in Denver, we rented a car and drove to Greeley, to visit our cousin, Patty, and her husband, Jack Noel. We all had dinner together at a nice restaurant called The Eatin' Place, in Eaton.

The following day, en route to Ft. Collins, we located the Dougherty place, where we'd lived when we first left Kit Carson County in 1934.

From Ft. Collins we drove up Poudre Canyon to visit Marge and Orville Hoffman, my college roommate and her husband, in the beautiful mountain-lodge home they built for their retirement years.

Saturday, the fifth annual get-together was even better than we had anticipated. That evening a group of us were at Maxine Iseman Chandler's home, visiting, reminiscing, and eating. On Sunday, an even larger group of us were at Isaphene and Ralph Lesher's home in Boulder. What a treat to be with lifelong friends. Vi Campbell Barr, my much-loved 5th grade teacher, was with us all weekend.

On Monday, Ella Storrer Lebsack met us at our hotel. We drove to Boulder, picked up Isaphene, and then drove on to Estes Park and down the Big Thompson Canyon. It was my first trip through the Canyon since the flood had devastated the area several years earlier. However, we saw little sign of the devastation.

The four of us enjoyed a long lunch at the Village Inn in Longmont before dropping Isaphene off in Boulder, and heading back to our hotel. It was a delightful day to add to my memory bank.

On our flight back to Ohio, Helen and I talked about what various ones of these childhood friends had done with their lives. We wished that we knew a lot more about them. I came up with a plan and sent the material to Isaphene for presentation to the group at the following year's get-together: each person would write a short "life story" of four or five pages, and send it to me. I would put them all on my computer, and eventually each one who participated would receive a booklet containing all the life stories. I prepared an outline for them to follow, listing some twenty areas of interest, and set a deadline for getting the material back to me.

One by one the "life stories" began to come in. It was fun reading about what each had done with their lives. The thing that amazed me, however, was how much traveling this group had done. I knew that Paul and I had traveled a good deal, but someone else had paid for much of our travel. These Colorado friends had been everywhere.

When Robert Knodel's material reached me, I noted that he had been a professional printer. I called and asked him how I should proceed in getting the life stories from my computer into booklet form. It was a most fortunate contact, as Robert told me that if I'd get the material on a disk compatible with Word Perfect, he'd do the set-up for me. He had lots of different styles of type, which I did not have on my computer. He did the set-up and sent me the master copies. I had them printed and put in binders. Thanks to Robert's expertise, the booklets are very attractive and a delightful keepsake for all those who participated. The many letters, phone calls, and gifts I've received, since I mailed them out, are proof that they are indeed appreciated.

Helen, who has spent years researching our genealogy, said that if she'd ever found anything like this booklet in the Archives, or in a library, she'd think she had found a gold mine. Therefore, I sent two copies to the Burlington Public Library and two copies to the Denver Archives. They each wrote very nice letters of appreciation.

Soon after the booklets had been mailed to each participant, in July 1993, the seventh annual First Central reunion was held at the Broomfield Park. Helen and I went. Ronda and Fred, bless them, took a week of their vacation to stay with Paul.

On Friday, we drove up Poudre Canyon to see Marge and Orville Hoffman, dear friends since college days, and enjoyed a beautiful day with them.

On Saturday we visited with all our old friends at the picnic. One sad note was that Bob Knodel, who had helped me with the set-up of the life story booklets, was in the hospital, undergoing by-pass surgery.

Vi Campbell Barr was there, eighty-seven years young. Again, we were at Maxine and Jake's for a Saturday evening smorgasbord. And on Sunday we were all at Isaphene and Ralph's in Boulder where Verlin Dunlap, who had lived in Kit Carson County his entire life, shared a lot of interesting information with us about people and places we had known years ago. It was a most enjoyable weekend.

As 1993 draws to a close, I sadly observe Paul's health failing almost daily. Between Thanksgiving and Christmas, I finally face the fact that I need help in caring for him. It is getting to the point that I can no longer physically do what needs to be done for him.

Our dear pastor, Michael Boys, referred me to Hospice. I knew nothing about Hospice. I find, however, that Hospice of Cincinnati is dedicated to keeping a patient in his own home, rather than in a nursing home.

An RN came to the house, made an assessment of our situation, and advised us how they could fill our needs. The result has been such a blessing I can hardly believe our good fortune.

A home health-care aide comes every morning from 9:00 A.M. to 11:00 A.M.. She massages Paul with a heavy Genie vibrator, gets him up, shaved, teeth washed, bathed, dressed, fed, and into his lift chair. He eats while sitting in his wheel chair, as he lists to one side and is in danger of falling from a regular chair.

Each week an RN comes to check his vital signs and consult with the doctor about his condition.

A Hospice volunteer comes one afternoon each week to stay with Paul while I run errands at the bank, library, post office, and grocery.

A barber also comes to cut Paul's hair while he sits in his wheel chair in our kitchen. A great weight has been lifted from my shoulders, not only because of the physical care Paul is receiving, but also because of the emotional support that I am receiving.

Earlier, I mentioned my "Memory Wall". Gladys Hartle's treasured oil painting of the Bavarian Alps is surrounded by mementos that fill the screen of my mind with happy scenes each time I look at them: the love chapter, 1 Corinthians 13, done in cross-stitch by Robin, as a thank-you for taking her on vacation with us. Mark's photo of California's Cronkite Beach signed M M Gettys. Phyl's hand-painted goldfinch, sent as an Easter card. Ronda's delicate floral in a lovely gold frame. A silk-screen print of Mt. Fuji, sent as a Christmas card by one of Paul's teachers. Reva's sweet little girl in pink. Two small gold-framed scenes, purchased on Guam, whose backgrounds are butterfly wings of iridescent blue. Irene's pretty Friendship plate. Juanita's letter paper, with seagulls flying over tranquil, blue water. The Last Supper, which I bought at a Goodwill Store for a dollar. All are treasured memories accumulated through the years, and which gladden my heart.

Someone has said that a true friend is one who inspires us to be more than we might otherwise have been, to develop the very best instincts in our natures, to mature into fine adult individuals. Paul and I have been true friends. I know that I am a better person for having met and married a man of very strong character, a straight-laced man of high standards, a man of real quality. Paul knew how to set goals for the future, and was willing to work hard to accomplish them.

We both came from homes where our parents epitomized character, hard work, and loyalty, in good times and bad. We started life together with very little except love for each other and respect for the vows we made to each other. We have raised three fine young folks, of whom we are very proud. If the measure of parents is the children they leave behind, then we have been good parents. They, in turn, are "passing it on" to their own young families.

Who dares compare a heritage of faith in God, steadfast love, honesty, loyalty, health, security, pride in good workmanship and achievement, and faithful service to one's community with an inheritance of only money?

It is undoubtedly true that some of the memories of over seventy years, detailed here, are less than one hundred percent accurate. However, the genealogy information has been taken from Helen's diligent research. And the records of our various trips have been taken from notes kept at that time.

Early in 1992, I started writing this memoir, not for publication, but purely for my own enjoyment and to leave an accurate record of our travels for our children. It is now the beginning of 1994. This would have been completed earlier had I not put together the First Central life stories booklet last year.

It is said that writing your life story helps you better understand yourself. I believe that is true. For years I shied away from even thinking about my childhood. I wanted to forget the drought and depression, the poverty, the soddy, the hand-me-downs, the barrenness of the eastern Colorado prairies. Writing about those years has been emotionally cathartic for me. Additionally, it has given me a much clearer picture of what is really important in the life of a child. Outer trappings may make life easier, and, therefore, more pleasant. But values instilled in the heart of a child are the gifts that are lasting and worthwhile.

Not until the advent of WWII did our country's economy begin a real upturn from the Great Depression years. Therefore, during the years of my childhood, most people were poor, as far as "things" were concerned. However, they were rich in the deep and abiding truths that give life its real meaning. At that time in our history, most parents, certainly those in our small community, were dedicated to passing on those basic truths as a legacy to their children.

Our parents were good parents. Re-living those years has given me a much greater respect for Mother's abilities and her efficiency as a homemaker. I'm sure that under similar circumstances, I would not have done as well.

Remembering Dad's happy personality has again verified the Biblical adage "A merry heart doeth good like a medicine," for he was a man of abundant health and energy. I recently read, "When you see a person who is a 'picture of health' you will no doubt find that the setting for the picture is a happy outlook on life." How true. A positive outlook is not only a wonderful gift to oneself. It is also a gift without measure to those with whom we come in contact.

These two good people, my parents, from very diverse backgrounds, experienced many years of deprivation and hardship, yet they endured. And eventually, they not only prospered financially, but left four very fine offspring to pass on their solid values and ideals to future generations. I am one of those offspring, and I do not consider it bragging to make such a statement. Who knows better than we ourselves, whether or not our hearts are good?

Life is like building a house. Each wall is made up of memories, which are a result of the decisions we make and the actions we take, as we go through life. We ourselves are the builders, and, eventually, we are the ones who have no choice but to live in the house we have built for ourselves. My "walls" embrace me with warmth and a great deal of love. I am a happy camper.

Paul passed away July 2, 1995 after many years of suffering. His mental abilities remained alert to the last, even though his physical body had become helpless. He was an outstanding, fine-principled man, a fine husband and father, and I have marveled many times that he, who had just graduated from Western Michigan, happened to come to the same school in Logan County, Ohio that I had come to from Greeley, Colorado! Talk about "the Hand of the Lord"!

The first year Paul was gone, I enjoyed a Tauk Tour to the "Canyon Lands" in our western states, with friend, Joy. We also went on a trip to the Greek Isles, ending in Instanbul, the only city in the world which lies on two continents!

On New Years Day, Helen and I flew to Acapulco and joined a Cunard Ship tour to Costa Rico, through the Panama Canal to Jamaica, returning to Key West and Fort Lauderdale.

Later Helen and I had a Tauk Tour to the Hawaiian Islands, I had been there a good many times, but she had not, and I wanted her to see that beautiful state. On our return to California, I stayed over a few days in San Francisco, where my two fine grandsons, Mark and Gary, escorted me around their beautiful city. What fine young men Rock's sons are!

One year I went with Helen on a trip to NYC, where we visited Times Square, Macy's, the Statue of Liberty, and saw a couple of shows.

Another trip that Helen and I enjoyed was a trip to the Lancaster, PA area where we saw the outstanding "Sight and Sound" production of "NOAH"----a production everyone should see! We also saw many historical sights in Philadelphis and Gettysburg, making this a very educational trip.

Helen was a master bridge player, having earned all those "gold points". I know nothing about bridge, as Paul and I were golfers. However, in September 2004, Helen was playing bridge with friends, had a brain aneurysm, and was gone at 89. When I called Marvin to tell him she'd died playing bridge, he said, "We can be grateful she didn't die crossing the bridge!" as she'd driven from her Lexington home to mine two weeks before and had crossed that Ohio River bridge going and coming! God is good!

Ronda's two daughters, Lia and Valerie, both graduated from Bowling Green University in Ohio. Valerie came to Arizona in 1995 and has been with Wells Fargo's main office in downtown Phoenix for many years. When Ronda retired from her position with Verizon in

Dallas, she moved to Arizona, as she did not want to go back to Ohio's cold weather, and had no family in Dallas.

The first year she was in Arizona, I sent John and Reva out to spend part of their Christmas vacation with them. John fell in love with Arizona. He had worked for 39 years for the same company in Ohio and started looking for something he could do in AZ while looking for a place to live. He found a job on the internet, retired, came to AZ and lived with Ronda while looking for a home for him and Reva. She stayed in Bucyrus and put their home on the market.

John had a very nice home built in Province, a new gated "55 and older" community, Reva loves it here. Their only daughter, Allison, graduated cum laude from Otterbein in Ohio, yet could not find a job as Ohio had put a curb on hiring. She came to AZ, found a teaching job immediately. She also found very quickly a fine young man, her husband Chase, whom we all love. They had a beautiful wedding last spring, have a new home, and are very happy!

Ronda's Lia, who taught Physics for many years in Ohio, also came to AZ to teach. And in December of 2006, I came out to spend Christmas with all my Arizona family. I had NO thought of making a home here, as Ronda had spent six weeks with me the year before and I'd completely re-done my Cincinnati home, thinking I was going to live there the rest of my life.

Well, when I was shown the large Villa here in the choices of models at Province, I fell in love with it. Jeannie Rieder, a dear friend, sold my Ohio home in a few weeks! As my brother says, "The Lord knew it was being readied to sell, even though I thought I was getting it ready for me to live in for years!" and since the end of February 2007, I have been a permanent resident of Arizona! SO time marches on!

I hated to leave my only brother, Marvin, who is 90, and my younger sister, Jean, who will be 80 in April. However, they have been out to see all of us recently and Ronda and I made a 10 day trip to Ohio to visit our Ohio relatives a couple of years ago.

I surely miss Rock and Dorothy, but they've been out to see us several times. Rock is a fine man, like his father was. Both of Rock's sons are fine men and now have beautiful little boys. Mark and Laura's Quinn, my first "great" is three, born on Allison's birthday! And Gary and Aggie's little Aiden will be two in June. Both are happy little boys and have fine parents. I recently read a line that I wish every parent could read: "Home is a child's first school. What are you teaching?"

I am loving it here in Province. I am remarkably well for nearly 94, so have been able to contribute in various ways to my new community. I've made hosts of new friends, as we have people here from most of the states and many from Canada. My next door neighbors are Scottish! If you are worried about having to make a change in your living situation, as you are getting older, please relax and realize that many new, good experiences lie in the future. Always remember, "The happiest people are not the people who HAVE the most, they have simply learned to MAKE the MOST of what the have!"

As 2012 gets underway, I feel that I am a very wealthy woman----wealthy in family, wealthy in friends, wealthy in health, and wealthy in memories. Life has truely been, as Henry Ward Beecher said, "an oratorio of melodies and harmonies of oft remembered joys."

Michelangelo, the masterful Italian artist, could look at a block of rough marble taken from the world famous quaries of Carrara, and see within it a beautiful Pieta. Many months, sometimes many years of back-breaking labor lay ahead of him before anyone else would be able to see the beautiful finished piece the he saw in the rough Carrara stone.

I like to think that back in 1918, the Masterful Potter saw in this two-and one- half pound "lump of clay"-----born prematurely, and, according to the doctor, with little chance at life----a Sarah, worthy of many years of patient effort in the turning, the shaping, the molding, even the firing. As I enumerate the prodigious ways in which God has poured out the evidences of His patience, His protection, His provisions upon this "prairie child", I am completely over-whelmed. Surely the many prayers of my good parents have been answered a hundred-fold!

gettys industries

©2012 & 2003 Sarah M. Gettys • smg1918@yahoo.com

Book Design: Mark M. Gettys • Gettys Industries, San Francisco